The Eaton Driv

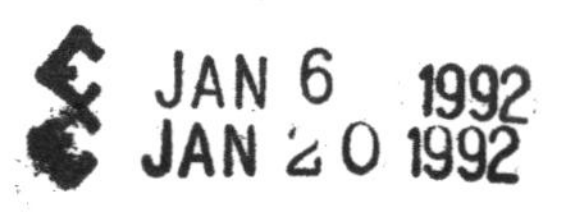

Pg. 19,

This book is dedicated to the late Mary Sutton whose enthusiasm and selfless devotion to Local 1000 was an inspiration to all who knew her.

The EATON DRIVE

The Campaign to Organize Canada's Largest Department Store 1948 to 1952

Eileen Sufrin

Fitzhenry & Whiteside
Toronto Montreal Winnipeg Vancouver

Printed by
the workers of
Éditions Marquis, Montmagny, Québec

Cover design: Don Fernley

Fitzhenry & Whiteside Limited
150 Lesmill Road
Don Mills, Ontario M3B 2T5

Canadian Cataloguing in Publication Data

Sufrin, Eileen Tallman.
The Eaton drive
Bibliography: p.
Includes index.
ISBN 0-88902-702-1
1. T. Eaton Co. – History. 2. Retail, Wholesale and Department Store Union. Local 1000 (Toronto, Ont.). 3. Retail trade – Ontario – Toronto – Employees – History – 20th century. 4. Trade-unions – Ontario – Toronto – History – 20th century. I. Title.

HD6528.M392R47 331.88′1138112′09713541 C82-094465-3

We would like to thank the Ontario Arts Council and The Canada Council for their kind assistance in the production of this book.

Contents

Tables

Appendices

Acknowledgments

FROM THE OUTSET, this book has been a co-operative effort. Over the summer of 1979 Wally Ross sat down with me a number of times to work up the first outline. That fall Art Kube had it run off and sent to a number of people interested in labour history for their reaction. The response from Morden Lazarus, Margot Thompson, Gower Markle, Nancy Stunden, Dan Moore and others was sufficiently encouraging to prompt me to seek assistance from the Canada Council's Explorations Program and from Labour Canada. Grants subsequently received from both enabled me to expand the resource material, initially a box of union leaflets distributed at Eaton's, to a file drawer eventually overflowing with information obtained at archives and public libraries in Ottawa, Toronto and Vancouver, as well as by correspondence.

An abundant collection of quotations to enliven the account emerged from a Local 1000 reunion in Toronto held on April 25, 1980. Ernest Arnold, Alex Gilbert, Olive Chester and Marjorie Chaussé headed a planning committee of such former staunch supporters of the Eaton Drive as Fred Dowling, Henry Weisbach, Moses McKay, Morden Lazarus, Jim Perna, Gwen and Stew Cooke and Iona Samis. Mary Sutton helped to locate and invite many former Local 1000 members and then, two weeks before the event, succumbed to a heart attack. Interviews with those who did attend were taped by Mary Eady, Larry Wagg and Margaret Dowling among others.

I am much indebted to Jim Whitridge, librarian for Labour Canada, and Garfield Clack, Ed Walker and Barry Maloney of the department, for forwarding information on labour legislation, working conditions in retail trade and data on union membership and collective agreements.

Policy and administrative decisions of the CCL Department Store Organizing Committee concerning the Eaton campaign were obtained from files at Public Archives in Ottawa, where Dan Moore gave me excellent co-operation in locating the records.

Hugh Buchanan supplied historical background on RWDSU in Canada, and Marjorie Whitten did likewise for the RCIA organizing attempt at Simpson's. Marc Zwelling, Wayne Roberts and Gene Homel suggested sources on Eaton's previous relations with unions and the press.

From the beginning I relied heavily on Ernest Arnold who was unfailingly prompt in answering a multitude of requests, ranging all the way from radio scripts used in the campaign to the direction in which the suspended geese in the new Eaton Centre are pointing. Many graphics included in the book were made available through Ernie's initiative.

As writing proceeded, Lynn Williams, without whose persistent urging it would not have been undertaken, and Wally Ross, the most vulnerable of former staff since he was closest at hand in Vancouver, read chapters, expanding and clarifying my recollections, as well as contributing more from their own experience. Two others, not previously involved in the Eaton scenario, read most of the manuscript and helped me to discard a good deal of irrelevant trivia. In doing so, Mary Millard buoyed up my spirits by her conviction that somehow, it would eventually emerge as *a book*, whereas my husband Bert shot holes in my English, mercifully suggested alternatives and admonished me to "polish it some more." Among others who read parts of the work and kindly offered comment were Marjorie Chaussé, Olive Chester, Margot Thompson, Morden Lazarus, Gene Homel and Edith Lorentsen.

Obviously, such an exchange entailed considerable photocopying. In this I had generous assistance from the CLC's western education department and the administrative services component of the B.C. Government Employees Union. Donations from the latter toward the expense of preparing the manuscript for submission to publishers enabled me to use the expert services of Susan Enefer, who often ran a shuttle service from her office to my home as deadlines approached. Mary Millard handled the mailing to eastern publishers, for which District 6, United Steelworkers' office contributed more photocopying.

Finally, working with Caroline Walker, editor for Fitzhenry & Whiteside, has been anything but the frustrating experience which I had been warned often characterizes relations between authors and publishers. Exercising minimal "red-pencilling" of content, Caroline improved its readability greatly by, in her words, "cleaning it up." The results reinforced my respect for the value of a good editor.

I extend apologies to those not named who responded to my inquiries by letter or telephone. While acknowledging the very considerable assistance received on this project, the responsibility for facts and opinions presented is entirely my own.

Eileen Tallman Sufrin
White Rock, B.C.

Preface

AFTER MUCH PERSUASION, Eileen Tallman Sufrin has written a volume which should be of immense interest to all trade unionists and persons interested in the social conditions of our time. Others, too, will find it to be a lively and absorbing documentary of an almost forgotten incident in labour history. It is a fascinating story and, as a former union organizer, I have not been able to read it without a lifting of the spirit and a quickening of the bloodstream.

This book is about a union organizing project, as the prologue says, but it is much more. It is a day-by-day, incident-by-incident account of life at the nerve centre of a long four-year campaign (1947-1951) against an employer using the most sophisticated weapons of industrial warfare, weapons refined by 100 years of testing and experiment. Mrs. Sufrin, with what amounts to total recall, has vividly and frankly described the campaign's high and low points, and is equally honest about its heartbreaking denouement.

The campaign was unsuccessful, but the activities of the planners and organizers, the strategy of the campaign, the role of individuals, and the virtually continent-wide network of consultation and participation are described in meticulous detail.

The Eaton Drive initiated new and modern techniques and ideas which have influenced every successful organizing campaign since that time. In terms of broad participation, collaboration and financial support, it has never been equalled. For enthusiasm and resourcefulness, it has never been excelled. The author has written a book which should become a primer for all union organizing planners, particularly in the white-collar field.

Why did the Eaton Drive fail? The reasons outlined by the author are undoubtedly valid. It is the age-old story of labour's endless struggle against the entrenched might of a great corporate empire, aided by the subservient media, the ubiquitous and parasitic so-called labour relations consultants and, above all, "the law's delay."

Perhaps it can also be said that the time for the campaign had not yet arrived. Since then, indications are that such bastions of anti-unionism as the public service, banks and insurance companies are slowly crumbling. Retail trade, including the department stores sector, has joined the march towards industrial democracy. The appropriate time may really be now, or soon.

But to my mind the most daunting message of this story is contained in the account by one Anne Stone of her canvassing experiences. She said:

> *Some of the places we visited were appalling, they were so poverty stricken. The poorer people were, the more they were afraid, even outside working hours, when we suggested that they join the union. I have crawled into cellars and climbed up to single rooms in attics. They were the people who were most reluctant . . . . they had so little and they didn't want to lose what they had.*

These are the people about whom Lady Eaton was later to say in commendation of the "Loyal Eatonians"; "They wanted their *company to be kept a family affair." Their company, indeed!*

As Ralph Chaplin, a famous bard of the labour movement, wrote in an earlier era:

> *". . . mourn the apathetic throng,*
> *The cowed and the meek,*
> *Who see the world's great anguish and the wrong*
> *And dare not speak."*

William Dodge, 1982

In 1974, William Dodge was awarded the Order of Canada, the year he retired from the CLC. During his term as executive vice-president (1958-1968) and secretary-treasurer (1968-1974), Dodge established the CLC's white-collar organizing committee and supervised its program for five years. Earlier, as a general representative of the CBRE, he borrowed some tactics from the Eaton Drive to successfully bring the large accounting staff of the CNR in Montreal into his union in 1950.

Prologue

THIS IS the story of one of the most intensive and sustained organizing campaigns in Canadian labour history: the drive to organize The T. Eaton Company Limited in Toronto some thirty years ago. It was a campaign which touched the lives of thousands of Eaton employees, and potentially had profound implications for the union movement across Canada. Yet it was virtually unreported in the Toronto daily press.

The purpose of this memoir is to record what happened in the Eaton Drive from a union point of view, and to describe some of its features which were unique in labour's efforts to extend unionism to the white-collar field. If it provides some insight into problems which were encountered, so that they may be overcome in future, it will have served its purpose.

The magnitude of Eaton's Toronto operations, dispersed as they then were over more than a dozen work locations, and embracing up to 16,000 employees at peak seasons, presented a formidable challenge to unionization. When Local 1000 of the Department Store Employees Union filed application for certification in October, 1950, the Ontario Labour Relations Board was faced with an application involving the largest and most complex bargaining unit ever to come before it.

Early on in the campaign, hundreds of Eaton employees became openly active and many maintained their commitment over five long years.[1] Their stamina and doggedness was equal to that of workers in industries with a much longer tradition of unionism. The determination of Local 1000 members was matched by the support given at every level of the Canadian Congress of Labour (CCL), from local union members to top-ranking officers of the Congress and its affiliates. Financial aid was only one form of such assistance, but a vital one and probably more generous than given to any other group of workers for organizing purposes.

This venture into the unorganized department store field held enormous potential for increased union strength, not only in retail trade, but for Canadian labour as a whole. With 30,000 employees, Eaton's was the country's third largest employer, surpassed only by the railways and the federal government.

Because its stores and mail order operations extended across Canada, Eaton's inevitably influenced the pattern of retail wages in the major cities, as well as in smaller ones. Throughout its history, Eaton's had successfully staved off unions. The Company had been equally successful in holding down wage levels. So notorious was their opposition to unions that marchers in the Toronto Labour Day Parade of 1934 dipped their flags as they passed Eaton's.[1] Thus, for unions in many provinces, the success of the Eaton Drive was considered vital to remove the threat to their wage standards of a large, lower-paid, and hence, constantly shifting work force. Across the bargaining table employers could always point to the fact that unskilled labour was available at lower rates.

Before starting the narrative of the campaign, a brief perspective is required of the labour history of the post-war period.

As is so often the case, union growth in Canada occurred later and was less spectacular than in the United States, where it exploded with the formation of the Committee for Industrial Organization (CIO) in 1935, and the passage of the Wagner Act that same year. Discontent had been brewing for some years in the American Federation of Labour (AFL). John L. Lewis, head of the powerful United Mine Workers, and other AFL leaders, were exasperated by the failure to tackle organization in the mass production factories. They blamed the craft structure of AFL affiliates which they felt was inappropriate and incapable of bringing millions of workers into unions. The CIO proposed an industrial union approach, bringing all workers regardless of occupation, into one union in a plant, so that maximum strength could be brought to bear to win recognition and to bargain with the employer.

In just a few turbulent years, the CIO approach was completely vindicated. Sit-down strikers in Akron, Ohio, and Flint, Michigan, led the way. Hitherto impregnable bastions of the "open shop" and company unions, such as Goodyear, Republic Steel, General Motors, General Electric and Ford, succumbed after bitter struggles, and signed agreements with CIO unions. Furthermore, white-collar workers in newspapers, department stores and government offices joined the CIO ranks.[2] By 1937, CIO membership had grown to 3.7 million.[3] A year later the Committee was expelled from the AFL and set up the new Congress of Industrial Organizations.

Many appeals to the CIO for help were made by Canadian workers in unorganized branch plants of American companies. The first breakthrough came at General Motors in Oshawa in 1937. Despite the vows of Premier Mitchell Hepburn to keep the CIO out of Ontario, the United Automobile Workers won a first agreement there after a short strike. CIO locals mushroomed and Silby Barrett of United Mine Workers District 26 in the Maritimes was appointed co-ordinator of a Canadian CIO Committee.[4]

In 1939, the convention of the Trades and Labour Congress (TLC) of Canada bowed to AFL headquarters' pressure and expelled the Canadian CIO locals. These promptly convened a conference which was attended by delegates representing about 55,000 members from 16 international unions and some purely Canadian locals.[5]

The All-Canadian Congress of Labour (ACCL), led by A. R. Mosher of the Canadian Brotherhood of Railway Employees, was about to hold its nineteenth convention.[6] Talks were initiated between its leaders and the CIO group. It was decided that differences over national and international unions were trivial compared with the greater common objective of "organizing the unorganized," the rallying cry of the CIO; they decided to amalgamate. In September, 1940, the founding convention of the Canadian Congress of Labour (CCL) took place in Toronto, with delegates representing an estimated 100,000 Canadians. It was anticipated that "the resources of the Congress, both in personnel and finances, will permit it to undertake an organizing campaign throughout Canada on a scale hitherto impossible."[7]

During World War II, Canadian unions experienced an unparalleled surge of growth. This was largely due to two factors: full employment and compulsory collective bargaining, introduced near the War's end under federal wartime emergency powers.[8]

Following its formation in 1940, the Canadian Congress of Labour set up a central fund and undertook a vigorous organizing campaign in many parts of Canada under secretary-treasurer Pat Conroy, who supervised the work of regional directors. CIO unions received generous assistance from C. H. Millard, head of the Steelworkers and Canadian coordinator for the CIO. By 1944, CCL membership had caught up with and slightly overtaken that of the older TLC.

In 1947, when the Eaton Drive began, union membership in Canada stood at 912,000, more than two and one-half times the pre-war level. Two years later, the milestone of one million members was passed. Even so, fewer than one in three Canadian workers belonged to a union (Table 1). By far the greatest proportion of the unorganized were to be found in the retail and personal service industries, as well as in the white-collar domain of insurance, banks and offices generally.

Retail unionism in the United States and Canada was minuscule in relation to the numbers employed. In 1935, the AFL Retail Clerks had about 7,000 members in all of North America.[10] It was common to find several AFL unions carving up department stores by employee occupations. In 1937, dissatisfied with this "craft" approach, a number of local unions (later to become the Retail Wholesale and Department Store Union, CIO) split away from the AFL and soon claimed 40,000 members, including a base in New York and Pittsburgh department stores.[11] Spurred on by this competition — and a new set of younger, more aggressive leaders — the AFL Retail Clerks had enrolled a phenomenal 100,000 members by the War's end.[12] In Canada, organization among retail workers, as in all other industries, never reached the momentum of its U.S. counterparts.

This, then, was the situation when the Eaton Drive started in 1947. Despite an abortive attempt a few years earlier by the Retail Clerks, and other AFL unions such as the Building Service Employees, to organize Simpsons in Toronto, there was a buoyant optimism in CIO-CCL circles: for them the tide of unionism was in full flood. Had they not trebled their membership in just six years? Could any employer be more intransigent than the Steel Company of Canada? The previous year, 1946, the Steelworkers had won a spectacular victory after an 80-day strike, during which they picketed the huge plant by land and patrolled it by sea and air.

When the proposed Eaton campaign was under discussion by executive officers of the CCL, the brief outlining the scope and requirements of the proposal contained this statement:

> There is always the possibility of failure. But no organization suffers as much from trying and failing, as in not trying in the first place.

CHAPTER ONE

The Department Store

IF YOU TAKE the Yonge Street subway and get off at Dundas in downtown Toronto, you will emerge at the entrance to the Eaton Centre. This is a huge commercial complex, the north end of which is occupied by Eaton's department store and a 21-storey tower which houses Eaton's administrative offices. Leaving Eaton's, you can browse through more than 250 shops of smaller merchants, in a galleria enclosed by an arched glass roof with 60 sculptured Canadian geese suspended from the ceiling, south to the overpass to Simpsons at Queen Street, Eaton's rival for more than one hundred years.

Since it opened in 1977, the Eaton Centre has reputedly been a bigger tourist attraction than the CN Tower or for that matter, Niagara Falls. Half a million people pass through it every week. Jointly financed by Cadillac-Fairview, Eaton's, and the Toronto-Dominion Bank, it is reported to have cost $265 million.[1] Before the turn of this century, Eaton's had already acquired much of the prime acreage on which the Centre stands.

To make way for the Centre, all Eaton's buildings in the area were demolished. There had been a large clothing factory and printing plant on Teraulay Street, mail-order buildings on Louisa and Albert, the Annex budget-priced store further south on Bay Street, and the Main Store occupying a city block north of Queen. Visitors today would not be aware, as they pass the huge bronze statue of Timothy Eaton at the entrance, that 30 years ago in those now-vanished buildings, thousands of employees fought long and hard to organize their union. Since 1950, Canadian retailing has undergone changes, which have had a major impact on the working conditions of department store employees.

In the Fifties and Sixties, as the urban communities spawned suburbs, neighbourhood shopping centres made their appearance, often anchored by food supermarkets. As they grew larger, the centres were frequently made viable by one or more department store branches, sparring off at either end. In the decade prior to 1971, department store locations more than tripled, nearly all the new sites outside downtown city cores. By 1975, when the number of shopping centres reached 1,800, it was thought that increasing rents, necessitated by skyrocketing land and construction costs, would curb expansion, but new plazas are still appearing.[2]

To make suburban shopping convenient, night openings were introduced by the food markets on one or two nights a week, with other stores following suit. Some now operate on a six or seven-day basis, and remain open six nights a week.

The decentralization of shopping patterns was advantageous to women employees, who have outnumbered men by about two to one in department stores; they could now find work closer to home. Further, they could work part-time in the evening, solving the problem of child care, provided there were husbands at home to babysit. Shopping centres have made department store employees shift workers. True, there has been no return to the inhumanly long hours of a century ago, for organized labour in general. Unionized supermarket clerks, in particular, have established the five-day week, usually of 40 hours or less.

Despite the increase in the number of locations and longer shopping hours, the department store share of retail sales in Canada has remained around ten percent. In 1977, out of $61.6 billion in retail sales, department stores accounted for $6.9 billion, or virtually the same proportion as in 1941. Food stores have claimed an increasing share of consumer dollars (25 percent in 1977) and Canadians are spending an even higher proportion on their cars. Automotive purchases amounted to 30 percent of retail sales in 1977 (Table 2).

Until 1951, Eaton's sales led all other department stores, totalling an estimated $500 million.[3] But when Sears Roebuck made its entry into Canada in 1953, and took over Simpsons' mail order business as Simpsons-Sears, Eaton's dominant position began slowly to be eroded. Its decline accelerated in the Seventies, particularly after 1976, when Eaton's, unable to turn around the losses it was experiencing, closed out its $300 million mail order business, leaving that field to Simpsons-Sears.

The climax came early in 1979 when, after a bitter war, the Hudson's Bay Company was successful in acquiring Simpsons, and altering the pecking order of the retail giants. For 1978, the ranking of the Top Five by sales volume was:[4]

1.	Simpsons-Sears	$2.1 billion
2.	Hudson's Bay-Simpsons-Zellers	2.0 billion
3.	Eaton's	1.4 or 1.5 billion (est.)
4.	Woolco	870 million
5.	Woodward's	780 million

In large cities, department stores intrude daily into our homes through the medium of TV or newspapers. The art of selling has been transformed into the "pop" art of creating demand. It has been taken from the salesclerk and become the domain of media advertising. One scarcely needs leave home, we are assured. Telephone buying is so easy! However, because this is an *urban* phenomenon, it obscures how much of our goods are still distributed through smaller merchants. Consider that, for the 1971 census, 156,532 retail locations were reported, of which 430 were department stores, representing only 34 companies.

Although they offer hundreds of other commodities and services, the mainstay merchandise of department stores is apparel and home furnishings. In these lines, department stores have always competed with a host of small merchants. In 1971, more than 20,000 shops were specializing in one or more types of apparel or shoes, and over 17,000 were offering home furnishings or hardware (Table 3).

Probably for quite separate reasons, trades unions and small merchants as early as 1904 voiced disapproval of department stores. The Toronto Trades Union Guide and Mercantile Directory referred to them as a "modern octopus," claiming that "they lower clerks' wages and tend to monopoly. With their bargain days, they hurt small merchants in outlying areas of the city. They have enough power to corrupt public officials and to escape factory inspectors' attention. By their advertising revenues they control the press."[5] The undeniable advantage of being big and powerful was spelled out in 1935 when the report of the Royal Commission on Price Spreads and Mass Buying examined the business policies and practices of major department stores.

Retail trade provides almost 15 percent of the employment in the Canadian industrial composite. About half of these 600,000 retail workers are in stores other than department stores and food chains, (Table 4), but because of the proliferation of outlets, the potential for unionism is decidedly less than the number of employees might suggest. First, one must eliminate family-operated groceries and other shops run only by working proprietors. In the vast majority of small stores there are few paid employees. Relationships in such stores are entirely different from those of a corporation employing hundreds or thousands, in which personnel policy is set by top management and an employee's grievance (and redress) is dealt with at the level of department manager.

Within the retail sector, about three out of ten are employed in department stores, and six or seven large firms account for the majority of these.

Department store employment has two characteristics: there are relatively more women, and more part-time employees, than in other categories of the retail business.

Even before the dramatic rise in female participation in the Canadian work force since the last War, about two-thirds of department store employees were women. These large stores provide opportunities for married women who wish to return to work when their children are in school, but do not want to spend time acquiring special skills. According to their family responsibilities, they can move in and out of department store work to earn income for specific purposes, a new stove or a new house, or simply to avoid boredom. For the employer, they represent a ready supply of cheap labour, either on a full or part-time basis. (This is not to dispute the fact that large numbers of women who work in department stores *do* depend on their earnings to maintain themselves and other members of their household.)

The actual extent of part-time employment in department stores bedevils statisticians because it takes such varied forms. Regular part-timers may work during certain hours each day, or full-time on certain days of the week, and share to some degree benefits applying to full-time staff. Non-regular part-timers may be on call in contingencies such as illness, or may be hired only for special sales or during rush seasons such as Christmas.

Two studies of part-time employment in department stores have suggested that *non-regular* part-timers — those who do *not* participate in usual employee benefits, vacations, pensions and so on — may out-number *regular* part-time employees. And together, regular and non-regular part-timers may equal or exceed full-time staff.[6] One study, in which 38 department stores participated in 1966-67, reported a total of 22,978 full-time and 25,035 part-time employees. A further breakdown by occupational group showed that the combined female sales staff in the 38 stores was made up of 6,387 full-time, 6,069 regular part-time and 8,726 non-regular clerks.[7]

The shift to self-service, which began in the Fifties, radically altered work in department stores. Salesclerks, skilled in the art of persuasion and knowledgeable about the product they were selling, were replaced by a cashier and wrapper working in a small enclosure in the middle of the department. There are still a few "salons" or specialty sections in most stores where a live salesperson can be found. In departments offering large durable items for the home, traditionally staffed by men, salespersons are still in evidence. These are the top-paying sales jobs in department stores.

Thus, management's constant drive to reduce payroll costs in order to offset the ever-increasing cost of new buildings and fixtures has had a profound effect on the skills, status and job satisfaction of saleswomen. It has been suggested that, just as union growth in supermarkets followed the increase in "blue-collar" type work brought about by automation and technology, so in department stores the less personalized, more rationalized system of distribution may make them more organizable.[8]

The characteristics of the female sales force have also undergone a dramatic change since 1951. At that time, more than half of the 95,000 women salesclerks in Canada were single and under 35; one-quarter were 45 and over. Twenty years later, 70 percent were married, widowed or divorced. Well over half were 35 years or older, and the proportion aged 45 and over had risen from 25 to 39 percent (Table 5).

An important feature of employment in department stores which has not changed, either within retail trade or as compared with workers in other industries, is the low level of wages. An observation made in January 1950 holds true today:

> "...A large percentage of the total female labour force is crowded into a relatively narrow range of lower-paid occupations, of which leading examples may be found... in retail trade..."[9]

In 1951, average weekly earnings in Toronto were 14 percent higher for manufacturing than for retail trade. By 1980 this gap had more than quadrupled. While it is true that the prevalence of part-time employment distorts average wage statistics, it does not account for the disparity, growing decade by decade, between the earnings of retail workers and others. Another example is the finance, insurance and real estate sector where a majority of employees are women; average earnings for this group in 1951 were 16 percent higher than in retail trade but by 1980, this differential had climbed to 50 percent (Table 6).

Within retail trade, the inordinately low level of department store earnings is even more striking. The categories with the highest percentage of female employees, department stores, apparel and shoes, and variety stores, have the lowest earnings. Nor can all the difference be attributed to part-time employment. Food stores, 44 percent of whose employees are women, also utilize part-timers, but their average earnings were 28 percent above department stores in January 1980, and are substantially more so in the unionized supermarkets. Automotive products and liquor stores, with fewer than 20 percent women employees, had the highest average earnings, fully 50 percent or more above those in department stores (Table 4).

Discrimination against women workers, in wages, job opportunities and promotions, is by no means a new phenomenon in retail trade, particularly in department stores. In the latter, it is surprising that so little has been done to achieve better standards through collective bargaining. Why does a cashier in a food store join a union while a cashier in a department store does not?[10]

Marianne Bossen, Professor of Economics at the University of Winnipeg and the author of a study on employment patterns and working conditions of Canadian department store workers, concluded that:

"...most women working there have an inferior position compared with men... in terms of lesser opportunities for development and use of talent, and in a consistent pattern of lower remuneration..." Along with her recommendations to employers and government, she had these succinct two words of advice to women department store employees: "Organize yourselves."[11]

This book is a case study of the efforts of men and women at Eaton's who had tried to do just that.

CHAPTER TWO

The Eaton Dynasty

IN JANUARY 1948, two hundred Eaton employees gathered in Toronto for their first union meeting. Their employer, John David Eaton, was the third generation to head the firm founded in 1869 by grandfather Timothy.

Two unusual and significant events had occurred the previous fall. In October, *New Liberty* magazine carried a rare interview with "Young Mr. Eaton," then 39, describing him as "Canada's richest man, 'boy president' of vast department store chain that's largest in Empire." Under a smiling, and indeed, very boyish picture was the caption: "John David fights unions with employee benefits, shorter hours."

A month later, Eaton's Toronto employees were astonished to receive an increase of $2.00 a week, the first *general* raise in their recollection. It was a unique departure from individual increases handed out with slips admonishing that they were "Private and Confidential." In fact, it smacked of the way things were done in labour negotiations. It also coincided with the recruitment of potential union activists nightly in the homes of Eaton employees.

There is no lack of books and articles eulogizing the merchandising genius of the Eatons, but very little is recorded about the curious mixture of parsimony and paternalism which characterized their employee relations.

In this, the *New Liberty* article was no exception. It gave an inventory of Eaton's operations, sprawling "like an octopus" over 200 communities and, through its huge mail order business, into virtually every Canadian home. It listed employee benefits, from employee discounts on purchases and low-cost life insurance, to a wide array of company-sponsored recreation facilities. It added fascinating tidbits about the Eaton family. The first car in Ontario, with licence Number One, was driven by Sir John Eaton. His son was taught to fly by war ace Billy Bishop and occasionally piloted his own plane on business. It was reported that John David's home on Dunvegan Road, which he termed "just ordinary," had cost several hundred thousand to decorate and equip with push-button controls in every room. It even cited the

Company's wage policy: 16-year-old males started at $16 a week, with an additional $1 per week for each year up to 25; females started at $18. Average pay for male salesclerks was $42, and for female clerks, $24, it was claimed.

One paragraph was devoted to John David Eaton's views on industrial relations:

> John David doesn't believe in unions. He says they are unnecessary for Eaton's. Except for a few employees like printers, Eaton's is not unionized although the unions have fought hard and long to get a foothold. Eaton's has fought just as hard to keep them out. In this they have followed the tactics of most non-union companies by anticipating the demands of their employees and giving them what they want before they ask for it. In general, today, employee-management relations at Eaton's are good, though pay is only average.[1]

Timothy Eaton, founder of the dynasty, was born in 1834 on a large farm in Ballymena, northern Ireland, the youngest of nine children. At 13, he was apprenticed as a draper to a cousin who had a large store and warehouse ten miles away. For a young boy it was a hard life. He worked 14 hours a day and longer on Saturdays, sometimes sleeping under a store counter. After seven years of this, he emigrated to Canada and ran a drygoods shop for several years with one of his brothers in St. Mary's, Ontario. At 35, Timothy decided to strike out on his own and, with his wife, moved to Toronto. He purchased a drygoods and haberdashery business for $6,500, and opened his shop at 176 Yonge Street on December 8, 1869.[2]

Toronto was then Canada's third largest city, populated by over 50,000, mainly of British origin, of whom a large proportion were wage earners. Timothy decided to woo the wives of this group of workers as his best prospective customers.

His advertisement in the *Globe* the day after the store opened startled his competitors by announcing a policy of cash only and fixed prices, an innovation in Toronto retailing.[3] Through his cash customers, wives of wage earners, he secured working capital to buy stock. Fixed prices ended the time-consuming haggling, leaving salesclerks free to concentrate on sales volume. The added promise of "Goods satisfactory or money refunded" soon attracted more customers.

At that time retail clerks worked as inhumanly long hours as Timothy. The shutters opened at 7:30 or 8:00 in the morning and didn't close until 10:00 at night. On Saturdays the store gaslights burned to midnight.[4] As proof of sound moral character (there was scarcely time for sin) the clerks were expected to appear in church on Sunday morning.

Tradesmen were more fortunate, usually working a 60-hour week. But *they* were far from content with their lot. They took up the agitation for shorter hours going on in Britain and the United States. In 1869, the year that Timothy Eaton opened shop, the Toronto Typographical Union asked its employers to reduce the work week from 60 to 58 hours, without success.

On April 14, 1872, a demonstration in support of the nine-hour day drew a crowd of 10,000 to Queen's Park in Toronto. Twenty-four printers' leaders were arrested and charged with "seditious conspiracy," but were soon released on bail. Shortly after, the Toronto Typographical Union won a 54-hour week. More important, before the year was out, legislation similar to the British Trade Union Act was brought in by the federal government which made union activity legal for the first time in Canada.[5]

Timothy Eaton could hardly have been unaware of the clamour for shorter hours by the husbands of his best customers. Perhaps it recalled his own youth when he toiled with no time for leisure and hardly enough for sleep. In any event, in 1875 he led the way among Toronto merchants by closing his store at 6:00 instead of 10:00 p.m., except on Saturdays. His 14 employees had the most favourable hours of any in the downtown area.[6]

By 1881 Toronto's population had doubled and Eaton's trade kept pace. In 1883 a move was made to much larger quarters on Yonge Street, north of Queen. Once renovations were complete, Eaton's boasted of being Toronto's first store with large display windows, electric lighting and — an elevator! The staff soon exceeded 150.

Agitation for shorter hours continued. In 1886 more than half a million workers in the United States took part in a wave of strikes to reduce the work week and end the arbitrary power of their bosses.[7] That same year, the newly-formed Trades & Labour Congress of Canada added its voice, when delegates to its convention in Toronto adopted the objective of a 9-hour day, 5½-day week.[8]

Timothy Eaton then made his next move in the Early Closing Campaign which he led among the merchants. He proposed closing at 2:00 instead of 6:00 p.m. on Saturday during July and August, and urged his women customers to use ballots placed in the store to vote in favour in order to "liberate your fellow creatures." Even in the face of a "no" vote by the majority who voiced an opinion, he went ahead, giving employees the half holiday on Saturday during the summer of 1886.[9]

Moreover, he proceeded to show his competitors that he could better them, despite shorter hours, by initiating Friday morning bargain sales, and by customer services such as rest rooms for women and restaurants in the store. In 1904, the daily closing hour was brought back another hour to 5:00 p.m.

The issue which led to the formation in the 1890's of the first retail clerks' unions in the U.S. was Early Closing; they campaigned for closing shops in the evenings and on Sundays.[10] There is no record of a clerks' union in Toronto during Timothy's time, nor would he have countenanced one in his store. He was adamant about his right to employ or discharge whom he pleased, a policy faithfully adhered to by his successors. One story of Timothy's time relates that "Employees could be instantly dismissed for gathering in groups while on the sales floor."[11]

Eaton's employed their own printers to produce their burgeoning mail order catalogue. On May 16, 1902, the Typographical Union "called out on strike two union printers employed by the T. Eaton Co. on account of the refusal of the firm to run their composing room under union rules. The men obeyed and the five pressmen employed by the firm also struck. Several bindery girls who were in the employ of the Company were asked to do the work of these men, and upon their refusal were discharged."[12]

Timothy Eaton was noted for acts of kindness and generosity to individuals, but as the staff grew to thousands — the opening of the Winnipeg store in 1905 added 700 more — the close relationships of the early days with employees, whom he liked to refer to as "fellow associates," became increasingly rare. It was ludicrous when his grandson, John David, in a letter to more than 10,000 employees at the time of the union vote 50 years later, addressed them as "friends and associates."

More and more Timothy had to rely on department managers to shoulder responsibility, including staffing. *Their* employee relations were apt to vary as widely as their personalities, but were always governed by the need to keep costs down in order to show as high a return as possible for their department.

Timothy Eaton died in 1907, leaving millions to his heirs, and a prediction which, though widely quoted, has yet to become a reality for retail clerks: "I may not live to see it, but some of you younger men, I hope and believe, will see the time when the world's business can be done in five working days, and better done than in six, and when Saturday will be given up entirely to recreation and Sunday to rest and worship."[13]

John Craig Eaton was 30 when he took over as president, already a millionaire many times over. As fun-loving as his fervently Methodist father was austere, he surrounded himself with the trappings of wealth: sports cars, stables, yachts, a private railway car, lavish trips abroad and *Ardwold*, the 50-room mansion near Casa Loma in Toronto where he and his wife, Flora, entertained.[14]

Despite the difference in life-style, he was in one respect very much his father's son, and Toronto was provided before long with another example of Eaton's intransigeant opposition to unions.

Much of the apparel sold in Eaton's stores and by mail order was manufactured in their clothing factory on Teraulay Street. Eaton's was the largest employer of Toronto's Jewish garment workers, who were then in the process of organizing to end the prevailing sweat-shop conditions in the industry. Although Eaton's was conceded to have better conditions than many others, grievances were not lacking.

Events leading up to the cloakmakers' strike in February, 1912, revolved around the management's demand that linings formerly sewn by hand were to be done by machine. Eaton's promised that no jobs would be lost, but the women wanted more than a verbal assurance. The spark which ignited the dispute was supplied when the men's tailors refused to work overtime to stockpile for the rush season and the company proceeded to lock them out. The cloakmakers walked out in sympathy, and "the public was supplied with a long list of grievances, ranging from low rates, and acceptance of graft by management personnel, to homework, unsanitary washrooms and child labour."[15]

In one account, the strikers claimed that when they applied for jobs, they were required to reveal how much they paid for rent and clothing and their living costs in general. This, it was charged, was to enable Eaton's to keep wages as low as possible.[16]

The major issue of the strike became recognition of the International Ladies Garment Workers Union of which most strikers were members. The Labour Council held rallies for their cause, placed Eaton's on the "unfair list" and castigated the press for not fairly reporting the labour side of the dispute. The Jewish community donated food and money. The ILGWU decided to hold its international convention in Toronto to lend support to the strikers.[17]

A committee of the mayor and other prominent community leaders tried to move "Jack" Eaton, to no avail. Finally, he privately agreed to settle, on the condition that no celebration mark his decision. A spontaneous celebration of jubilant supporters dashed this possibility. Eaton's next offer was to reinstate the strikers with no concessions, providing they "apologized!"[18] Fifteen weeks later, defeated, they returned to their jobs. Toronto garment workers did not recover from this setback until after World War I.

The cloakmakers' dispute also exposed Eaton's attitude to the press. When he lost an argument with Joseph Atkinson, publisher of the *Star*, over an editorial concerning the strike, Jack Eaton pulled his back-page ad from the paper.[19] Atkinson filled it with pictures until it was once again occupied by Eaton's ads.

Like his father, Sir John (he was knighted for his contribution to the war effort) could be magnanimous. To help recruitment, he had the company make up army pay to full salary for married employees, and to half for singles.

To mark Eaton's Golden Jubilee in 1919, Sir John announced to his 18,000 employees that henceforth they would have all day Saturday off in July and August; the 5½-day week would be in effect for the rest of the year, except prior to Christmas. With hours still more favourable than his competitors, Sir John said he was merely "carrying out my father's wishes."[20]

Three years later, after a brief illness, he died at the early age of 46, leaving Lady Eaton to raise their six children. She became a vocal and active director and later vice-president of the company, a matriarch in her relationship with female employees as well as with her children.

Despite her wide travels, Flora Eaton's perception of the world around her was surprisingly naïve. To friends she described Quebec's anti-conscriptionists in 1917 as "sheep without a shepherd . . . (or) even a sheep dog to keep them straight." Women's suffrage she regarded as a "nuisance," that "complicated the problem because it is not restricted to intelligent women." Returning from her villa in Italy in 1927, she made headlines in the *Star* with her praise of Mussolini for making the Italian people "happiest in the world" and for ending the sight of "beggars in the streets and around the cathedrals."[21]

Her views on employee relations, as expressed in her memoirs, were equally vapid. She wrote: "I believe I am right in saying that Mr. Timothy Eaton was the first man in Canada, or for that matter on this continent, to concern himself with the lot of the workers."[22] It goes without saying that Local 1000 was anathema to her.

In the interim, before one of Sir John's sons became old enough, the reins were taken up by a nephew and protégé of Timothy, Robert Young (R. Y.) Eaton, who, like his uncle, was austere, conservative and a shrewd businessman. During his 20 years as president, the Company went through two contrasting periods, great expansion in the Twenties, and severe retrenchment during the Depression. Stores had been bought or built in eight cities across Canada and in 1930 the College Street store opened in Toronto, specializing in quality home furnishings. It was dubbed "the white elephant" partly because of its white limestone exterior, but also because of its losses when customers continued to comparison shop between Eaton's and Simpsons in the downtown area. The added costs of expansion were accompanied by a severe drop in sales as the Depression deepened. Some customer services were cut, but Eaton employees bore the brunt with layoffs, wage cuts and short time. When the government appealed to the Company not to swell the ranks of the unemployed, about 800 were kept on but this meant more wage cuts for everyone.

In 1934, for the first and only time in its history, Eaton's was required to open its books to public scrutiny. In that year the Stevens parliamentary committee began its inquiry into price spreads and mass-buying practices of giants such as Canada Packers, Dominion Textiles, Eaton's and others, and the effect on small business, prices and wages. Committee auditors examined in detail the financial affairs of ten department stores. They found that in 1929 Eaton's accounted for 58 percent of all department store sales and did seven percent of Canadian retail business, a share unmatched by any company in the United States.

The Committee turned the spotlight on the mechanism by which the Eaton family, and the large shareholders of Simpsons and Hudson's Bay, amassed millions. The leading role was played by the department manager. His was the responsibility for running "his own little store." He was in charge of the buying, advertising, merchandising and staff. For this he was paid a good salary and, as well, an annual bonus commensurate with the profit his department showed for the year.

Centralized services such as rent and interest (Eaton's Realty Company made millions from property charges levied on its parent), maintenance, delivery charges and so on, were charged to the department at more than actual cost, a common practice known as "loading." Even the amount charged to the department for its purchases of stock was "loaded," or higher than cost. This accounting sleight-of-hand lowered the apparent profit margin of the department, justifying a higher mark-up to arrive at the retail price for the merchandise.[23] The Committee found that Eaton's mark-up of 47.9% was higher than any other stores examined with the exception of Dupuis Frères in Montreal.[24]

To protect his bonus, or even his job, the manager was compelled by the practice of "loading" to drive as hard a bargain as he could with his suppliers, and to keep payroll and other employee costs to a minimum. The incentive obviously worked in controlling wage costs. The Committee learned that 68.7 percent of Eaton's female salesclerks in Toronto made less than $13 a week (April, 1933). Across the street, 51 percent of Simpsons' women salesclerks received $12.50

(January, 1934) which was then the Ontario minimum wage for a 44-hour week.[25]

Worse than the low wages were the conditions employees had to endure under some managers. To testify to this, the International Ladies Garment Workers Union brought witnesses who had been employed in Eaton's garment factory before the Committee. The women told of having their work timed with a stopwatch, of being subjected to speedup that had them in tears or hysterical. They gave examples of how much piece work rates were slashed on certain garments, yet they were required to produce enough to make up the $12.50 minimum wage or be sent home for as much as a week. "...So I asked him how he thought a girl was going to live if she was going to be sent home every time she fell down on her money," testified an employee with 18 years' service. "He said it did not matter to him, none of his business and got very angry over it."

In the spring of 1934, women in one department formed a local of the ILGWU (although told by their manager they didn't need a union) and asked for better piece work rates on the dresses they made. The manager told them that if they did not decide to accept the going rates by 5:30, they were fired. They got passes to leave to consult their union official, who advised them to return to work and press for better rates without striking. As their department was already closed for the night at 5:30, they went back next morning, to find their time cards removed from the rack and themselves locked out. Eaton's had rid itself of another union group.[26]

When the *Telegram* reported that autumn that labour Day marchers "dipped their flags in sorrow as they passed Eaton's," R.Y. Eaton demanded a retraction. When this was refused, R.Y. henceforth would have no dealings with reporters.

In 1935, the Royal Commission (which assumed the earlier work of the Committee) on Price Spreads issued its report, a monumental contribution to the record of our Canadian corporate history.

Commissioner Stevens resigned from the cabinet to form the Reconstruction Party, but he had not heard the last word from department store workers. A letter received from a Winnipeg employee read in part:

> I am employed like thousands more here in Winnipeg in a large department store, & sorry to say that I have seen the day when its Executive body... fell away from its high and honorable place, by repudiating the sacred solemn pledges of those... now dead, until now we are suffering under greivances *(sic)*... brought about by greed and selfishness of the few. Just recently we had the yearly handout of Bonus to the managers, immediately followed by the short time to the sweated workers who are

> at their wits' end to know how to make ends meet... this morning I, an 8-hour day worker commenced at 7:30 a.m. and continued until 12:45 p.m. & got credit on my pay for 4 hours, this is a regular practice and no isolated case.[27]

John David Eaton, who served *his* apprenticeship with the company during the Thirties, recalled those years later in a somewhat different light: "Nobody thought about money in those days because they never saw any. You could take your girl to a supper dance at the hotel for $10, and that included the bottle and a room for you and your friends to drink it in. I'm glad I grew up then. It was a good time for everybody. People learned what it means to work."[28] How true! One could work a whole week for Eaton's and earn little more than the price of a night's outing!

By the time John David assumed the presidency in 1942, the staff numbered more than 30,000. His grandfather's paternalism was now dispensed by the Welfare Office, which assisted employees with health or other personal problems, usually on a department manager's recommendation. As in Timothy's time, such assistance was not to be considered a right, but a privilege earned by loyalty to the Company.

The personal touch evaporated even further in 1950. After Local 1000 applied for certification, John David retained professionals to deal with the thousands of his employees who had joined the union.

As Eaton's position in the retail field declined in the Sixties, John David Eaton was reported to be under heavy pressure from financial institutions to institute modern decision-making criteria in company policies. When, in failing health, he decided to retire early in 1969, his empire was estimated at $400 million.[29]

At that time, John David Eaton was asked if he had ever used his influence to suppress newspaper stories. Instead of answering directly, he countered: "Wouldn't you?" There were all sorts of things from their private lives that people wouldn't want to see in the paper![30]

Following 1969, a period of re-organization took place in which hundreds of long-service managers were eased into other jobs or retirement to make way for younger men recruited from universities or from competitors. Top executive posts, held for the first time by other than the Eaton family, changed hands several times in a number of management shuffles. However, by 1977 a fourth generation of Eatons was in command. Two of John David's four sons, Fredrik Stephan and John Craig II, became president and chairman of the board respectively. The day the Eaton Centre opened, Fredrik added a homey touch of good public relations by standing at the entrance to shake hands with customers.

The Eaton brothers are included in the group referred to by Peter Newman as the "New Boys" in *The Canadian Establishment.* He describes them as "more aware than their predecessors of the social environment in which they operate, international in their outlook, relentless in their dealings, unsentimental and tough."[31]

From his office on the twentieth floor of the tower adjoining the Centre, Fredrik Eaton is reported to be more friendly and open (without revealing matters financial) with the press than his predecessors. On the subject of unions, one article reports: "Management says that they are still 'welcome to try.'"[32]

CHAPTER THREE

Why Toronto?

IN THE YEARS following its formation in 1940, the Canadian Congress of Labour and its affiliates made great strides in building membership in the new industrial unions. This expansion, however, was not without its growing pains, and Congress officers were soon under pressures from two sources.

Contributions from affiliates to the CCL's Special Organizing Fund proved quite inadequate to maintain the field staff across the country. Annual organizing expenses were running three to five times more than receipts, and had to be met from general revenue. This provided an inducement for the CCL to issue charters directly to locals organized by its staff, as the per capita tax in such cases was more than the few cents per member paid by the national and international unions.

On the other hand, when the list of newly-chartered CCL locals came before the annual conventions, sparks flew. Spokesmen for international unions protested being asked to help CCL locals whose members belonged within the jurisdiction of an established union.

It may have been that both these pressures were at work when, in 1945, the Congress extended an invitation to the CIO's Retail, Wholesale and Department Store Union to organize in Canada. Making inroads into the large and unorganized retail and wholesale field called for resources beyond the Special Organizing Fund. Moreover, the entry of RWDSU into Canada would avoid inter-union squabbles, since distribution workers, other than those in trucking and railways, were clearly within its jurisdiction. At least, that was the theory!

Following a meeting between Pat Conroy, the CCL's director of organization, Tommy MacLachlan, a staff member who had previously organized a number of locals of retail employees, and Sam Wolchok, RWDSU international president, Wolchok agreed to establish a Canadian headquarters. Existing locals including employees of dairies, bakeries and the Dominion Store food chain, were to be transferred from the Congress to RWDSU to provide an initial operating base.

That same year, Norman Twist of RWDSU's St. Louis staff was appointed Canadian director, with MacLachlan as assistant, and an office was opened at 1207 Bay Street in Toronto, the building occupied by the national headquarters of the Steelworkers, Packinghouse Workers and some other CIO-CCL unions.

Before long, Twist was turning his attention to organizing department stores which, because of the numbers employed, held out the best hope for union growth on a large scale. Although under no illusion about the difficulties of organizing a department store, he knew that they had been overcome elsewhere. Such famous stores as Macy's, Gimbels, Wanamakers and others had collective agreements with his union in the United States. He also fully realized, as did the Congress, that RWDSU could not go it alone, and would need financial and other assistance from the larger unions in Canada. Fortunately, Twist was able to discuss his problems almost daily with men of broad vision like Charlie Millard and Fred Dowling, Canadian directors of the Steelworkers and Packinghouse unions, from whom he received encouraging promises of support.

The Robert Simpson Co. Limited, across Queen Street from Eaton's in Toronto, employed many thousands in their store and mail order whose wages and working conditions were reported to be inferior to Eaton's. However, organizing prospects there were bleak because of the failure of a campaign begun in 1943 by the AFL Retail Clerks.

Several of the most active union members had been fired, and much time and effort was spent seeking their reinstatement. Another AFL union, the Building Service Employees, siphoned off blue collar maintenance men, caretakers and elevator operators but it too failed to obtain certification. After persisting for three years without securing a majority and in the face of employee turnover claimed to exceed 50 percent, Local 540 of the Retail Clerks Association disbanded in 1946.[1]

There was the option of taking advantage of Saskatchewan's labour legislation, the most favourable in Canada, which had been introduced by the CCF government. Eaton's had stores in Regina, Moose Jaw and Saskatoon. There also was the alternative of starting in a city with a high proportion of unionized industrial workers, such as Hamilton or Windsor, Ontario, who could be counted on to support the store clerks. Would it not be easier to obtain a union majority in a store or branch employing a relatively small staff? But what then? The task of concluding an agreement might be more difficult in a branch of a large company whose personnel policies were set by head office. In industrial relations, it is rarely easy for the tail to wag the dog. (Bank employees were to learn this lesson many years later.)

Eaton's Toronto staff included a strong mix of blue-collar workers and white-collar salesclerks: a large caretaking and maintenance group; elevator operators and restaurant workers; delivery and warehouse employees; and a wide variety in workshops employing various skills. While Mail Order was essentially a selling counterpart of the stores, the assembly-line nature of its clerical and shipping functions should make its employees more receptive to the idea of a union than those working behind a store counter. Therefore, in an industrial-type union embracing all occupations, the militance of blue-collar workers should offset the timidity of the salesclerks.

Also significant was the list the RWDSU had acquired of several hundred Toronto employees of Eaton's who were said to be interested in organizing a union, an invaluable asset in starting a campaign.

Pleasing the customer has always been more important to the retailer than keeping employees happy. Where a high percentage of the customers came from union families, this could work to the advantage of a union by bringing consumer pressure to bear. In this regard, the officers of the Toronto Labour Council were aggressive and efficient, and could be counted upon to mobilize rank and file support among the CIO-CCL locals in the city.

Early in 1947, Norman Twist began discussions with Congress president A. R. Mosher and top officers of affiliated unions to enlist their support. Eventually a memorandum outlining the potential and plans for the Eaton Drive was prepared and discussed at a meeting of the Congress Executive. As a result, they appointed a Department Store Organizing Committee (DSOC-CCL) and set up a special fund for contributions.

Making good their offer of support, Fred Dowling and Charlie Millard agreed to act as chairman and vice-chairman respectively of the DSOC-CCL. Pat Conroy, secretary-treasurer of the Congress, agreed to act in this same capacity for the Committee. Other leaders of major unions who served on the Committee were:

George Burt	Canadian director	United Automobile Workers
J. E. McGuire	Secretary-treasurer	Canadian Brotherhood of Railway Employees & Other Transport Workers
Sol Spivak	Manager, Toronto Joint Board	Amalgamated Clothing Workers
Sam Baron	Canadian director	Textile Workers Union of America
Silby Barrett	Canadian director	District 50, United Mine Workers

As RWDSU director, Norman Twist was automatically a member, and when he returned to the United States in 1949, T.B. MacLachlan replaced him on the Committee.

CHAPTER FOUR

The Team

WHAT DOES IT take to make a good union organizer? While there is really no stereotype, and performance varies widely depending on the individual, two or three attributes are essential.

Above all, an organizer must be able to communicate: the primary function of the job is to persuade workers to join and become active in a union. As well as being able to put one's prospective members at ease, it is important to win their trust and respect. It is not enough to be armed intellectually with all the reasons for forming a union; the organizer must be able to impart them to members, and to inspire as many as possible to assist in signing up their co-workers.

In addition there are occasions when an organizer will have to address informal groups or business meetings where a working knowledge of the rules of order is required. All skills come with practice, but it is best to have developed them earlier through participation in other organizations.

The organizer's day-to-day work is generally unsupervised. This calls for a realistic approach to planning work. The art of delegating to others is neglected at the risk of failure and early exhaustion. Hours of work are always irregular, and often excessive; strained domestic relationships are all too common.

Full-time union work demands a greater degree of commitment to the job than most occupations. In its fullest sense, commitment goes beyond the periodic rounds of bargaining for higher pay and other economic gains. It is nurtured by a belief in the longer-range goals of the labour movement: the attainment of industrial democracy and a more equitable society generally. The depth of this commitment will be an important factor in determining how long an organizer lasts in full-time union work.

In 1946, when the search began for a team to undertake the Eaton campaign, it was no easy task to find organizers not already employed by other unions. There was the added qualification that those selected be able to relate to white-collar workers.

Writing of the formative years of the Canadian Congress of Labour in the Forties, Professor H. A. Logan observed: "A problem of the

Congress... that it has not altogether overcome is to find organizers capable of the great task it has undertaken. Industries have had to be attacked in which there was no tradition or knowledge of organization... by outsiders with experience only of other industries or by inexperienced insiders fresh from the work bench. Both types have been used as organizers and not always with good results."[1]

Later on, local union officers were a source of organizers, but there had hardly been time for these to develop. Then, there was the problem that if they undertook union work without seniority reinstatement clauses in their contracts, and proved unsuitable, they might not be rehired or might be blacklisted in their industry.

With this brief indication of the dilemmas faced by the Retail, Wholesale and Department Store Union, let's see how Norman Twist made out.

During the CCL's 1946 convention in Toronto, Murray Cotterill, Steelworkers' public relations director, introduced me to Norm Twist over dinner. We talked about Norm's plans for organizing Eaton's and he inquired if I would be interested in heading the campaign. This took me quite by surprise, as my experience in organizing white-collar workers was very limited. I suppose it was not easy to find anyone, even with a slight acquaintance with the special problems posed by white-collar employees, who could be persuaded (or was foolhardy enough!) to agree to direct an undertaking of that magnitude. I returned to Vancouver, promising to think it over.

My organizational training had been acquired in the Co-operative Commonwealth Youth Movement during the Thirties. My contact with unions started as secretary of the CCF Trade Union Committee in Ontario, of which my friend, Fred Dowling, was chairman. We rallied whatever help we could for the new CIO unions in leaflet distributions or during strikes. I became convinced that a solid base of organized workers was a prerequisite to the success of a socialist political party.

In 1940, the year the CCL was founded, Charlie Millard offered me my first full-time union job. Bank clerks had been asking him for help in forming a union. The Office and Professional Workers Organizing Committee (OPWOC) was created for this task, with Millard as chairman and myself as secretary.

Bursting with grievances and given the opportunity, locals of bank clerks in Toronto, Ottawa and Montreal had a meteoric rise in 1941-42 to almost 900 members. Bank employees joined OPWOC by correspondence in Vancouver and other cities. The organization collapsed almost as rapidly when a three-week strike in early 1942 by Banque

Canadienne Nationale employees in Montreal was lost when the management obdurately refused to meet with the union.[2]

My next assignment was the contest between the Steelworkers and Machinists to obtain recognition at the John Inglis munitions plant in Toronto, with 17,000 workers, about half of them female. As well, I helped to organize the large office staff, and when Local 2900, USWA, won the vote, worked with their committee on contract proposals and assisted in negotiating their first office agreement.

During several wintry months I worked with a group of office employees at Algoma Steel in Sault Ste. Marie to sign up a majority into the OPWOC. We succeeded, but at the time there was neither the statutory obligation on the employer to bargain, nor were these workers militant enough to strike for recognition.

In May 1943, I was off to the Steelworkers' Vancouver office with the less strenuous assignment of starting a monthly tabloid for our B.C. membership, to provide an alternative to the policies advocated by the Labour Progressive Party, the wartime name used by the Communists whose party was illegal. By 1947, an end to the domination of the B.C. labour movement by the LPP was in sight.

Charlie Millard had agreed to lend me to the Eaton Drive, maintaining my salary as part of the Steelworkers' contribution. Although I had close friends in Vancouver, particularly Bert and Mary Gargrave, at 34 I was not ready to settle down, and the Eaton campaign presented an intriguing challenge. I agreed to report for work in Toronto that August.

At the CCL's first summer school at Lake Couchiching in Ontario, I met Lynn Williams and his new bride, Audrey. Lynn was the second organizer hired for the Eaton Drive, on the recommendation of Howard Conquergood, educational director for the Steelworkers and later for the Congress.

Although only 23, Lynn was already a veteran in community activity, having worked as a volunteer under Howard Conquergood at the Hamilton YMCA during his senior high and McMaster University years. His "Y" work took him into the Hamilton Mountain area where he came to know many union and CCF members. At 16 he worked for the CCF in his first election campaign. Years later he ran unsuccessfully as a candidate in West York in Toronto. Lynn's conviction that society needed a radical change "was moulded in my home, in my reaction and response to my father's experience in the Depression as the minister of a church with a working-class congregation."

In 1943, Conquergood left the "Y" to work for the Steelworkers, and Lynn spent a year in the navy. But this was not the end of their association. During the Stelco strike in 1946, Lynn showed up again to volunteer assistance to his friend. By then he had made up his mind to work in the labour movement and, when Norm Twist offered him the opportunity, he accepted "without any hesitation whatsoever."

Our first chore was to find a union office conveniently located for Eaton employees who worked in buildings that sprawled over the area between College and Queen streets. Lynn and I combed the district and early in September were fortunate in finding a tiny office at 572 Bay Street near Dundas, a few minutes' walk from Eaton's factory and mail order buildings and central to all three stores.

The two-storey building was owned by Al Good, and appropriately, the pub which occupied the ground floor was called "A Good House." One entrance from the street into the pub also led upstairs to a number of offices, including ours, an excellent arrangement for employees who might not wish to be seen coming to the union office. Local 1000 had the home it was to occupy for the next five years. As other tenants moved, we gradually took over the whole floor.

Shortly afterwards the third member of our team arrived, sent by the International Office of RWDSU on a temporary basis. This was Angus Sumner, then also in his early 20's. The son of a Florida district attorney, Gus had quit his law studies to become active in left-wing activities in the southern States. In 1947 he was working for RWDSU in New Orleans. Gus was a willing worker with an engaging personality, even if at times our political arguments became heated and we had trouble understanding his southern drawl.

Marjorie Gow, a diminutive elf with several years' union work behind her, was next to join us. She also had been involved in the Stelco strike, handling union publicity, and had left to rest on her sister's farm in Haney, B.C. Norman Twist contacted her there and hired her to do publicity for the Eaton Drive.

Her mother had been left a widow in Prince Albert, Saskatchewan, when Marjorie was a year old, with three other children to raise, "without widows' allowance, no social services, no nothing in those days." Eventually, the family moved to Vancouver where Marjorie finished high school.

Her first job, doubling as a store clerk and waitress in a combination shop and night club, was so strenuous and demeaning that she took up stenography. At the outbreak of World War II, she was working at the Shaughnessy Hospital in Vancouver, ostensibly as a stenographer, "but in reality interviewing applicants — or their widows — about war pension claims (from WWI) and preparing a précis on each case for hearings before the Canadian Pension Commission's travelling tribunal."

In 1943 when she saw history repeat itself in the way discharged veterans were being treated, she took a leave of absence in Toronto, during which she decided "to get into some work which might more directly help people to stand up for their rights." At the suggestion of a friend, she contacted Sedgewick at the Steelworkers' national office, and spent the next three years working for that union in Toronto and Hamilton.

During the preliminary discussions on the Eaton campaign, it had been suggested that at least seven organizers would be required, and that it would take about 18 months to reach the application for certification stage, after which, with the start of dues collections, the organization would become self-sufficient. We never did have seven full-time staff, and the estimate of the duration proved several years short. However, after the first few months, realizing the magnitude of the undertaking, Lynn and I were clamouring for more help. In January 1948, Wally Ross, another protégé of Howard Conquergood, was added to our staff.

Wally had attended Trinity College School in Port Hope, near Picton, Ontario, where he was born, and later the University of Toronto, one year in applied sciences, and two in maths and physics at Trinity College. He recalls that his interest in academic courses was secondary to swimming, rowing, football and skiing.

While employed in the early Forties as an instrument technician at Research Enterprises, a Toronto war plant, Wally had acquired his first union experience as recording secretary of Local 1039, United Steelworkers. Through the influence of Conquergood and men he met in the local union, he became active in the CCF. In various capacities, he participated in election campaigns for Ford Brand, Eamon Park and Andrew Brewin.

After leaving the war plant, Wally sold insurance for Confederation Life for several years. At the time he joined the RWDSU staff, he was 28, married, with a year-old son.

Next to our office was Angelo's restaurant, run by the Fazzari brothers, where we ate our evening meal, five nights a week, before taking off to make our first call on an Eaton employee by 7:00 p.m. Considering the highly-spiced pasta consumed nightly, it is a wonder that we did not all develop ulcers. These meal hours were spent in shop talk or political arguments, relieved by pranks Gus and Wally played on the waitresses. One time Wally, who carried a spare for his artificial eye, deposited it in his soup and summoned the waitress to remove the foreign object!

Olive Richardson, whom I hired to manage our office, added wit and beauty to our group. Her family had inherited strong labour convictions, as well as the gift of musical talent, from their Welsh forebears. With others in the East York Workers' Association, during the Depression, the Richardsons had often helped to prevent evictions, carrying furniture back into a house when it was put on the street.

At 13, Olive joined the CCYM and played an active part at both local and provincial levels. With her friend George Luscombe and her sister, Gwen, they produced an annual musical review of left-wing skits and songs.

When she came to work with us at 22, Olive already had six years' office experience, including several years as secretary to the manager of Hudson's Bay buying offices in Toronto, which gave her an insight into the department store business. Our office was run efficiently and, as important in a union campaign, cheerfully. Members who dropped in were made welcome and put at ease. By 1950, Olive's ability was given wider scope and she was added to the organizing team.

At the end of 1948, Gus returned to the United States, and we began to look for a replacement. Ernest Arnold was hired the following April. Like Wally, his union experience had been gained in wartime, in the machine shop of DeHavilland Aircraft at Malton. In 1942 the United Automobile Workers were trying to oust a company union there, and Ernie became active in the UAW. But he also took issue with the "non-partisan" political stance of LPP members in the UAW, and helped to build support for the CCF in the plant.

On the farm where he grew up near the town of Ivy, Ontario, Ernie recalls the "little red school house," the chores to be done morning and night, and then a four-mile walk into Barrie to attend high school and later to take a business course. His one ambition after finishing his education was to find a job with *shorter hours*. However, finding any job proved an elusive goal. In the late Thirties, he applied for a job at Eaton's where he knew the employment manager, but his friend told him, "Eaton's is no place for you, Ernie. You'd be wiser to go back to the farm."

Layoffs at DeHavilland came with the War's end, and Ernie worked at a variety of jobs, including a short spell in Simpsons' Mail Order. In his spare time he worked for the CCF in Toronto's East End. Going from door to door for subscriptions to the paper or memberships taught him a great deal about human nature. In April 1949, when he came to work with us, Ernie was 39, married, with three children, which put him at the top of our list for family responsibilities.

There were two peak periods of activity when our staff almost doubled on a temporary basis: prior to applying for certification in 1950 and again before the vote in 1951. Alex Gilbert and Mrs. Mae Coulston, who both started in the summer of 1950, stayed on until after the vote, and came to be a part of our regular team.

Alex Gilbert grew up in the area now known as Kensington when it was the heart of Toronto's Jewish community and its garment workers' unions. Outside of school hours, his spare time was spent adding to the family income, selling papers on the street-corner, working weekends in a garage and as pinboy in a bowling alley, and summer holidays in a can-making factory.

After obtaining a motor mechanic's certificate, Alex could not find work in his trade and, in 1931, took a job in the radio manufacturing plant of Rogers Majestic. There he helped to organize a local of the All-Canadian Congress of Labour, but "as soon as the warehouse was full of radios, everyone was laid off, and when I got called back, a company union had been formed." An avid reader, he was a self-educated democratic socialist when I first met Alex in the CCYM.

His first assignment for us in 1950 was lining up people for leaflet distributions several times a week, "a chore I really hated, but which had to be done." And, typically of Alex, it was well done.

Mae Coulston was among the first Eaton employees I called on after we began home visits. She asked intelligent questions about the general objectives and approach of the union, agreed to act on the organizing committee, provided we gained sufficient support, and volunteered names of others whom we could contact. Having been the cashier in the College Street Employees' Cafeteria for quite some years, she was on friendly terms with almost everyone.

Although approaching retirement, Mrs. Coulston was an outspoken and active member of Local 1000 right from the first meeting. In the summer of 1950, after she had retired from Eaton's, she agreed to work as a part-time organizer. Mrs. C, as we affectionately called her, was highly regarded by her former colleagues and used her soft Scottish brogue to good advantage. We kept in touch until her death in 1966, but not until I started this memoir, and asked her son about her background, did I learn how fascinating it had been.

"Born 1889 at Kilmarnock, Ayrshire, Scotland. Early interests: trying to get out of Scotland. After trying shopwork, housework, factory work, at the age of 19 she indentured herself to a family in New Brunswick. When their advance for the fare to Canada was repaid, she moved to Winnipeg and married in 1914. Papa was American, very fond of poker. Shortly after I appeared in mid-1915, Papa got killed in a street accident... God knows how, as there must have been about one car in Winnipeg then. Mother went back to work. At the end of the War we went to Scotland, but in a couple of years she got restless, returned to Canada, married again and moved (illegally) to Detroit where I joined her in 1925. That day she met me at the Windsor-Detroit ferry, strode through customs pushing me ahead, and said she had been shopping in Windsor. Resolute little woman! From there we moved to Toronto in 1931.

"Her interest in the union at Eaton's probably came from working there at low pay from about 1932 on, as well as from her mother, who, a generation earlier, had been active in forming the Scottish Wholesale Co-operative Society.

"Mother had held some very good jobs. She managed the dining room of a classy hotel in the Scottish Highlands, and a private dining club in Detroit. She could have run both the (Employees') Cafeteria and the College Street Round Room at Eaton's."

I have never worked with a group who possessed so much commitment. In my work experience, by no means confined to labour unions, most organizations encounter staff problems arising from drinking. Also, if union organizers become personally entangled with members in the local union, it often leads to family difficulties that rebound on the organizing effort. Neither problem presented itself with our group: they were self-disciplined.

We were fortunate in having tolerant and understanding wives and friends who, patiently or otherwise, put up with having very little of our time.

No orders were handed down from above. Decisions about our work plans were made at staff meetings and disagreements were talked out until there was some consensus.

The intangible glue which prevented our team from becoming unstuck was a good sense of humour. Even in our most disheartening moments, someone would see the droll or absurd side of the situation and we would soon be sharing a laugh over our predicament.

It is obvious that, despite diverse backgrounds, we had all come to share the same political philosophy and, in my opinion, that explains the dedication we felt for our work. We believed that unions had a vital role to play in the democratic achievement of social and economic change in our society.

Eaton's impugned other motives. In the vote campaign, to drive a wedge between the members and staff of Local 1000, they told employees, "You can turn your future over to these professional organizers whose main interest in you is what you mean in terms of dues and power — or you can retain your future in your own hands . . ."[3] They also wondered what we would do with $200,000 a year in union dues. "Local 1000 already has a staff of seven. If they average about $75 a week, the annual salary bill is running around $25,000.... Let's double it to be on the safe side.... What do they propose doing with the rest of the potential $200,000...?"[4]

Crass statements from spokesmen of a multi-millionaire family, whose fortune had been amassed through low wages and high mark-ups! Furthermore, they were misleading. At no time did Local 10000 have seven organizers "averaging" $75 a week. When the drive began, organizers received $50 a week which had increased to $60 at the time of the vote; my differential for directing the campaign was an extra $10 per week. On an hourly basis, we earned less than most Eaton employees.

After the Eaton Drive, the staff continued to make distinguished contributions in the field of labour and politics. (Appendix C). Lynn Williams is now international secretary of the United Steelworkers of America, the first Canadian to be elected as an international officer. He describes the Eaton Drive as "the fundamental occupational and, in many ways, political and ideological experience of my life. While my general sense of social direction was already established, it was during the Eaton Drive that these ideas were tested and given substance."

"The work experience of the Eaton Drive has been the basis for everything I have done since. It was there that I learned what union work really involved," Lynn remembers. "Nothing else I know requires such an unusual mix of imagination, inspiration and practical understanding. Hardly a day goes by in which I do not reach back to the associations and experiences of that campaign as a prime source of all three."

CHAPTER FIVE

Laying the Foundation

IN SEPTEMBER 1947, when we began visits to the homes of Eaton employees, we had discussed how best to allay the fears which we knew would be the biggest obstacle to be overcome. We decided to assure everyone whom we visited that there would be no overt union activity until at least 200 Eaton employees, representing all main divisions, had indicated a willingness to help with the campaign. Until such time, we would not ask anyone to sign a membership card, nor would we hold any meetings.

Where the initial list of contacts came from is not certain, but almost without exception it led us to people with more than a passive interest in seeing Eaton's unionized. From them we secured more leads in their own or other departments. A file card system for prospects was started, addresses looked up in the city directory, and the cards area-coded for making up visiting routes. We also obtained valuable information about wages and working conditions and identified grievances so that Marjorie Gow could begin work on union publicity material.

Every evening, from Monday to Friday, we set off, each with seven or eight prospects to visit. We were lucky to find three at home, but three meant an evening well spent as most of these initial contacts lasted an hour, more or less, by the time we put people at ease and got them talking about conditions at work. None of us had a car then, and Lynn recalls "all the careful planning to make the best use of streetcars and buses" as we made up routes. Even then, Toronto and suburbs covered an immense territory.

As anticipated, the first reaction of most was a mixture of caution and fear. As we chatted, this became tempered by the obvious desire for a better standard of living. It was apparent from the homes of these workers, or the rented rooms they lived in, that they were having a struggle to make ends meet. There weren't many like the belligerent driver who practically threw Lynn off his doorstep shouting that higher wages would only "bring on another Depression."

Some visits turned out to be hilarious, like the one Lynn and I paid to a warehouse employee, a "key" contact, but timorous due to approaching retirement. While Lynn talked to him, I chatted with his wife.

Before leaving we had to admire the tricks their dog could perform, culminating in a game of the dog chasing him around their dining-room table. Once out the door, we ran down the street before giving way to howls of laughter. That Christmas we bought his dog a toy bone, but it was a long time before our warehouseman joined the union.

Norm Twist had told us how fascinating it was to organize a department store. It was like having dozens of businesses under one roof. We soon found this out as Lynn and I walked around the stores, familiarizing ourselves with departments and merchandise, and locating them on floor maps. Although most space was given over to apparel and home furnishings, all three stores had a multitude of other departments, selling everything from candy to cameras. Interspersed with the merchandise departments were service facilities which made it hard for small merchants to compete: restaurants, travel bureau, post office, beauty salon, shoe repair, rest rooms, wedding bureau, lending library, dry cleaning, budget plan offices (credit cards were still to come), to name but a few.

As we pieced together the scope of the departments, as well as the mail order, factory and other operations to which we did not have access and had to rely on employee information, our objective of 200 activists appeared to be a bare minimum.

To obtain certification, a union needed a majority of employees in the bargaining unit as members (Chapter 6). Thus, accurate information as to the number of employees, department by department, was essential. Due to high turnover and seasonal fluctuation, keeping employment data up to date through stewards was a continuous exercise throughout the campaign. Eventually, we were able to arrive at approximate figures for all main divisions, as follows:

	Number of employees as estimated by the union
Stores:	
Main	4,000
Annex	700
College	1,350
including, for all stores:	
Restaurant workers	900
Caretakers	360
Elevator operators	140
Maintenance trades	210
Delivery-Dispatch (all depots)	800
Warehouse	220

Mail Order	1,900	
Factory	1,000	
General and Administrative offices	1,000	12,580
Non-regular employees considered to be ineligible for bargaining unit (estimated):		4,000

Week by week throughout the fall, the list of potential members for the organizing committee of 200 grew. We kept in touch with all of them regularly by phone and, as well, Marjorie mailed a weekly bulletin to their homes dealing with aspects of union organization.

At the same time we gathered ammunition for publicity from problems and grievances as well as examples of favouritism and arbitrary treatment by some managers. It became apparent that the common denominator propelling Eaton employees toward collective action through a union was bargain basement wages and a pay policy that discriminated by age, sex and marital status.

Eaton's had heard grumbling over wages throughout their corporate history, even if their commissioned chroniclers had failed to report it. Now it had undoubtedly reached their ears that once again a union was at the door. And, with reports of wage gains by unions in other industries, might not Eaton employees forsake their practice of touching the left toe of Timothy's statue "just for luck" and join the union instead?

In November 1947 the Company reacted. Employees received the first *general* increase in their memory: $2 a week. Previously, individuals were notified of a raise by a white slip marked "Private and Confidential" in their pay envelope, when and if their department manager felt they merited one.

Immediately we were on the phone to our contacts to see what effect the increase was having, as we knew an organizing campaign could be nipped in the bud by such management tactics. To our relief, we found "it would take a lot more than $2 to satisfy Eaton employees."

By mid-December we had our network of more than 200 and were planning the first organizational meeting and the first general leaflet distribution for Monday, January 12, 1948.

Much effort went into finding a suitable meeting place. We finally settled on the Wakunda Community Centre, an ivy-covered building on Bloor Street, not far east of Yonge, formerly a private mansion. Folding doors enabled half the meeting hall to be closed off between what once had been the living room and dining areas. In case of a poor turnout, this would be advantageous. We also decided to hold three meetings: an early one in the evening for store employees; followed by one for delivery and warehouse workers, and an after work meeting the next day for mail order and factory employees.

Invitations were mailed out, to serve as admission to the meetings, and were followed up by phone. On January 10 we invited the press and radio stations to a news conference at our office to announce the Eaton Drive. Reporters took copious notes, but not a word appeared in the three daily papers. There was a brief mention on radio newscasts — Eaton's did not advertise on the air.

January 12 would test the effectiveness of our work to that point. How many would attend? To our surprise and gratification, it was not necessary to close the folding doors at the Wakunda Centre.

Norman Twist spoke to the meetings as Canadian director of the Retail, Wholesale and Department Store Union. Self-assured, and dressed impeccably but not flamboyantly, Norm was equally at ease talking to teamsters or white-collar workers. He described the gains, monetary and otherwise, made by department store employees through their union in the United States. It was low-key, but inspired confidence, matching the subdued atmosphere of the meeting. The men and women present were more interested in looking around to see who else was there than in participating in the question period. But they were serious. When they were invited to sign membership application cards at the conclusion of the meetings, we had the first 176 members of Local 1000. It was a most exhilarating experience for our small staff, vindicating our judgments made in hundreds of home calls the past autumn. The men and women we had talked with not only sounded sincere, *they were sincere*. Fred Dowling, chairman of the Department Store Organizing Committee, CCL, was able to report that "The meetings exceeded expectations in attendance. All present signed application cards and took a quantity to enroll others." The Eaton Drive was off to a good start.

CHAPTER SIX

The Law Says...

LABOUR RELATIONS LEGISLATION, designed to protect the right of workers to organize for collective bargaining, has been the subject of controversy ever since the first union was formed in Canada. The initial hurdle was surmounted in 1872 when a federal law exempted unions from being liable, through their mere existence, to charges of criminal conspiracy in restraint of trade. Thereafter, a worker could participate in a union, and even go on strike, without the risk of being thrown in jail.

However, as early unionists soon found out, there was no law to protect them, while they sought to organize, from espionage or physical violence by hired agents of employers, or from imported strike-breakers and police brutality during a strike. Governments, federal and provincial, saw their role as one of preventing industrial conflict and, if it did erupt, of helping the employers to settle the dispute with every means possible. While this accommodated the employers' interests, it did little to encourage the development of unions as equal partners in the industrial process.

Through political action, labour had some success in procuring legislation to set minimum wage standards, paid vacations and holidays, factory acts, workmen's compensation for accidents, and so forth. But not until the country was well into World War II was there legislation to compel an employer to bargain with a union once it represented a majority of his employees. In industry after industry, union recognition was won only after long, bitter and costly strikes — or lost when the employer's ability to hold out surpassed that of the strikers.

In an attempt to avoid interruption of the war effort, and using its emergency powers to override provincial jurisdiction in labour matters, Mackenzie King's government issued guidelines on June 19, 1942 for employer-employee relations during the War. Order-in-Council P.C. 2685 contained the pious wish that employers *should* recognize and bargain with unions of their employees' choice, a suggestion which many proceeded to ignore. (In my own experience the Montreal bank strike in 1940 was a case in point.) Unions were also incensed that employee associations, often sponsored by the employer to fend off a legitimate union, were given equal status under P.C. 2685.

Not until February 17, 1944, almost ten years after the Wagner Act was passed in the United States, did the Canadian government pay more than lip service to collective bargaining. As of that date, another wartime Order-in-Council, P.C. 1003, was issued. It prohibited certain unfair practices by employer or union. A Wartime Labour Relations Board was established with power to certify bargaining representatives of the majority of employees. Government conciliation officers were to be made available should the parties be unable to conclude a collective agreement.

This Order applied to all establishments designated as essential to the war effort. The provinces were expected to adopt similar measures and set up provincial boards. Ontario did so on April 6, 1944. The provisions of P.C. 1003 were adopted and the Ontario Labour Relations Board was established. With minor amendments, this legislation continued in force until April 1948, when it was replaced with a provincial Labour Relations Act, which set out the powers of the OLRB in greater detail.[1]

By this time Local 1000's campaign at Eaton's was out in the open. From the first meeting in January 1948, the committee of local union activists had grown to more than 350. Relatively, this group was exposed to much less risk in attempting union organization than the majority of Canadian workers who preceded them. For the core of young veterans on the Committee, to be fired for union activity was almost trivial compared to their experiences in the War said to have been fought for democracy.

It was quite another matter for the Local 1000 Committee to convince their co-workers that the law was now on their side. The greatest deterrent in signing up members was fear, ranging from being passed over for promotion to being discharged on some other pretext for joining the union. The relevant provisions of the law were quoted in one of the first union leaflets distributed at Eaton's, and were repeated time and again during the campaign. The prohibitions stated that no employer, or person acting on his behalf, should:

a) refuse to employ any person because the person is a member of a trade union . . .

b) impose any condition in the contract of employment seeking to restrain an employee from exercising his rights . . .

c) seek by intimidation, by dismissal, or any other kind of threat, by the imposition of a pecuniary or other penalty, or by any other means whatsoever, to compel an employee to abstain from becoming or

> continuing to be a member or officer or representative of a trade union...[2]

To what extent Eaton employees were impressed by these legal assurances is difficult to say. If John David Eaton was powerful enough to keep any unfavourable publicity out of the newspapers, could he not find ways to flaunt the labour law as well? If employees instinctively felt that their own department manager could find ways of getting around the law if he were against the union, who could blame them? Because, in truth, they were quite right. The process of fighting cases of discharge for union activity was so long and arduous that even if the persons were reinstated a year or more later, they might well find that the union had collapsed because of the very fear created by their dismissal!

This is not to say that the unfair practices section of the law was worthless. It had a psychological value in persuading employees to exercise their rights, and undoubtedly had a restraining effect on some employers. This was particularly true in the case of Eaton's department managers. As soon as one spoke openly against the union, he would find his remarks publicized in a union leaflet, thereby not only reaching the ears of every employee, but also those of John David.

One such incident occurred in the Hosiery Department of the Main Store. The morning after Mrs. Kay Hunt, a sales clerk in the department, had participated in a Local 1000 radio broadcast, Mr. C.D. Palmer, the manager, asked a counter head if any employees in her section were in the union. When she replied that she didn't know, he persisted: "There must be. One of the girls from this department did a radio broadcast last night," at which point Kay Hunt spoke up, "I did." Incensed, Mr. Palmer fumed: "We don't want a union at Eaton's, and we don't want anyone working for us who belongs to a union." Mrs. Hunt informed him that she had been a member of the Retail, Wholesale and Department Store Union at her last job, and joined Local 1000 when she started at Eaton's. Going further out on the limb, Palmer then asked: "Why didn't you tell us that before we employed you?" and delivered a lecture on how well Eaton's looked after their employees.

Our leaflet, needless to say, had some questions to ask Mr. Palmer: had he read the unfair practices sections of the Ontario law; did he know that Eaton's veterans had fought for democratic rights, including those of unions; did he realize he might embarrass top management who had so far been neutral in the campaign; since when did the Employment Office begin inquiring into union affiliation?[3]

Mr. Palmer was by no means the only manager who had no use for unions, but most found more subtle ways to express their antagonism. Years later, another Main Store member recalled her experience:

> I was quite young when I started at Eaton's as a parcel clerk — I think it was 1942. I was only getting $12.50 a week which wasn't much money. Then I went into selling stationery in the Main Store. When the union came along, I thought it could better the wages and also some working conditions, which was much needed. I helped to get new members. You had to ask a dollar and they had to sign a card. I got many new members.
>
> They knew in the department that I was doing all this for the union. They used to joke... like if (someone) was beefing, the boss would stand right there and say, "Well, get Olive to sign you up in the union." He was the one that was against it. They knew what I was doing because one would tell the other, you know.... They didn't keep quiet enough. *(What reason did people give for not joining?)*.... It was fear, I really think so. They were afraid of losing their jobs.

For unions in the position of Local 1000, the most important part of the Ontario Labour Relations Act was the procedure whereby a union could obtain recognition, or be "certified," as the exclusive bargaining agency for the employees.

The Ontario Labour Relations Board was the agency given authority under the Act to deal with applications for certification by unions. The Board consisted of a chairman and four members, with equal representation from employers and employees, and an administrative staff. It had power to decide if the bargaining unit of employees, as stated in the application, was appropriate, or in other words, would lend itself to collective bargaining. (In the case of Local 1000, this is more fully discussed in Chapter 15.)

Once the appropriate unit was defined, the OLRB proceeded to determine whether the applicant union had a majority of the employees as members. The procedures to be followed, including the criteria for union membership, were contained in the regulations to the Act. These could be amended more easily than the Act itself and were largely influenced by the recommendations of the OLRB.

In 1948, according to the Regulations, a signed application for membership was sufficient proof of union membership. Two years later, the Act underwent an extensive revision, adding more detailed provisions concerning unfair practices, certification procedures, the negotiation and the content of collective agreements, and conciliation measures which were to precede the right to strike.[4] Since this legislation was in effect when Local 1000 applied for certification in October 1950, it is helpful at this point to refer to changes from the previous Act which were pertinent to our campaign.

The new Act defined a trade union as "an organization of employees formed for purposes that include the regulation of relations between employees and employers." An employer was not to participate in or give financial or other support to the formation of a union.

The list of unfair practices set out in the previous Act was repeated, with others added. No person, acting on behalf of an employer or a union, was to use intimidation or coercion to prevent employees from exercising their rights under the Act. No person was to "attempt at the place at which an employee works to persuade him *during his working hours* to become, or refrain from becoming or continuing to be, a member of a trade union" [*emphasis mine*]. If our members did not always follow this to the letter, neither did Eaton's supervisors and managers. As for our organizing staff, we were careful to arrange to meet store employees in the public restaurants during their coffee break or lunch hour.

Another new section prohibited an employer from altering wages or other conditions of employment, without union consent, from the time notice to bargain was given by a certified union until conciliation procedures were completed.[5] We publicized this provision to allay fears that Eaton's might, for example, discontinue "privileges" like the employee discount on purchases.

Among its powers the OLRB had exclusive jurisdiction to determine "whether a person is a member of a trade union." In other words, the Board could establish its own criteria for union membership. As already mentioned, when the Eaton campaign began, a signed application for membership in a union was acceptable as evidence of membership. But by September 1949, the Board had developed a *policy* governing proof of union membership. This policy did not become part of the Regulations under the Act until 1951, but had already been stated in 1949 in the reasons for dismissing an application for certification.[6]

Evidence of union membership, according to the Board's policy statement, now required that the person had, in addition to signing a membership application, paid on his own behalf at least $1 "in respect of the prescribed initiation fee or monthly dues" of the union concerned. As an alternative to such payment, the person could present himself at a union meeting to take "the members' obligation" or "by doing some other act which, in the opinion of the Board, is consistent only with membership in the applicant [union] and [has] been accepted into membership..."

The alternatives to the payment of the $1 minimum fee might have been practical in a small craft union. For Local 1000 they were out of the question. Therefore, at the end of 1949, with more than 5,000 signed application cards, and in the face of our repeated assurances that no money or dues were required until Local 1000 was certified, it was a severe blow to our campaign to have to collect the $1 fee.

It was not the prospect of getting members to part with a dollar that was so upsetting. It was all the wasteful duplication of effort for our stewards to retrace their steps in contacting every member, the added paper work of receipt books, and a heavy load for our union office staff in recording the payments and matching them with application cards.

I would estimate that compliance with the change in the Board's policy represented several months of effort which might have been spent more usefully in getting new members. Right up until we applied for certification, teams of Local 1000 members spent evenings trying to locate those who had signed a card but not yet paid the dollar fee.

The 1950 Act also introduced some changes in the simple majority previously required for certification. If a union could show membership of 45 percent in the bargaining unit, it would be entitled to a representation vote. With 50 percent plus one membership, the Board could certify without a vote if they felt "that the true wishes of the employees are not likely to be disclosed by a representation vote." And if 55 percent or more were found to be members, the Board was also permitted to certify the union without a vote.

The catch was that, should a vote be held, the union had to secure a majority of *all those eligible to vote*. Clearly, if such a stipulation had governed elections for public office, very few politicians would have been seated in any of our governing chambers. At the time of the Local 1000 vote, Eaton's endeavoured to justify this arrangement by saying that, while it was obviously necessary to have a mayor in Toronto, it was not necessary to have a union.

Not until 20 years later was the Act amended to provide for certification if a majority of those casting ballots voted for the union.[7] In 1960, a provision was added to the Act whereby, upon applying for certification, a union might request a pre-hearing representation vote.[8] Had this been in effect at the time of Local 1000's application, it would not have been necessary to wait 14 months for a vote to be held, and the results could well have been vastly different.

CHAPTER SEVEN

Leaflets: The Vital Link

IN ANY UNION CAMPAIGN, leaflets play an important role. At Eaton's they were the *only* practical means of communicating with the huge and widely scattered work force. The leaflets were designed to arouse interest and start discussions and to urge action: filling out the membership application form on the leaflet and mailing or bringing it to the union office. They exposed and sought to counteract company manoeuvres, reported progress in organizational activity and generally provided a vehicle for union education among a class of workers which had no traditional roots in the labour movement. The bulletins of Local 1000 quickly became a medium through which employees could voice grievances anonymously. This greatly increased readership — by department managers as well as employees!

By far the most common complaint was low pay and salary inequities. Many of our early leaflets were devoted to Eaton's wage policy, which varied with employees' age, sex and marital status. In 1947, it was customary for women to start at $20 a week. Boys were hired for less, and single men for $24 to $26 a week. Married men started in the range of $28 to $32. This application of Marxist dogma (to each according to his need) by the archetype of capitalist enterprises, was, to say the least, ironic. In typical Eaton paternalistic fashion, employees were not asked to define their needs.

I recall the story told by a widow who approached her boss in the Advertising Department for a raise. The exchange went something like this: "But Mrs. Blank you've already had a raise." "Yes, but I need more." Boss: "The other girls don't make as much as you do." Mrs. Blank: "Yes, but they're either living at home or maybe they're living in sin!"

Length of service was ignored in the pay envelope, and old-timers would often discover that the newcomer they had just trained was getting a higher salary than they were.

Commission sales people had higher earnings, depending on the season, but here too there were numerous inequities based on sex and the type of merchandise sold. Mail order employees in general were paid less than their counterparts in the Stores. For some there were "production" bonuses above a quota of orders handled.

At that time, the Toronto Welfare Council periodically compiled what they considered to be a minimum budget to maintain a family in good health and decency. In January 1948, their minimum for a family of five called for weekly earnings of $44.45. A large proportion of Eaton's breadwinners earned considerably less.

Overtime pay was another sore point. There was much avoidance of pay for overtime, and then it was only at straight time whereas time and one-half for overtime work was general for union workers in Toronto. Our leaflets called for an end to "free" overtime, and for pay at time and one-half.

A brochure, entitled "I Know from Experience," was made available to committee members to hand to long-service employees. In it, "Mr. Old-Timer" recalled sharing hardships in the lean years through wage cuts and layoffs, but believed:

"Our years of service have been an investment [resulting in] substantial profit for the firm," and inquired if it was "unreasonable to want a pension plan, contributory if necessary, in which we will have some say, to take care of our needs when our working days are over . . .?" Many a gold watch holder in Eaton's Quarter Century Club was now 50 or over with no formal pension plan, no seniority protection, and very little chance of finding a job elsewhere at that age. Old Age Security was $40 per month at age 70 in 1948. Small wonder that many older men and women hesitated to join Local 1000 for fear of losing their job.

In several leaflets, the union voiced the worries about the insecurity felt by long-service employees, and called for an equitable pension plan for all retirees. The recommendations of department managers influenced the pension an employee would receive, and none were large enough for subsistence. On the other hand, the pensions of the managers themselves were known to be substantial.

To supplement general leaflet distributions, there were special pamphlets, easy to fit in a purse or pocket, addressed to groups such as salesclerks, restaurant workers, or delivery employees.

Our literature had to be well-written and attractive to pass the scrutiny of articulate and advertising-conscious department store employees. The facts had to be accurate to maintain the credibility of the union. Because we doublechecked information given to us, we did not make many gaffes. When brought to our attention, they were scrupulously corrected at the first opportunity.

Marjorie Gow and the organizing group would discuss the content of forthcoming leaflets at Saturday morning staff meetings. The quality of

her work set high standards for our publicity and was invaluable in promoting the growth of Local 1000. For the first year, Marjorie wrote, typed and pasted-up the copy for the leaflets, and then churned them out on an ancient multilith, aptly named "The Monster."

"I don't know where we got The Monster. I believe it was there, leering, when I arrived at 572 Bay Street," Marjorie recalls. "It was simply not suitable to handle the runs. For the first few thousand, it behaved beautifully but from there on [10,000 were needed for a distribution] it started to balk like hell and threw paper all over the place." When this happened, the sight of Margie pulling levers to stop the chaos was enough to send us scurrying down below to Angelo's. Miraculously, not once did we face distributors in the morning with no leaflets.

During the Drive a succession of talented young men added flair and satire to our publicity by contributing illustrations and cartoons for very little remuneration. Most were students or unemployed, and worked with Marjorie for an hour or two each week. The first of these, Ron Parker, was with us until mid-1949. He created a cartoon strip on life in a department store, "In Lower E-E-E-Tonya" (cribbed from the currently popular comic strip, "In Lower Slobovia").

Ron also invented the Mugwump, a character who was to remain with us for the rest of the campaign. This unique species, sitting on the fence with its mug on one side and "wump" on the other, typified the sort of employee who was heard to say, "Oh sure, I'm all for the union. Hope it gets in soon and does something for us," but, in the next breath, "Sign a union card? Who? Me? I haven't decided yet."

Ron was followed by George Luscombe,[1] enlisted by his friend Olive Richardson. George remembers doing art work on a volunteer

basis "until Eileen broke down and decided I should be paid something." In 1950, Bill Newcombe, a professional artist, added his inimitable style to our leaflets. Later that year Hugh Webster took over the art work. Hugh spent his evenings at our office, after attending theatre school during the day.[2] He enlivened many of Local 1000's events with skits which he wrote and directed. Prior to the vote campaign, Hugh became assistant editor of *Unionize*.

The first issue of *Unionize*, the weekly bulletin of Local 1000, appeared on April 6, 1948, with the headline: "*It Pays Off — Right From The Start.*" The article reminded Eaton employees that even without a union contract they had all benefited from Local 1000's efforts. First, there was a general increase of $2 a week in November, followed by further $2 increases early in 1948 for most employees upon authorization of department managers. The second concession to union standards was the payment of time and one-half for overtime. But in order to achieve greater job security, an end to arbitrary discharge and favouritism in promotions, the article stressed that a union contract was needed to provide grievance procedure and seniority protection.

As a comparison with salary policies under a union contract, the same issue reported gains in RWDSU's latest agreement with Lerner stores in New York. These included a $5 a week general increase, establishment of uniform starting rates of $35 a week for salesclerks (supplemented by commission) and $37 for non-selling staff, plus coverage extended to employees' families under the health plan.

After the first year, we decided that Marjorie and The Monster had endured one another long enough, and had our leaflets printed by Syd Robinson at Thistle Printing. Syd was a CCF member who had extended credit to many a struggling new union when the CIO-CCL was getting a foothold. He ran a business-like shop, producing high quality work. Delivery on time was of major importance to us, and in the four years he printed our leaflets, never once did Syd fail to meet our deadlines.

Arranging for the distribution of *Unionize* and other special leaflets was an onerous task. To cover all Eaton operations required 10,000 leaflets, and even then we relied on members to pass their copy on to a part-time employee. A minimum of 15 people was required for a distribution so that, apart from our small staff, we had to rely on volunteers. As I remember, office employees of other unions were among the most dependable; Iona Samis and Mary Gilchrist of UPWA were "regulars." Some organizers were especially co-operative; Henry Weisbach and the late Jim Murray never turned us down if they were in Toronto. Some had a regular "stand" like Marty Levinson, a law student, at Christie Street. Warehouse, or my friend, Jack Jolly, at Hayter Street Delivery-Dispatch. As well, we combed the CCF and CCYM for distributors, especially if some conference had brought them in numbers to Toronto.

It was asking a lot of people to get downtown by 6:30 a.m. on public transportation, and stand around for two hours or so handing out leaflets, particularly in winter. Therefore, arranging distributions was a chore none of us relished, so we rotated it, offering up a silent prayer that those we contacted would show up. Ninety-nine percent of the time they did.

To lighten the tedium, we formed the Polar Bear Club and issued membership cards to distributors in Local O. In time, it grew to quite a size. Over the years I have run across people in various parts of Canada who greet me with: "Don't you remember me? I handed out leaflets in the Eaton Drive." The latest such occasion was when I was asked that question by the admitting clerk at a Surrey hospital in B.C. She had once belonged to the Toronto CCYM.

At first, Eaton's placed wastebaskets inside the entrances to catch discarded leaflets, but a year later these were superfluous. A tally taken one morning in 1949 revealed that of 10,360 leaflets, only 415 were refused. In that year, members of Local 1000 began to participate in distributions, and by the end of the campaign, well over half of the distributors were Eaton employees.

Among the first employee distributors were a husband/wife team, Art Boxall, a roast cook in the Georgian Room restaurant, and Olive who sold stationery in the Main Store. Art recalls being questioned by his supervisor, one of the dietitians:

> "I hear you're handing out leaflets for the union," she says to me, and when I admitted it, she asked me why. "Because we all want more money." Then she says, "You can get fired for that. You had better watch your step." But I wasn't afraid of being fired. I was a good worker. I was a good roast cook. I was on several [Local 1000] committees.

Tom Pezzack, who retired after 40 years' service from Mail Order Hardware, used to show up to hand leaflets to former associates and urge them to join the union.

As all those thousands went in to work, there was no doubt that Eaton's hiring policy was preponderately WASP. I do not recall blacks or Asiatics, although Wally Ross claims he remembers one "token" Negro. Toronto had become notorious for anti-Semitism; by then Anglo-Saxons outnumbered Jewish employees even among Eaton's clothing workers in the Factory.

However, anyone from Northern Ireland, particularly from County Antrim, generally could get a job at Eaton's. Sid Moffat arrived in Canada in 1949, and after being laid off from a construction job, went to work for Eaton's the next year. He soon became a regular distributor and recalls one day very well:

> I used to start work at 11:00 at Hayter Street Dispatch, so I could go early in the morning and help out with the distributions. This one morning — it was around St. Patrick's Day — all of us handing out leaflets were wearing shamrocks.
>
> This one fellow heard my brogue, and being from Northern Ireland himself, he thought what I was doing was disgraceful. Here I was, going against Timothy Eaton so to speak. He called me for everything.

After distributing to early shifts at various buildings, I used to end up around 8:30 at the Yonge Street entrance to the Main Store. By this time, the salesclerks with whom I was involved in organizing were going in. Reading facial expressions was a good barometer of union acceptance or otherwise. This would swing all the way from an icy stare and refusal of the leaflet, through apprehension, indifference or curiosity to a pleasant smile, and as the Drive progressed, a friendly greeting or hurried request for more application cards. I would try to remember such reactions and match them with salesclerks' faces when I saw them in the Store.

Ernie Arnold's best distribution story is about one morning when he and Larry Nielsen, of the Hayter Street Upholsterers, were on duty at The College Street Store entrance. A long black chauffeur-driven limousine drew up and an elderly lady, whom Ernie thought rather dowdy, got out. When offered a leaflet, she gave them a withering look and swept past into the store. In his usual low key, straight-faced manner, Ernie asked Larry: "Who was that coming to work in a limousine? I thought the cleaning staff had already gone in." Larry replied: "That was Lady Eaton." Her director's office was in the College Street building.

On another occasion, when an employee gave John David Eaton a copy of *Unionize*, he handed it back with the quip: "You need it more than I do."

To our profound regret, ill health forced Marjorie Gow to withdraw from the campaign in April 1950. We were unable to replace her; publicity was added to my other duties and my work week stretched to seven days. Although we had several editorial assistants for short periods in 1951, this was a responsibility that I was never able fully to relinquish from then on.

The leaflets constituted our single most important tool in the long struggle to organize Eaton's. Next to staff salaries, the printed publicity material accounted for the largest item of expenditures. From 1948 to the end of 1951, printing and distribution cost less than $20,000, probably not as much as one week's advertising by Eaton's in the Toronto newspapers.[3] In that length of time, we put out more than two million pieces of literature. A representative collection of Local 1000 publicity is now on file in the Labour Section, Public Archives, Ottawa.

CHAPTER EIGHT

Collars, White and Blue

EARLY IN 1948, membership in Local 1000 reached the level where we could begin to build a structure of union committees. These were based either on occupational groups such as drivers, caretakers or restaurant workers, or on departments located on the same floor in the Stores and Mail Order. The objective was eventually to have a steward for every department, or location, as for example, one for each warehouse.

In union terms, a steward is the person who looks after the interests and general welfare of a group of fellow employees. During the organizing period, it is the steward's function to enroll employees in the union. Once a collective agreement is in place, the emphasis changes. It may still be necessary to collect dues and sign up new employees, although union security clauses, such as union shop and checkoff provisions in agreements, minimize or eliminate these chores. But the new and more important role is assisting employees to process grievances at the first level of management. As far as the members are concerned, the union steward is the centre of information. In large enterprises, where attendance at union meetings is sporadic, he or she *is*, in fact, the union. Thus, stewards form the vital link between the membership and the union executive.

By now, responsibility for Eaton's various divisions had been allocated among us. Lynn Williams and I had the three Stores with some 6,000 employees. We divided the work on the basis of floors. In the Main Store each floor covered an area equivalent to a square city block. However, there was a good deal of flexibility depending on whether the departments were staffed by men or women. We shared departments which served all floors; Lynn was assigned to caretakers, parcel wrap and elevator operators, while I had the cafeterias and restaurants.

Wally Ross was in charge of Mail Order, with about 2,000 employees in three buildings. Delivery and Warehouses, a homogenous group of about 1,000, were Gus Sumner's responsibility, along with the 12-storey Factory on Terauley Street.

Eaton's Factory posed several organizational problems. Clothing workers predominated in the building which manufactured a variety of goods. However, they were still not covered by contracts with the garment unions. Another large department was composed of several hundred printing trades employees, producing Mail Order catalogues and the Company's printing. They too had no formal union contract. We had no wish to infringe upon the jurisdiction of these established unions.

On the other hand, there were workers engaged in manufacturing luggage, boxes, thread, etc. who might wish to join Local 1000. Since there was no way to sort out these different groups when leafleting at the Factory, we decided to test the response from all and worry about jurisdiction later.

Daily meetings of department committees were held at our headquarters, after work or in the evening. On free evenings, we continued home canvassing and met prospects during the day on their coffee breaks, but activating the department committees was now our priority. Involvement as a group gave committee members more confidence and a sense of accomplishment as progress reports were given at these meetings.

Specific problems of departments were raised at meetings and then aired in *Unionize*. In turn, this led to discussion at work and opened the way for the committee member to invite other employees to come to the union office to talk the matter over. For many who attended, it was the first time they had considered what might be done about their "beefs" through collective action. The groundwork was being laid for general meetings when contract objectives would be voted upon.

Among the most vocal groups were employees whose duties revolved around delivery to the customer. They all shared the same frustrations due to Eaton's policy which required salesclerks to promise the customer delivery the next day on most items purchased before 5:00 p.m. This created a speed-up at the end of the day when everyone was tired, and necessitated frequent overtime for those who wrapped and labelled parcels and for dispatch workers who sorted them into city delivery routes.

Complaints of dispatch workers at Hayter Street appeared in *Unionize*, April 27, 1948. According to them, "Day in and day out [we] work at high speed. During the last hour of the day with the rush of last minute packages, we are expected to do what would normally be a half day's work." Working conditions were poor, "cold, drafty and dirty buildings," and the pay low — $30 to $32 a week. They proposed that customers be advised that purchases made after 3:00 p.m. could not be delivered the following day.

Parcel wrap employees put forward the same suggestion, but it was not acted upon by the Company. Due to the build-up of work in the afternoon, this group was allowed a 15-minute relief only in the morning, whereas sales personnel had one in the afternoon as well. After this was raised in *Unionize*, the morning rest period for parcellers was extended to 30 minutes.

Within a few months, Hayter Dispatch provided another example of job insecurity at Eaton's and the need for grievance procedure. The normal shift was 11:30 a.m. to 7:30 p.m. but employees were expected to work until all packages had been routed. One day a week, they were expected to report at 7:00 a.m. On September 16, it was George McDougall's turn to start at that time. When he asked his boss for permission to leave at 7:30 p.m., he was asked to stay until everything was cleared up. McDougall protested that he was too tired, whereupon he was told to go home, but "don't come in here tomorrow." By the time customers got their parcels next day, George McDougall was another addition to Eaton's turnover statistics.

At the end of the process, drivers felt the lack of rationale in Eaton's delivery policy. They were obliged to finish deliveries, regardless of the number, in all kinds of weather. Drivers were responsible for large amounts of cash from C.O.D. orders. Further, they did not receive any overtime pay until their work week exceeded 48 hours. Although their pay had been raised from $38 to $40 a week, these drivers considered themselves poorly-paid compared to union truckers in Toronto.

Needless to say, under such conditions, employees in delivery-related sections joined Local 1000 in substantial numbers.

It is generally true that interest in a union varies in inverse proportion to satisfaction with earnings and working conditions. On both counts, Mail Order workers received less favourable treatment than their counterparts in the Stores. For some unperceived reason they worked a 5½-day week of 42 hours, two hours longer than Store employees, and took home less pay.

Working conditions were intolerable in many parts of the dilapidated Mail Order buildings: lighting was inadequate for close clerical routines; ventilation was poor; and it was cold in winter and stifling hot in summer. According to one clerical worker, "Desks were only for managers. We clerks were lucky to have a table with four legs on it." Elevators in the Albert Street building were decades old, and although classed for freight, regularly carried employees. *Unionize*, February 27, 1951, reported two incidents of these elevators falling to the basement with employees aboard.

Four times a year, more than a million Canadians received Eaton's Catalogue. Orders flowing back from this immense volume of advertising were filled by assembly-line techniques. Batches of orders came through on moving belts. The process was described on one of Local 1000's radio series by a member from the Mail Order Copy Department, as follows:

> When we get the order... it has already been through the hands of the cashiers, has been marked for shipping instructions, and an address label attached. We copy the items on a sheet, or sheets, if the goods are from different departments. We work on a bonus system. If we type more than 1,250 a day — that's about 200 an hour — we get 38¢ for every 100 after that. But few of us make any bonus. I can usually keep up to that pace because I've been there a long time. (How long, if you don't mind telling us?) Over 20 years in this same department. [1]

Orders were hand-copied by some employees, but the quota and bonus were based on typing which, of course, was faster.

The arbitrary powers of management led to a widespread feeling of insecurity. The case of Ernest Manning, related in *Unionize* (June 29, 1948), under the heading, "Eaton's Looks After Their Own," made a mockery out of their vaunted paternalism.

During the War, when Eaton's was badly in need of help, Manning, then over 60, was employed as a trucker in Mail Order Assembly Packing. As well as trucking, he threw parcels on the conveyor belt, wrote up C.O.D.s at busy periods, and performed other routine clerical tasks. Fellow employees said Manning was an able and willing worker, with "no black marks" against him.

Then on March 29, Manning took ill and was off work for eight weeks with bronchitis and pleurisy. For a couple of weeks after his return, he was assigned to writing C.O.D.s or other light work, and allowed to go home an hour or so early. However, when he again tried tossing heavy parcels onto the conveyor belt, he found it too strenuous, and one of the managers suggested that he retire. His question, naturally, was "on what?" Why could he not continue to write C.O.D.s? Well, as he was told, this was "girls' work" and the Company could not pay him $29 a week for doing *that* job!

On June 12, despite his plea that he be allowed to work until July 1, Ernest Manning received two weeks' vacation pay and a week's additional salary. As a last resort, he contacted Eaton's Welfare Office, only to be assured, "This is the best thing that could happen to you, Manning. You are going to get a much-needed rest."

This was not the end of the story. Through Tommy MacLachlan, Manning was placed at General Bakeries, under contract with Local 461, RWDSU. He was hired at $5 a week more than his final pay at Eaton's.

Manning was not a member of Local 1000. But his story pointed up the need for grievance procedure and greater job security provisions through a union contract, and brought us many new adherents.

Mail Order and Stores were under different management for the same merchandise departments, but the annual bonus based on performance applied to both. The length to which some managers would go in cost-cutting was set out in a letter to the editor printed in *Unionize* (March 27, 1951) as follows:

> Not only do Eaton employees have to buy their own pencils to write company orders, as you wrote in *Unionize* two weeks ago, but the Mail Order office I work in makes a profit on them. Pencils are bought at 39 ¢ a dozen, and sold to employees, three for 10¢. We understand that ink is bought for our department from the profit on pencils.

Out of such ingrained attitudes and practices came the Eaton mansions, yachts, planes and tax deductible charity donations.

And from these employer-employee relations came strong committees of Local 1000 members from Mail Order.

At all committee meetings we inquired about personnel changes. Keeping our records up-to-date absorbed a good deal of time, but proved its worth when we had to gauge our membership percentage before making an application for certification.

Records of Eaton employees were maintained in a metal file cabinet of sliding trays, each accommodating several thousand small file cards. It was our most-used piece of equipment throughout the campaign. As well as Local 1000 membership application cards, it contained a card file for every department. Pink cards were used for members, blue for prospects, yellow to denote those definitely anti-, and white for status unknown. Changing the colour of these department file cards was part of the daily routine, so that the organizer responsible could have a current picture at all times.

Lynn recalls what painstaking work it was to build up the complete department lists from which our file system was constructed, and then to keep it revised. When the bargaining unit was under investigation in 1950, it enabled us often to be more informed than Company officials. "When I've been talking with organizers since, sometimes confused as to how many were eligible for the union in plants of three or four hundred," Lynn commented later, "I regale them with how we struggled — successfully — to build up accurate information about more than 10,000 at Eaton's." In later campaigns in which he was involved, Wally Ross made use of the same system.

From RWDSU organizing experience in American department stores, shoe salesmen were the first to show interest, and this was borne out

at Eaton's. Anyone who has observed customers' habits (not to mention malodorous feet) would no doubt understand how a shoe salesman's day can be fraught with frustration. Earnings in Eaton's shoe departments, selling men's, women's and children's shoes in a large area on the second floor of the Main Store, were a combination of salary and commission. The latter was a percentage of sales exceeding a quota set by management.

It must have been very trying to remain affable with a customer who, after trying a dozen pair, left with the well-worn phrase, "Sorry, but I'm just looking." To be assigned stockroom or other work while others were making commission on the selling floor was another irritant. Considering the effort required in selling shoes compared with other merchandise, these salesclerks felt they were underpaid. This feeling was enhanced during visits from sales representatives of shoe manufacturers, when Eaton salesmen could not fail to note the contrast between the life style of these men and their own.

There were not many women salesclerks in the shoe departments. One of them related why she joined Local 1000:

> The men in my department signed me up. I thought it was a good thing. When I first started at Eaton's I was getting about $12 a week. It went up to $18 and stayed there for about ten years. Men's wages were terrible, for men with families. I lived with my mother and dad. So I got to thinking about these people. They couldn't afford a car. They had no money to

> spend. They were just able to come to work and go back home. It was an awful way to live.

On one of his home calls the previous fall, Lynn had contacted a "natural leader" who agreed to get some others to have a beer after work. By the time the committee structure was being developed, there was enough leadership among shoe salesmen to have organized a dozen other departments.

An important factor in making the shoe departments a union stronghold was their habit of socializing as a group after work. As one member explained, "There was a bunch that stuck together at dances and parties...

There were only two in my section who didn't belong to the Union. They didn't come to the parties." Later, some of these members were among the most active on Local 1000's Social Committee.

In bedding and linens, also on the Main Store second floor, two salesmen who were close friends took the lead in signing up others. On the other hand, some months passed before any progress was made in men's clothing on that floor. Here, commission arrangements were better than average, and salesmen felt more prestige. However, it took only one well-respected, long-service employee to get things moving. And so it went. Employee leadership was the key. Eventually, the second floor committee could boast of the highest union percentage of any selling floor in the Main Store.

On floors staffed mainly by women selling female apparel, it was a much different story. A comparison of the earnings of women employed in department stores with those in other sectors of retail trade has already been noted (Table 4). Most women at Eaton's were well aware of the fact that compared with men they were second-class salesclerks in pay and promotional opportunity. But it was another matter to persuade them that they could begin to alter this relationship through a union. The majority of full-time sales-women worked because they relied on their earnings to maintain themselves or contribute to family support, and they thought they might risk losing their job by becoming active in Local 1000.

When we began organizing, the weekly salary for most women salesclerks was $20. In some, but by no means all, departments this was augmented by a commission paid on sales exceeding a quota set by management. One member from the Main Store who did not have commission arrangements wrote out her weekly budget which we published in *Unionize* (April 13, 1948). From her gross of $20, deductions for income tax, unemployment insurance and 10¢ for charity, came to $1.20, leaving her a net of $18.80. She lived in a rented room and cooked

Unionize

Vol. 3, No. 27

DEPARTMENT STORE EMPLOYEES UNION
Local No. 1000

July 11, 1950

Here's Why

MRS. ANNE STONE is employed in Eaton's Mail Order Adjusting office. As Chairman of Local 1000's Publicity Committee, she takes an active part in the Union. Here's why Mrs. Stone thinks a woman's place is in the union:

"Most women work of necessity. It may be, for the very young, that our present job is merely a stepping stone to something better. It may be that there is a hope chest to be filled, or the down payment on a home to be gathered together. It may be an education for our small fry that is our goal. Maybe we have an idea that when our job is done we would like to enjoy the fruits of our labor in pleasant, modest, independence. It may be merely that we are trying (cont'd on page 3.)

Part-timers often say, "The union is all right for full-timers, but not for me". MRS. NELLIE JAMES is a part-time waitress in the College St. Round Room, and Steward for her department. She disagrees with this view, and says:

"Every married woman at Eaton's should be interested in Local 1000. What we do affects the livelihood of all the men who are heads of families.

Whether we intend to stay indefinitely or not - and one never knows when plans to stop work may not materialize - we owe it to every self-supporting employee in Eaton's to (continued on page 3.)

Women Join Local 1000

most of her own meals. Weekly expenses came to $7 for rent, $10 for food including lunches, and 75¢ for carfare, leaving a balance of $1.05. Timothy Eaton would no doubt have been pleased that this "surplus" ruled out tobacco or liquor. But what about clothes? Or medical bills? Or a summer vacation? Of course, she could always have gone to the

Eaton Girls' Camp at a very low charge, and if she were really ill, the Welfare Office might take care of her doctor's bill.

Timothy Eaton's tradition of assisting employees faced with illness or other major problems was carried on by the Welfare Department. (Blue Cross and hospital insurance were yet to come.) The Company maintained hospitals in the Main Store, College Street and the Factory with a nursing staff, who also visited employees in their homes.

After six months' service, employees became eligible for assistance with certain health bills at the discretion of the Welfare Office. They also received part pay from the fourth day of absence. However, while the duration of this sick pay was related to length of service, it varied a good deal depending on the individual. Thus, employees dreaded illness since they were never sure of their entitlement. In any case, for most employees part pay was insufficient to take care of living expenses, let alone medical bills.

Large numbers of part-time employees worked in the selling departments under a variety of schedules. Some worked regularly 20 hours a week, others only on Saturdays or on special sale days. A Reserve Staff was on call as needed. "Casuals" might work full-time for several weeks before Christmas. The regular part-time employees were the only ones which we felt might be included in the bargaining unit, and we confined our efforts to this category.

The full-time women salesclerks were difficult enough to interest in the union, but the part-time employees in this occupation were even more so. Less dependent on their earnings, they were more apathetic about doing anything to improve them. We had to rely on full-time members to approach the part-timers to join, and they, in turn, often regarded the part-time staff as too transient to bother with. Furthermore, where employees worked on salary and commission, it fostered competitive rather than co-operative feelings within the group.

In such a work environment, it is not surprising that the women who became active in Local 1000 had strong personalities, were angry about salaries and the arbitrary powers of managers, and courageous enough to become identified with the union.

The departments staffed by women in the College Street and Annex Stores were smaller, and thus more closely under the eye of supervisors. The fear of being seen having coffee with a union organizer limited our opportunities to approach them.

Another element which affected the salesclerks' attitude toward the union was the value of the goods they sold. In departments offering prestige merchandise — fine china, silverware, diamonds, furs, *haute couture* salons — salesclerks acquired a reflected status from the customers. Those who sold can-openers in housewares or thread in the notions department were far more receptive to the union.

Similarly, the salesmen of quality furniture at College Street were less attracted to Local 1000 than their counterparts in the Annex Budget Store. Higher-priced merchandise resulted in higher commission earnings. This was even more the case among the salesmen who worked on straight commission. They received an advance or "draw" rather than a salary, and earnings were determined by the value of merchandise sold.

The men who sold refrigerators or stoves or radios on straight commission were inclined to regard themselves as entrepreneurs rather than employees, with results determined by their own initiative and talent. It was Lynn's belief that once the idea took root that through a union, commission rates and conditions were *negotiable* with the employer, a floodgate of complaints would open up.

For example, it was a very long time before we had enough members in the radio department to attempt a meeting. Finally, in arranging an after-work meeting at our office, Lynn recalls, "One of the inducements was that I promised it would not last more than an hour. When this time passed, their problems had just begun to emerge, and they insisted on carrying on for another hour. When they finally broke up, it was after deciding to meet again the next week." However, individualism was stronger than collectivism among most of these salesmen and our strength in the straight commission departments remained minimal.

In his classic work on white-collar workers, C. Wright Mills came to the conclusion that their claims to prestige rested not only on the merchandise sold or the "exclusiveness" of the store, but on "their style of appearance [as] their occupations enable and require them to wear street clothes at work."[2]

Eaton's expected salesclerks to be well-groomed. For men, this meant wearing a suit with a shirt and tie and making sure one's shoes were shined. The standard attire for women was a black dress, although navy or dark brown were countenanced. The most common accessory was a simulated pearl "choker." Good grooming also entailed at least a minimum of cosmetics, hair shampoo and the like. In Toronto's climate, seasonal changes in clothing added to the expense.

As Mills pointed out, in North American society, status, the barometer of self-esteem, tends to rest on conspicuous consumption. When consumption is limited by income, "clothing expenditure [becomes] merely an index, although a very important one, to the style of appearance and the life-ways displayed by the white-collar strata."[3]

For Eaton employees the limitation on consumption was stringent indeed. In recognition of this, and to offset the required clothing expenditures, employees were allowed a ten percent discount on purchases, which rose to twenty percent twice yearly at the time seasonal clothing was needed. One of the anti-union rumours was that these discounts might be discontinued "if the union got in." To dispel this fear we pointed out that employee discounts were still in effect in unionized stores in the U.S.; that employee purchases added up to considerable sales volume for the Company, and that according to a survey of retailers, nine out of ten granted discounts to employees.[4]

Regardless of discounts, Eaton employees were fighting a losing battle in trying to manage on their incomes due to the rapid rise in post-war prices. Many were forced to moonlight in the evening or on weekends. Organized industrial workers had overtaken any advantage white-collar workers might have had, not only in higher wages, but in new benefits such as health and pension plans. Periodically, we published statistics on average earnings in manufacturing and other industries. Invariably, retail trade was near the bottom of the wage ladder.

Despite these economic pressures, the white-collar workers in office and sales jobs at Eaton's were slower than the rest in seeking relief through a union. Perhaps it was true that, as one writer observed, "The Eaton family was far more real and interesting to many of them than their own..."[5] It must have been titillating to be entertained at Eaton Hall, Lady Eaton's huge Norman castle built on 600 acres, with its private lake, near King, Ontario. If I recall correctly, the elevator operators were one group so entertained, but their hostess would have been horrified had she known that nearly all of them were members of Local 1000!

At the time, Eaton's was the largest employer of restaurant workers in Toronto. An estimated 900 men and women prepared and served food in cafeterias for customers or employees, a number of coffee shops, and two prestigious restaurants, the Round Room at College Street and the Georgian Room downtown. They also operated a large baked goods counter, one of the busiest spots in the Main Store.

The skilled jobs — chefs, cooks, bakers — were nearly all performed by men. Preparation of vegetables, salads, sandwiches and desserts was done by women, mainly on a part-time schedule of six hours a day, 30 per week. Waitresses too were employed part-time to cover the noon-hour period. Unskilled work such as washing dishes and pots was done by men or women, depending on physical demands.

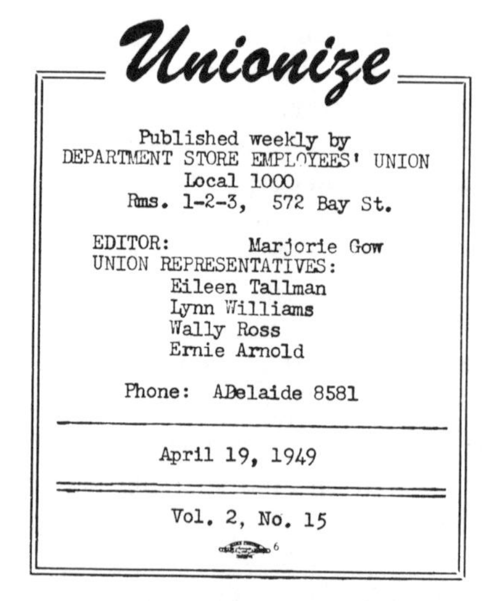

Unionize

Published weekly by
DEPARTMENT STORE EMPLOYEES' UNION
Local 1000
Rms. 1-2-3, 572 Bay St.

EDITOR: Marjorie Gow
UNION REPRESENTATIVES:
Eileen Tallman
Lynn Williams
Wally Ross
Ernie Arnold

Phone: ADelaide 8581

April 19, 1949

Vol. 2, No. 15

HI YA! COMING TO THE SEMINAR? YOU'LL LIKE IT!

EXPOSES FIRE HAZARDS
(cont. from Page 1)

spirits in bulk and the use of such substances as gasoline and amyl acetate in unprotected areas, where a spark from a match or electric motor could result in an explosion that would mean death and maiming to employees and public alike - to say nothing of the damage to property that would result.

■ In spite of the fact that his reports were frequently ignored and his recommendations rarely acted upon (since keeping down costs in the department appeared to be Mr. Smith's main concern) Mr. Farley went on doing his job and reporting dangerous conditions where he found them.

■ In the latter part of February, Farley who was the second senior man in the department was given an open transfer. The reason given was "reduction in staff", in spite of the fact that six weeks earlier a new man had been taken on and a week after he was let out another employee was put in his place.

(cont. Page 3)

Food workers were subject to the same low pay and inequities as prevailed throughout Easton's, but behind-the-scenes pressures and indignities were more powerful catalysts than wages in inducing them to organize. They were under the immediate supervision of dietitians.

Evidently, training in nutrition and food preparation did not extend to the art of good employee relations. Becoming a dietitian, or even a chef, was out of the question for nearly all food workers, and their attitude toward a union was therefore not inhibited by career aspirations.

Grievances of restaurant employees appeared in the second issue of *Unionize* (April 13, 1948), a forerunner of many more to follow. The item accused the manager of the food departments, Miss Violet Ryley, of cutting costs at the expense of employees. "Waitresses are having to do all manner of work not connected with their occupation, such as scrubbing floors, washing walls, painting chairs....

Older women are being let out, or transferred, in spite of seniority, to be replaced with younger and lower-paid employees," the article claimed, concluding that union grievance procedure was sorely needed. Three weeks later we were able to report that employees in the "Beanery," as the Employees' Cafeteria on Louisa Street was known, were no longer required to wash walls and mop floors.

It seems there is a general opinion that restaurant cooks are an eccentric, temperamental lot. More likely there is a physical explanation, stemming from speed-up and oppressive temperatures at work. The discharge slip of a young pastry cook, laid off without notice in January 1949, was changed from "shouting at employees" to "lack of work." The employee in question was a recent English immigrant with a wife and two children. The Company's Employment Office did not even tell him the procedure to apply for unemployment insurance. He was replaced by two part-time women. He had received $38 for 40 hours, but the women were both hired at $16 for a 30-hour week. Thus, the food departments gained an extra 20 hours of work for $6 a week less pay.[6]

Full-time restaurant workers received a $3 weekly allowance toward meals at Eaton's. However, they reported that there was seldom any choice; they ate the left-overs from the previous day. And if they were off work a day or so, the food allowance was deducted pro rata from their pay.

When the Hub in the Main Store basement was converted to a cafeteria, employees took a pay cut from 50¢ to $1 a week, because their work was downgraded from waiting on customers to clearing tables. "Beanery" part-timers called it adding insult to injury when they were advised of a salary increase of 50¢ a week by means of a "Private and Confidential" notice in their pay envelope. It was no secret to them that 50¢ would not buy a pound of butter or a dozen eggs or even a movie ticket.[7]

This sort of penny-pinching in a company run by a multi-millionaire family who lived lavishly produced a militant group of men and women as leaders of the Local 1000 restaurant committee, including the only part-time employees who were consistently active in the union. Pointing out that part-timers would benefit proportionately in wage gains won by the union, as well as have access to grievance procedure, the steward for the Round Room waitresses urged:

> Every married woman at Eaton's should be interested in Local 1000. What we do affects the livelihood of all the men who are heads of families. Whether we intend to stay indefinitely or not... we owe it to every self-supporting employee in Eaton's to join the Union and take an interest in its affairs.[8]

We were never able to understand why Eaton's factory departments, which one might expect to be the easiest to organize, proved to be the least interested. Possibly it was due to memories of the harsh treatment meted out to clothing workers in past organizational attempts. Perhaps the variety of goods being manufactured, and the differences in production quotas and operating conditions, made for less cohesiveness than in a factory producing cars or packing meat. The proportion of long-service employees was large. Younger people gravitated toward unionized factories where the pay and benefits were better.

During the drive, individuals who were solidly behind Local 1000 emerged in a good many Factory departments. However, they were, in general, unable to form effective committees to complete organization.

Before Eaton's found this out we were instrumental in correcting one inequity relating to Factory workers. They had to work five years before getting a second week's paid vacation, whereas the rest of Eaton employees became entitled to a second week after two years' service. It was usual for the Factory to shut down for two weeks in the summer. Thus, those not entitled to vacation pay for both weeks lost a week's income. This was publicized in *Unionize*, and rectified in the summer of 1948. Due to the number of long-service Factory employees, the change to two weeks' vacation after two years would not have been a costly item for the Company, but it represented one more example of what even the threat of a union could do.

In June at the end of the first six months of the open campaign, a confidential report to the Department Store Organizing Committee of the Congress summarized progress to that point, with a comparison of gains over the first quarter of 1948. Local 1000 now had members in more than a third of the 294 store departments, in almost half of 96 in Mail Order, and in 15 of 42 factory departments. Two-thirds of warehouse employees and about one quarter of delivery workers were members. However, of the 10,000 potential, Local 1000 had less than 15 percent signed up. Both the membership and the number of departments with members had almost doubled in the second quarter, but obviously, a 51 percent majority was still a long way off. The report concluded:

> The spirit among the committee of more than 300 and the members themselves is quite optimistic. The amount of union talk in the departments has led them to believe that the union is actually much stronger than it is. No figures have been released, of course, and the information herein is strictly confidential.

It was equally obvious to our staff that four organizers were spread far too thinly over so many departments, especially with the inexorable turnover of workers. We were learning that speed is of the essence in department store unionization. We could have effectively utilized three times as many organizers. Unfortunately, that level of staff was not achieved on a regular basis at any time during the campaign.

As the membership grew and the committees became more active, Eaton's reacted by continuing to raise salaries. The weekly minimum for women with a year or so of service was moving to $25. This was increased in some departments by discontinuing commissions and incorporating the average commission for the previous year into the basic weekly pay. Caretakers could now reach a maximum of $36 a week after one year, instead of $35 at the end of two years' service. Eaton's were under pressure not only from Local 1000 but because union wages in Toronto were making it difficult to hire men. For example, In June 1948, Leaside Warehouse receivers were making $28 to $30 a week. Although help was badly needed, the Company had no luck in recruiting at that wage. When eventually a new man was hired, the receivers found out that he was getting $34 a week, and immediately sought an increase.[9]

Membership rose steadily through the summer, and significantly in September, after the announcement of a pension plan. There were no longer many refusals as *Unionize* was offered to employees. Department news items created interest and, knowing that everyone enjoys a joke to brighten the day, we tried to inject as much humour as possible into the leaflets. Cartoons were invaluable for this, and so was Marjorie Gow's witty way with words, as illustrated by what she made out of an item in *Flash*, Eaton's employee magazine. The poem, entitled "Your Job," read in part:

> Don't ever belittle the job that you fill;
> For however little your job may appear,
> You're just as important as some little gear

That meshes with others in some big machine,
That helps keep it going though never is seen.
They could do without you, we'll have to admit,
For business keeps on when the big fellows quit!
But always remember, my lad, if you can,
The job's more important — (Ah, yes!) than the man!

Marjorie's satirical parody, which follows, hit a responsive chord with Eaton employees, and was passed around and taken home to show others.

I'M A QUEER LITTLE GEAR
AND MY LIFE IS IN AN AWFUL MESH

Can't you work a little faster,
said the straw boss to the gear,
There's a manager behind me, and
he's treading on my rear;
He says that sales are lousy and
he's crying in his beer —
And he wants all gears to mesh!

He says the job's important — more
important than a gear —
He says that gears know what to do
if they don't like it here;
If you don't increase production
you'll land out on your ear —
And he wants all gears to mesh!

The season soon is coming when his
bonus will be here;
And the big shots want big profits
at the ending of the year;
First they milk the public dry —
then they strip a gear —
So we gears had better mesh! And how
(Ah, Yes) *But fast — GET UNIONIZED!*

CHAPTER NINE

Pensions: A Plan at Last

ONE CAN PICTURE John David Eaton's chagrin, and the irritation in the executive suites, that September morning in 1948 when Local 1000 "scooped" the Company by announcing: "Pension Plan Slated Oct. 1st." We had worked into the early hours of the morning to get a short statement run off on The Monster for distribution with *Unionize*, and would have been less than human not to gloat over management's discomfort.

Even since our first leaflet the previous January, Local 1000 had been calling for an equitable pension plan to end the uncertainty beclouding the future for large numbers nearing the end of their working days. Salaries were too low to enable employees to purchase annuities or put aside savings. Retirement allowances were a haphazard affair, dependent on recommendations of department managers who could also dismiss an employee at any time before retirement.

There were never answers to the questions of how much, when, or for how long, but one fact was clear: except for managers, Eaton employees then in receipt of retirement allowances were living in penury. The federal old age pension at the time was $40 a month, at age 70, and it was paid only after a means test.

According to our information, the directors of Eaton's had been considering a contributory pension scheme as far back as 1940, but shelved it during the War. We claimed that the proposal was resurrected only when it became apparent that Eaton employees were in earnest about the union. Along with the wage increases and other concessions granted since Local 1000 appeared on the scene, the pension plan represented more "jam today" in the hope that long-service employees would forget the union tomorrow. Later, the Company asserted it had taken three years to develop the plan. As we discovered, the wheels grind slowly if that is to the Company's advantage.

Although not yet officially announced, the plan was to be effective October 15, and booklets for employees were already printed. In the September 21 issue of *Unionize*, we were able to reveal highlights of the plan. It provided that after 25 years' service, a pension for life would be paid to men at 65 and women at 60. The employee's contribution would amount to five percent of earnings from date of entry in the plan to retirement. Should an employee leave before retirement, any contributions plus interest would be returned or could be left on deposit toward a smaller payment at retirement age.

Participation in the Eaton Retirement Annuity Plan was limited to full-time employees, aged 30 years or over, upon completion of five years' service. The amount of pension was based on a formula of 1 3/4 percent of future earnings, and a lower percentage on past earnings, the cost of the latter to be born by the Company.

Not a word about the plan, now known to all Toronto employees, appeared in the dailies until October 13, the date on which the well-orchestrated announcement by John David Eaton was scheduled.

In the meantime, *Hush Free Press*, a scandal sheet sold outside Eaton's and Simpsons, came out on October 9 with a story under a large heading: "T. EATON'S vs UNIONS," with a sub-head which proclaimed, "Union's Long Drawn-Out Battle with Toronto's Merchandizing Prince Comes to An End: John David Finds a Solution." Buried in the garbled account were a few lines of superlatives describing the Eaton pension as "the greatest mass pension... ever put forward by any company or any government." Apart from this, the lengthy article was given over to union-bashing, and extolling free enterprisers like the Eatons, who could be counted on to stave off unions and those twin evils, socialism and communism.

On October 13, the Toronto dailies snapped to attention and printed almost identical, lengthy news stories about Eaton's pension plan, apparently taken verbatim from a Company hand-out, along with a Karsh photo of John David. The headlines in two papers were curiously similar even in their inaccuracies: "T. Eaton Co. Announces New Pension Scheme for Every Employee" *(Toronto Star)* and "All Eaton Employees in New Pension Plan" *(Globe & Mail)*. By no means *all* employees were covered; thousands of regular part-time workers were excluded; thousands more would leave Eaton's before becoming eligible to participate in the plan.

On October 15, the *Globe & Mail* eulogized Eaton's president and the plan in a fawning editorial, which read in part:

> It [the plan] gives positive answer to those who claim that relations between a huge corporation and its staff can never be anything but impersonal. This plan is not coddling and is not presented in answer to an organized demand. It came spontaneously and, for this reason, deserves special recognition as a contribution to the general betterment of employer-employee relations....Tens of thousands of families throughout the country will be given a feeling of security they have not had

> before.... It is natural to expect that... the bonds of loyalty between the company and its staff will be further strengthened.

The veiled reference to Local 1000 was ironical, coming from editors who had not considered the start of a union drive at Eaton's newsworthy enough to warrant an inch of space in January, or at any subsequent time.

Nor were its editors disposed to allow the employees' union to express any views about the pension plan. Some of these were set out in the following letter to the editor of the *Globe & Mail*, dated November 1, which was never published:

> Many Eaton employees, who are members of Local 1000, Department Store Employees' Union, affiliated with the RWDSU, CCL-CIO, have mentioned that the editorials and newspaper accounts of the Eaton Pension Plan were more glowing than accurate.
>
> The Plan is undoubtedly an improvement over the old hit-or-miss charity system the Company previously employed. The Eaton workers have been in need of a pension scheme for many years, and the Company has been discussing pension plans for many years, but it was not until the employees began organizing themselves into our Union, that a plan was finally put into effect.
>
> The *Globe and Mail's* headline says, "All Eaton Employees in New Pension Plan," a statement which was misleading to the Eaton workers and the general public. To qualify for the pension plan an employee is required to have worked for the Company for at least five years and to have reached 30 years of age. This means that a great number of employees who started to work at Eaton's in their teens, say 18 years of age and are now around 24 or 26 years of age, cannot enter the plan for another four, five, or six years, in spite of the fact that they have been full-time employees for six or eight years.
>
> Another group of employees who do not quality for the Plan are the part-time workers, many of whom have worked with the Company 15 and 20 years, 4 or 6 hours a day.
>
> There are many other objections to the Plan, but one of the most general is that there is no employee representation in its administration.
>
> In fact, the Eaton Retirement Annuity Plan would appear to be just an average company pension plan. It may be as your editorial says, "A model for other employers, both large and small," but from the employees' point of view it leaves much to be desired.
>
> Norman G. Twist, Canadian Director
> Retail, Wholesale and Department Store Union

Women restaurant workers, most of whom worked a 30-hour week at Eaton's, were the most vocal in complaints about the pension scheme. A cafeteria employee who had started with the Company in 1928 and worked through the Depression voiced her disappointment at being left out of the plan after 20 years' service. She had clipped the editorial praising the plan as "an investment... in human well-being, in human dignity, and therefore in the security of the business itself." As she told *Unionize*, she was filing this clipping in her bureau in an envelope marked "Human dignity deferred."

A rumour was spread among some departments that the government would not approve a pension plan which included part-time employees. We checked this with the Annuities Branch of the Department of Labour who refuted the story, and we were able to advise in the next *Unionize* that no government rule prevented part-time workers from coverage, and in fact, some companies had extended benefits to this category.

A year later in October 1949, part-time employees were permitted to participate in Eaton's pension plan, under the same eligibility provisions (age 30 or over with five years' service) and could retire after completion of 25 years' service. In welcoming this amendment to the plan, *Unionize* drew attention to the five issues in which admission of part-timers had been urged.[1]

Upon examining the fine print, more defects were revealed and publicized. Broken service due to layoffs during the Thirties was commonplace; in calculating past-service benefits, time worked prior to a layoff was not linked with years of service after recall. Another point which caused anxiety for some employees was that the formula for calculating past-service benefits was based on the employee's 1947 earnings. The plan did not state the effect of absence without pay during part of that year due to illness. And, after all they had been through, veterans resented having to wait until age 30 before participating in the plan.

However, it soon became apparent that by far the greatest shortcoming was the meagre pension those close to retirement age would receive. This must have sent a chill down the spine of thousands in the Quarter Century Club who had little time left to build up future benefits. As mentioned, the pension was based on a percentage of earnings, with no minimum amount. Consequently, the discrimination women employees encountered in the pay envelope prior to retirement was carried over for the rest of their lives. Moreover, while pensions for male retirees were also inadequate, they could work until age 65, whereas women had to retire at 60 on even lower incomes.

What this meant to some women was told by the daughter of a former Local 1000 steward:

> After my father died, my mother had to go back to work (as) there were three of us kids. She started at Eaton's in the Millinery department

> at $12.50, the minimum wage for women [in Ontario] at the time. She retired at 60 because women had to. Men retired at 65. So after 20 years of working there, [her pension] was about $52 a month. She had been underpaid all those years. She was the buyer in the Infantswear department, and I used to tell her that she should try to get a job somewhere else because she had lots of ability.

The dilemma of such women, and Eaton's remedy for it, were aired on one of Local 1000's radio series: "Since they (women retirees) can't starve for ten years until they become eligible for government old age pensions... some are starting back to work at Eaton's, *as new employees*. This makes a farce of the whole plan."[2]

In typical Eatonian fashion, there was no uniform policy governing retired-rehired employees, other than to accommodate departmental staff requirements. Some former salesclerks were rehired part-time in selling departments. But restaurant workers found it almost impossible to return to their former, or any other, job. Undoubtedly, the speed-up and physical demands of the food sections had taken their toll, but they knew of younger women being taken on for lighter jobs that they might have filled. A former employee confided to one of our members that she didn't know how she was going to make ends meet: her pension was $35 a month (after 33 years' service!) and the Company had declined to rehire her.[3]

We urged the retired-rehired employees to join Local 1000 to press for improved pensions for themselves and future employees, but I cannot recall that any of them were active in the union. They were too much at the Company's mercy.

None of these problems arising out of the pension plan were noticed by the press that had so lauded its introduction. One story that did circulate, and was perpetuated by company historians, was that John David Eaton had dipped into his own pocket to the tune of $50 million to cover past-service benefits. For example:

> The President [John David Eaton] is generally conceded to be Canada's richest man, and this opinion became a fairly substantial fact in the year 1948 when he made his own personal contribution of $50 million to the launching of the Eaton employees' contributory pension fund — a gift which enabled payment of immediate benefits to men and women approaching retirement age. It is doubtful if any other Canadian citizen could approach that scale of wealth-sharing.[4]

This writer and others appear to have missed the point that, being a private, family-owned concern, all net proceeds of the business accrued to the Eatons. Thus, the decision to build Timothy Eaton Memorial Church, or a wing of the Toronto General Hospital, or to return withheld wages in the form of pension benefits to their employees, was largely a matter of from which pocket to take the funds so as to obtain the maximum tax advantage, either for personal or business reasons. And stated in terms dear to corporations when they discuss profits, the $50 million toward past-service pensions was probably no more than *one percent of Eaton's sales volume* for one decade or so out of its 80 years of existence.

Despite employer resistance to the inclusion of pensions within the scope of collective bargaining, CIO unions in the United States were negotiating better pensions for mass production workers than AFL craftsmen had ever dreamed of. In 1949, the United Steelworkers won pensions of $100 a month, fully company-financed, for workers in a number of major U.S. steel corporations.

In Canada, the breakthrough came in the spring of 1950 when the United Auto Workers, representing 12,000 Ford Motor employees in Windsor, Ontario, negotiated a *company-paid pension* of $55 a month, after 30 years' service, at age 65, with the possibility of continuing to work to age 68. This settlement was reportedly based on assurances that the means test would be eliminated in federal old age pensions within two years, at which time Ford workers could anticipate an additional $40 a month at age 70. As we pointed out, if Ford workers chose to put five percent of their earnings into annuities, as Eaton employees were required to do under their contributory plan, they could have a pension in excess of $55 or $95 a month as the case might be. The UAW was to be equally represented with Ford on the board of trustees administering the plan. Another important feature was that service broken due to layoffs could be connected for pension calculation.[5]

When Local 1000 members were formulating contract proposals in 1950, the May membership meeting was devoted to pensions. To start the discussion, Wally Ross, the most knowledgeable of our staff in this area due to previous work experience, compared a number of pension plans with Eaton's. As well as the Ford plan, and the employer-paid, union-administered one covering members of the Amalgamated Clothing Workers, features of others were presented. Simpsons permitted participation in theirs after one year's service, Canada Packers, after two years. The highest level of benefits were provided under the Bank of Montreal's retirement scheme.

The pension objectives set by Local 1000 members at this meeting included a minimum pension of $100 a month after 20 years' service, retirement at age 60 or after 30 years' service, regular employees to be eligible after one year's service, with no age limit. They called for the plan to be company-financed and jointly administered with the union.[6]

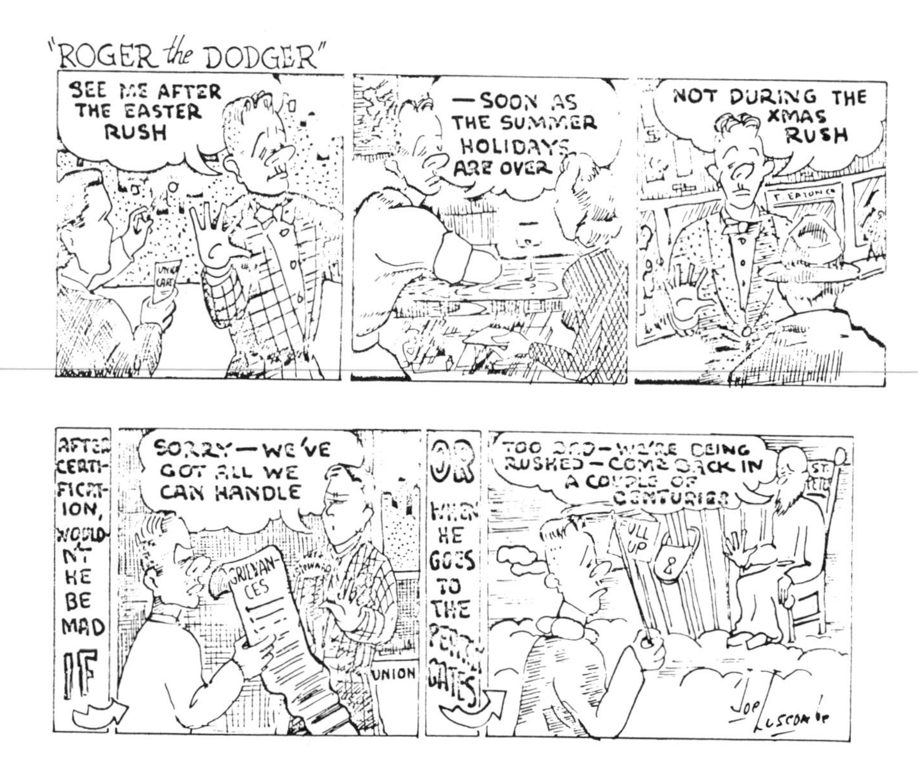

CHAPTER TEN

Helping Hands

SIMULTANEOUSLY with the start of the open drive at Eaton's, the Department Store Organizing Committee of the Congress went into action. On January 5, 1948, Pat Conroy wrote to all affiliated locals, advising that the Retail, Wholesale and Department Store Union was "now undertaking the organization of the T. Eaton department store chain across Canada, with concentration... on Toronto... which affects between ten and twelve thousand employees." Terming it "one of the biggest jobs facing the Congress," he proposed that each local set up a committee "to collect individual donations from members... so that the campaign will have the support of the rank and file of our unions throughout the country." Contributions would be earmarked for a special "T. Eaton Fund."

At the Toronto Labour Council's meeting on January 13, a report was given of the successful organizational meetings we had had the previous evening. Delegates passed a resolution pledging all-out support to Eaton employees. Like the news release we issued announcing the start of the campaign on January 12, there was no mention of the TLC resolution in the daily press.

An early leaflet combined messages of support and encouragement from DSOC members on behalf of their organizations. Conroy promised "The CCL stands four-square behind the campaign...." Spokesmen for two of the largest affiliates, J. E. McGuire of the Canadian Brotherhood of Railway Employees and C. H. Millard of the Steelworkers, pledged assistance and Millard offered the resources of his union in other industrial centres as well as in Toronto. F. W. Dowling of the United Packinghouse Workers spoke of the broader social goal: "Today the organized labour movement is the most articulate voice in the country for a better world.... We look forward with pleasure to having Eaton employees join with us in making democracy work for themselves and for others." It was pointed out that the men and women handing them leaflets every week were volunteers from other unions, a practical gesture of solidarity.

In the months to come, Local 1000 members had the opportunity of hearing at firsthand a number of these union leaders. Notwithstanding the never-ending pressures of their work, we were able to secure a succession of outstanding speakers for our monthly membership meetings, and thus, to give Eaton employees some insight into the ideals of the labour movement, and the dedication of its leaders.

To reach individual members of other local unions, quantities of large buttons imprinted: "I Am Helping to ORGANIZE EATON'S" were made available for sale, proceeds to the T. Eaton Fund. From then on, these buttons were much in evidence at union conferences. In turn, by means of regular circulars to all CCL locals, and reports to the Labour Councils across the country, members were kept posted on the campaign.

Over the summer we put much effort into the construction of a Local 1000 float to be entered in the Labour Day parade, the annual event when members of the two labour congresses managed to forget their differences and march together. Participation not only gave us a chance to inform the general public of our campaign, but to acknowledge the support received from Toronto unionists. Our float turned out to be quite elaborate and colourful. At one end, a tumbledown shack depicted Eaton's outmoded employee relations, contrasted with the facsimile of a modern dwelling, bedecked with union objectives. The panel skirting the truck proclaimed that Local 1000 was organizing Eaton's, and the theme "We're Moving into a Union House" to tie in with the display.

The fine, sunny weather that Labour Day brought out crowds to see the floats and watch 25,000 unionists march to the Exhibition Grounds to hear speeches from union officials. Speaking for the CCL, president A. R. Mosher called for labour unity, a low-cost housing programme and the re-imposition of price controls. "The workers are blamed for endeavouring to keep up with price increases," he protested, "but they find that every wage increase . . . is offset by a corresponding or greater increase in prices." Thirty years later, Mosher's words still have a familiar ring.

Our first banquet for committee members was planned for September 17, with Pat Conroy as the main speaker. The timing could not have been better, as we had just "scooped" the Company by announcing their forthcoming pension plan, and union talk at Eaton's was at a high point. The Chez Paree banquet hall on Bloor Street was packed to the doors.

Conroy was in top form, and delivered a spirited address. He told the gathering, "The welfare of all people demands that white-collar workers cannot remain in a groove by themselves . . . . We are not doing you a favour.... We need your hundreds of people of intelligence and good education to help us strengthen the gains we have made. Collective bargaining would bring monetary rewards, "but the greatest [gain] of all is in self-respect, the right to decide your own destiny. That cannot be calculated in terms of money." He concluded with the appeal, "Your staff cannot do the job alone. They need your help and lots of it. Let's get on with the job tomorrow morning!" This the committee members did. More cards came in during September than in any previous month of the drive.

The next month, the CCL annual convention opened on October 11 at the Royal York Hotel in Toronto, giving us a chance to acquaint delegates from right across Canada with the progress of the campaign. Using the display from the Labour Day float, we set up a booth in the lobby where we chatted with delegates, passed out copies of *Unionize* and sold "Organize Eaton's" buttons.

Eaton's delivered a quantity of printed leaflets for convention delegates, welcoming them to Toronto, and thoughtfully included a map showing the route to their stores. More thoughtful still, they refrained from saying how unwelcome they found the attentions of Local 1000!

Since I had attended every CCL convention since it was founded in 1940, and knew delegates from various parts of the country, it was agreed that I should report to the conference for Local 1000. The news of our progress to date was received with heart-warming applause.

Local 1000's membership meeting was scheduled for October 13, and despite the pressure of convention business, A. R. Mosher took time to officiate at the presentation of the charter of the local which had been received from RWDSU, and to briefly address the meeting. The day before, his own union, the CBRE & OTW had had its fortieth birthday party under his leadership.

Mosher, always a forthright speaker, told Eaton employees, "I would not make you a single promise. Whether your union will be of value to you or not, whether it will advance your economic welfare, will depend far more on *you* than on anybody else." He reminded them that railway unionists "have been paying dues all these years, while you have been paying yours to the boss — and he has built up a pretty nice bank account compared to any one of you."

"A lot of people working for low wages still seem to think the labour movement is just a rabble where people get together to make trouble, to organize strikes, to fight industry," Mosher went on. "The moment you start to enquire, you realize this is a fallacy.... As individuals we are powerless... the world is organized, employers are organized, and we must pay the organized price for all our needs. We should organize so as to charge the organized price for the services we render.''

Howard Mitchell and Jimmie James, RWDSU representatives in charge of Saskatchewan and Manitoba, were also in attendance, to stress how important the success of the Toronto campaign was to department store workers in their provinces. Earlier in 1948, a contract had been signed between Local 468, RWDSU, and the Hudson's Bay Company in Winnipeg, covering some 500 employees in the restaurants, bakery, delivery, maintenance department and coal yard, which along with other gains, included a 5.7 percent general increase in wages.

In mid-November, the Eaton Drive became the focal point of discussion at another conference, this time the fifth biennial convention of the International RWDSU, in Grand Rapids, Michigan. The union's organizational efforts in the next period were to centre on the southern United States, where the CIO was conducting a vigorous campaign, and in Canada. Lynn Williams reported on the Local 1000 campaign, and again our booth was a gathering point for delegates, who made their good wishes tangible by buying ''Organize Eaton's'' buttons like hot cakes. A unanimously-adopted resolution promised ''full financial and moral support.''

Through conversing with delegates, Lynn brought back a wealth of information to pass on to our members. For example, shoe salesmen from New York told of their long struggle to organize their local and of their conditions under the present contract. They earned $61 per week, plus 2 percent commission on all sales, plus ''spiffs,'' to average between $75 and $80 a week.[1] When they heard this, our shoe committee members redoubled their efforts!

Meanwhile, Eaton employees were bracing themselves for the annual bedlam of the Christmas rush, and working all day on Saturday, starting November 6. Final touches were being added for the annual Santa Claus parade, an event which had attracted huge crowds of Toronto's children and their parents since 1905 when Timothy Eaton originated the parade. After complimenting all the staff who worked so hard to create the story-book procession, Marjorie Gow found the similarity between the illusory father figure of St. Nick and Eaton's paternalism too much to resist, and commented in *Unionize* (November 23, 1948):

> Santa Claus is a wonderful idea — for children. When the belief in a portly giver of gifts outlasts childhood, it's a pathetic spectacle. A

> corporation conducted on paternalistic lines is a hang-over of the Santa myth.
>
> Santa Claus in a business suit likes to fancy [himself] in the role of St. Nick.... Employees are expected to act like well-brought-up, old-fashioned children, seen and not heard... grateful for any little charities and "privileges" — but never, never insisting on having any rights of their own.
>
> Employees in unionized companies have grown up. They are no longer standing around imitation Christmas trees, waiting to have their little noses wiped. They sit down together and decide what things they can justly claim to be their rights... and then bargain collectively with management.

The time was approaching when the managers could expect their annual bonus (that is, if they had demonstrated their ability to cut costs) a bonus which had been a sore point with employees over the years. To appease this resentment, Eaton's came up that year with the incredibly clumsy formula that all those earning more than $50.60 a week would also have a bonus amounting to two weeks' pay. Since very few below the managerial level earned that much, it appeared to be aimed at enhancing the loyalty of some supervisors and straight commission salesmen. Interestingly, what sharpened the employees' ire was not the amount of $50 but the additional 60 cents. It was never explained to them by what niggling feat of bookkeeping legerdemain this precise amount was arrived at.

December was dreaded as the worst month of the year. As well as the six-day week with no overtime for Saturday afternoons, there were the exhausting night openings before Christmas. Further, the sales-clerks and others regarded much of the extra work caused by the crush of last-minute shoppers as an exercise in futility, as mountains of exchanges piled up when the holiday was barely over. The employees paid a heavy price for the commercialism of Christmas.

According to a former Mail Order employee, frustration reached a peak in 1950, when employees received two Christmas cards, one from John David and one from Lady Eaton. She recalls: "The message on Lady Eaton's card came across that we should all thank God that we had jobs. We had worked that Christmas Eve till the last dog was hung. What the employees did was carry those cards out of the building and discard them. You should have seen the streets around Eaton's.... (They had) the street cleaners out on Christmas Day."

Several times during the year, Local 1000 membership meetings had gone on record in favour of a five-day week, reported in *Unionize* with the oft-repeated quotation from Timothy Eaton, in which he hoped his employees would live to see the day when Saturdays would be devoted to recreation and Sundays to rest and worship.

From the outset, it was my view, not shared by all of our staff, that Saturdays off for department store salesclerks was not a realistic bargaining objective. When were industrial workers on a Monday-to-Friday schedule to shop? If the membership did not see it that way, perhaps it was because they were inclined to take the Eatons at their word. In any case, one can hardly blame them if, in the midst of the seasonal bedlam, they decided to reiterate this goal and take it one step further. At the Local 1000 meeting on December 6, after a lengthy discussion, the following resolution was endorsed with the instruction that it be sent to John David Eaton as president:

> WHEREAS the needs of the shopping public can be filled in five days as well as in 5 1/2 or 6, and
>
> WHEREAS the general trend of organized labour is to work a shorter week in the interests of the health and welfare of the individual worker and in a more equitable distribution of work among all employable people;
>
> THEREFORE BE IT RESOLVED that Local 1000, Department Store Employees' Union... forward a request to the T. Eaton Company to establish a year-round five-day work week with a maximum of 40 hours, Monday to Friday, with no reduction in pay.

This last membership meeting for 1948 was a very full one. As well as the lengthy discussion on the five-day week, Larry Sefton, then in charge of the Hamilton area for the Steelworkers, was our guest speaker, and extended best wishes from these locals who were actively supporting our campaign. The evening came to a close amidst bursts of laughter as members performed a zany skit entitled "Adventures of P. Ulysses Clutterbuck in Toyland."

CHAPTER ELEVEN

Orphaned by the Storm

THE DELEGATES at the Grand Rapids convention of the RWDSU could not have had an inkling when they voted full financial and other support for Local 1000 that a month later, on December 15, 1948, the jurisdiction of their union in the department store field would be lifted by the CIO. For some time, our staff had been aware that there was a row going on in New York between the International and leaders of the department store locals. However, we didn't know that when Sam Wolchok was re-elected president, unopposed and with a standing ovation, it was due to the fact that the opposing dissident locals had seceded from RWDSU not long prior to the convention.

It might be useful to digress long enough briefly to review the early background of the CIO's retail union.[1] Following the formation of the CIO, the United Retail Employees of America was established, not by organizing the unorganized, but by splitting off a sizeable portion of the New York membership of the Retail Clerks, AFL. Its founding convention was held in 1937 at which time Sam Wolchok was elected president. That same year the CIO named a Department Store Organizing Committee, as it was felt that the task of organizing millions of retail workers called for more resources than the new retail union could muster. The DSOC-CIO was to be headed by Sidney Hillman of the Amalgamated Clothing Workers, with Wolchok as assistant. Hillman was one of CIO's most experienced and trusted leaders. Further, his union had long been a power in New York City, which had the largest concentration of retail stores in North America, and like Philip Murray and other top CIO officers, Hillman could be relied upon to deal with the Communist factions which were causing problems for the CIO in some quarters. Unfortunately, Hillman became ill, and the DSOC-CIO never functioned effectively; in 1940 it was dissolved, leaving the retail field to Wolchok's union.

Over the next few years, URWDSE[2] made substantial gains in New York department stores. Contracts were signed between Macy's, Gimbels and Bloomingdales, and the International's Locals 1, 2 and 3 respectively, each of which had more than 2,000 members. Another large store, Hearns, became part of Local 1250, a composite incuding the Oppenheim-Collins shoe chain and others. Except for the Macy local, the leadership which emerged in the others toed the Communist Party line, and friction soon developed between them and Wolchok, especially when they set themselves up as an unofficial "union within a union," calling it the "United Department Store Employees."

In 1941, most New York store employees were working a six-day, 45-hour week. In negotiations that year, Local 1250 asked the Hearns management to reduce hours to a five-day, 40-hour week, along with a salary increase. A strike was averted by a compromise agreement: the 40-hour week would be lengthened at peak selling season and shortened during July and August. No pay increase was included, but the local officers felt this could be re-opened if others won the 40-hour week plus an increase.

The next contract negotiations were between Local 2 and Gimbels, with the union making the same hours-and-increase demand. Also the Local 2 committee proposed that the contract be signed only with the local, instead of making the International a party, as required by the union's constitution. Naturally, both Wolchok and Gimbels rejected this idea, but before the issue had to be resolved, a compromise basis for settlement was reached, to be put before the members: employees who preferred a 45-hour week would get a larger wage increase than those whose work week was reduced to 42½ hours. Local 2 members voted in favour of this proposal, but within a few days, under pressure from Local 1250 and others, the president of Local 2 repudiated the tentative agreement, and negotiations became stalemated. In mid-August, Gimbel employees struck, and for the time being, differences between the International and local officers were shelved. After mediation through the CIO, an alternative was worked out, calling for either a 42½-hour week with a $1.50 per week raise, or a 40-hour week with no increase. The strikers voted overwhelmingly for the shorter week, and the strike ended on September 11. It was a major victory for the union, and the five-day, 40-hour week soon became the pattern in union and unorganized stores alike in New York City.

The strike settled, quarrels resumed between Wolchok and the left-wing local leaders until Pearl Harbour and the Nazi invasion of the USSR dramatically changed the tactics of the Communists in unions, both in the U.S. and Canada. From being super-militants, they became fervid supporters of the "no-strike pledge," regardless of the trade union issue. The steady stream of slander against union leaders who did not share their political views was dropped or soft-pedalled. Although New York was centre stage for the protagonists, the URWDSE was making substantial gains among wholesale, warehouse and dairy workers in cities such as St. Louis, Toledo and Detroit, and department stores in Pittsburgh and Boston.

The most protracted and costly struggle in the union's brief existence was with Montgomery Ward in Chicago, the longest-established mail order house in the U.S. After winning a representation vote in 1940 for Ward's warehouse employees, a year went by without a contract in sight. Then, early in 1942, URWDSE won a vote at the Chicago store, only to again reach an impasse in negotiations. When a strike seemed imminent, it took a directive by the National War Labor Board and two personal orders from President Roosevelt before Ward signed a contract, but when it expired a year later, union-busting tactics were resumed. Sewell Avery, Board Chairman of the firm, in charge of labour relations, adamantly refused to renew the contract despite more NWLB directives until, in April 1944, the employees struck.

Again, Roosevelt stepped in, placing the U.S. Army in control of Ward's operations in order to end the strike. This sent shock waves through the business community as the press photographed Sewell Avery being carried from his office by burly soldiers. This "occupation" was relinquished at the end of the War, at which time Ward's promptly renewed its unremitting attack on the union. The dispute devoured funds and manpower and weakened both the International and local alike until, eventually, the latter disintegrated from sheer exhaustion.

The passage of the Taft-Hartley Act in the United States in 1947 rekindled the dissension in RWDSU (the name was changed at the 1946 convention). Under this legalized witch hunt, any union official who refused to sign an affidavit that he or she was not a member of the Communist Party could not be a party to a collective bargaining agreement. Furthermore, a union whose officers had not signed the affidavits could not appear on a ballot in a representation vote. Two incidents arising from this law brought matters to a head in RWDSU.

The executive of Local 3 suspended three Bloomingdale members who had been trying to oust them from office on the grounds of "being Communists," and asked the company to dismiss them. The International Board ordered the local to reinstate the three members. While this was still up in the air, the contract between Oppenheim-Collins and Local 1250 expired, and the employer refused to renew it, since the local officers had declined to sign the Taft-Hartley affidavits.

A strike, unauthorized by the International, ensued. Finally, as the employees still wanted a union, the National Labor Relations Board conducted a vote which was won by the Retail Clerks, AFL; Local 1250's officers had forfeited the right of RWDSU to be on the ballot.

This was more than Wolchok and his executive could swallow. They made it mandatory that the local officers involved sign the affidavits required under the Taft-Hartley law or hold new elections. Both sides were rigid. The officers in question still refused and the International placed their locals under its administration, thereby removing their authority. But before this could take effect, these locals were persuaded to secede from RWDSU. The Macy local, not directly involved in the political infighting, decided to become independent. Thus, prior to the Grand Rapids convention in 1948, on top of the drain of the Montgomery Ward ordeal, RWDSU had just lost a large bloc of its New York membership.

Phil Murray, by now CIO president, had backed Wolchok in this internecine struggle. However, when he saw that the fracas had reached the point where it seemed improbable that RWDSU under Wolchok's leadership could maintain or increase its strength in the retail field, Murray publicly suggested that its International officers resign. This time Wolchok and his cohorts were on the defensive and declined. Moving swiftly, on December 15, the CIO transferred jurisdiction for the organization of department and men's wear stores to the Amalgamated Clothing Workers of America (ACW).

Perhaps Norm Twist, RWDSU Canadian director, who must have known how serious the situation was in his union, did not wish to upset our group with the details, or perhaps we were just too busy to delve into the matter. More crucial from our viewpoint, we were not aware that the T. Eaton Fund was depleted, and the salaries of Lynn, Marjorie and Wally were being paid temporarily from the general funds of the Congress. In any case, the disarray of RWDSU in the United States was very soon reflected in its Canadian operations.

Gus Sumner, the only organizer on our staff paid by RWDSU, had returned to the U.S. at the end of 1948. Early in 1949, Twist departed for St. Louis and we heard that both he and his former director, Harold Gibbons, had moved over to jobs with the Teamsters' union. Tommy MacLachlan took over as Canadian director, but had cutbacks in staff, particularly in Western Canada. Wolchok was replaced by Irving Simon, leader of a strong shoe salesmen's local in New York, who began the long process of rebuilding the shattered union.

By now Local 1000, Department Store Employees Union, was a healthy year-old infant, nearing the 3000-mark in membership. With that many cards signed in a RWDSU-chartered local, a new foster parent prior to certification was out of the question. But who was going to look after the baby's room and board, now running around $2,500 a month? On behalf of the CCL's Department Store Organizing Committee, Dowling, Millard and Conroy lost no time in impressing upon the ACW's New York headquarters that as well as the department store jurisdiction, they had inherited a campaign that was well under way in Toronto, Canada, and in dire need of financial assistance.

In March 1949, a three-member team from the ACW arrived to assess our operation. They were thorough and business-like in their investigations, which lasted the better part of a week. On the basis of their report, the ACW decided to contribute $2,000 a month to the Eaton campaign, and re-examine the situation around the end of the year. There would be no change in the status of Local 1000 as far as affiliation was concerned — that could be dealt with after certification — and the DSOC-CCL would continue to raise further funds and exercise general supervision over the Drive.

With all this new turn of events, we had not skipped an issue of *Unionize*. The campaign had simply been given added impetus, as we announced on March 29, by the decision of the ACW, one of the CIO's most successful unions, to "contribute substantially to the Eaton Drive." Naturally, we lauded their considerable achievements in providing pension and welfare benefits to their members, paid for by the employers, and in maintaining harmonious union-management relations in the clothing industry. Ironically, however, it was this same union that for almost half a century had not succeeded in bringing clothing workers in Eaton's Toronto factory under a collective agreement.

At 572 Bay Street, outwardly oblivious to this intra-union change in scene, daily activities carried on as usual with department meetings, training new stewards and so on. With the regular ACW monthly donation, it was possible to plan our work for the rest of the year and we began looking for a replacement for Gus Sumner. Clearly, however, unless our budget was substantially increased, members of Local 1000 would have to shoulder an ever-increasing share of the organizing work, and to this end we directed all our efforts.

CHAPTER TWELVE

Gaining Momentum

NO SOONER WAS the Christmas gold rush over than the January slump-cum-sales became the order of the day, redoubling employees' insecurity and fear of layoff. The casuals had gone before year end, but at the start of 1949 layoffs cut deeper, extending to regular staff. As well, the practice prevalent in the Thirties of asking employees — married women in particular — to "take a few days off" was revived in many departments. Full-time workers with some years' service were sent off for three days to a week without pay, while part-timers, with lesser pay and benefits, were kept on. Since each department manager made his own personnel decisions it led to some chaotic situations. One day the main switchboard was left with insufficient operators to take care of numerous department sales, and the manager had to scramble around for help while full-time operators lost pay.[1]

Our claim that a union contract was the only way to protect seniority in layoffs, whether temporary or permanent, took on added meaning. Besides, what kind of paternalism was this, we asked, if Eaton's couldn't afford to keep on its regular staff for a few slack weeks right after their most lucrative season?

Membership in Local 1000 was growing at a steady pace, if not as fast as we had hoped. The first time we announced how many had enrolled was at the March meeting, headlined in the next *Unionize*: "OVER 3,000 SIGNED Local 1000 Over Half-Way Mark."

The general committee suggested we adopt the slogan, "Every Member Get A Member," a logical proposal which, if acted upon, would produce enough to apply for certification, and we commenced using this in all our leaflets. Unfortunately, as in most organizations, only a small minority responded, and the stewards had to continue taking the initiative in signing up co-workers.

Two events in April sparked a good deal of interest. As guest speaker at the April 5 membership meeting, we were able to secure Gladys Dickason, the personable and dynamic vice-president of the Amalgamated Clothing Workers in New York, and one of the team sent to assess our campaign the previous month. A former economics

Unionize

Vol. 2, No. 11

Issued by Department Store Employees' Union, Local 1000
Affiliated RWDSU, CCL-CIO, 572 Bay St. Toronto 2, EL. 7539

March 22, 1949

EVERY·MEMBER·GET·A·MEMBER

Since the announcement was made last week that over 3000 Eaton employees have signed up in Local 1000, congratulations have been coming in from many quarters.

There is good reason for this. The eyes of department store workers all over Canada are upon the Eaton organizing campaign. Unionization is still in its infancy in department stores and other white-collar groups in Canada, so there is, naturally, intense interest in the Toronto venture.

Another reason is that 3000 sounds like a lot of people. A 3000 membership would mean, in most places, a whopping big local union and people outside are

(cont. on Page 4)

DISMISSED WITHOUT WARNING

EX-EATON EMPLOYEE CHARGES MRS. HOMUTH WITH HARSH AND UNFAIR TREATMENT

(See story on Page 2)

lecturer and now research director of the ACW, Miss Dickason had acquired much practical organizational experience in her 15 years with that union. She had been involved in the campaign to organize Cluett Peabody's (overalls) factory, a 100-year old firm which, like Eaton's, had a long tradition of bucking unions.

Relating the story of the clothing workers' union from its beginnings in 1910 when they earned $4 and $5 for a 72-hour week, Dickason said there had never been a time when organizing was easy, but at least now Eaton employees had the law on their side. The health, insurance and retirement plans, employer-paid and union-administered, enjoyed by ACW members were outstanding in North America. Just at that time, the union was sponsoring a slum-clearance programme and $10-million co-operative housing project in conjunction with the City of New York. In concluding, she did not have to refer to the president of Eaton's by name when she told the members:

> It may seem wonderful to read the career stories of a Rockefeller or other multi-millionaire... but the success story of the Clothing Workers' Union is a greater story than that of any man who has succeeded in piling up millions for himself... You can accomplish through the labour movement so much more than you ever dreamed... all it takes is faith and courage.

On Saturday, April 23, the first Local 1000 Seminar combined education and entertainment. It was held in the remodelled Memorial Hall, operated by the Canadian Legion, at 22 College Street. The afternoon was given over to group sessions on the conduct of meetings, rules of order, how to report union news, and public speaking. A registration fee of $1 included dinner and an evening of entertainment, with extra dinner tickets available for members' spouses or friends.

Our after-dinner speaker was Miss Agnes MacPhail, CCF MPP for York East, who delighted the capacity audience with her dry humour, as she likened the position of the individual employee at Eaton's to the story about the elephant trumpeting "every man for himself" as he danced among the chickens. Participation in unions, Miss MacPhail had found, led workers to become interested in provincial laws that affected them directly and then in legislation designed to improve the lot of all Canadians. To illustrate, the CCL had just presented its annual brief to the federal government, urging action on low-cost housing, pensions of $60 a month and a national fuel policy.

In mid-April Ernest Arnold joined our staff, so that the work load could be redistributed. The Mail Order division, which was making good progress, was assigned to Ernie, while Wally took on Delivery, also nearing its majority, and the Factory departments, the weakest of the lot in terms of members.

Two or three department meetings were held every day at our office, and when a department had a substantial number signed up, a steward was elected, with assistants, if the size of the department warranted.

Most often the same person who had been doing the organizing was elected steward, but to be chosen by co-workers provided a new sense of commitment. Apart from organizational purposes, these meetings gave employees an opportunity to discuss problems specific to their department, and to work out proposals for solving them through collective bargaining. For example, in selling departments there was a widespread trend from salary-plus-commission to straight salary. To determine if they were winning or losing on this new basis, employees had to break the "private and confidential" bugaboo about earnings and discuss them openly at union meetings. Out of such meetings came examples of the inequities in Eaton's wage policy which we publicized in *Unionize*; in just one issue, May 10, 1949, we cited four:

> MAIL ORDER DRESSES: Girls hired a year ago at $19 have now been raised to $20, but new help is being taken on to do the same work at $21.
>
> COMMISSION SALESPEOPLE: When commission people are changed over to straight salary, seniority allowance is not taken into consideration when adjustments are made.
>
> RECEIVERS: At Fraser Ave. there is a variation of $10 a week for receivers doing the same work.
>
> BASEMENT GROCERIES: Stockmen are (hired) anywhere from $24 to $30, all doing the same work.

As well as salary inequities, more ammunition was provided to stewards and members by our exposure of unjust treatment in three cases of severance of employment.

The union office received numerous complaints about Mrs. Dorothy Homuth, in charge of female personnel in Eaton's Employment Office.[2] When a department manager decided to dispense with an employee's services, Mrs. Homuth's role was to finalize the matter. (Incidentally, Lady Eaton's memoirs refer to Mrs. Homuth as a personal friend and travelling companion.[3]) Her manner in dealing with employees was often heartless and demeaning, as in the case of Isabella Honeyman.

On her arrival the morning of March 9, 1949 at the Mail Order Files office, where she had worked for four and one-half years, Isabella Honeyman was told to see Mrs. Homuth at the Employment Office. Due to a heart condition, Miss Honeyman had lost time but her supervisors had never complained about her work. Mrs. Homuth informed her that, as her department was slack, she was arranging a transfer, but in the meantime Miss Honeyman was asked to sign her severance slip. Greatly upset because she was self-supporting, she told her friends in her office what had happened and, as she was well liked, considerable indignation was expressed. It reached the ears of

Mrs. Homuth, who ordered her to return to the Employment Office. There, in front of others, Miss Honeyman received a tonguelashing from Mrs. Homuth for repeating their "confidential" conversation, and was told: "I don't like your attitude... Don't think you're going to dictate to me." The hapless employee was then informed that any transfer was out of the question and advised not to return to her department again.

In April we reported the treatment received by Mrs. Grace Keener, an experienced saladmaker in the Louisa Street Employees' Cafeteria, who had worked for Eaton's in Montreal and Toronto for 13 years. Speed-up was the order of the day in restaurant departments, but when it reached the point of dietitians standing over employees checking and recording the time spent on every operation, nerves became even more frayed. One Saturday morning, the dietitian in charge of Mrs. Keener's section told her that her work methods were being changed, that she was to throw out the salad moulds she had just made, and in future would work from a menu. On Monday morning, no menu or other instructions were provided and, in a burst of irritation, Mrs. Keener was heard to remark, "I guess I'll have to get a transfer out of here." No sooner said than done. Asked to report to the Employment Office, she was handed an "open" transfer, Eaton's gutless way of saying "you're fired," and subsequently received one week's pay in lieu of notice — after 13 years' service! She was replaced by an employee with no saladmaking experience.[4]

The discharge of G.A. Farley provided an even greater element of drama as well as injustice. For more than a year, Mr. Farley was employed on the fire inspection staff, responsible to Mr. Walter Smith, chief engineer. He had good credentials, having trained with the London, England, fire brigade, and later having had charge of two fire stations. During his year at Eaton's, his reports drew to Mr. Smith's attention many shortcomings in the Company's fire prevention measures, as well as hazards involved in the storage and use of flammable materials by various workshops and departments. By and large, his suggestions were ignored. At the end of February 1949, Farley was given an "open" transfer by reason of "reduction of staff," although he was the second most senior man in his department. However, a new man had been hired six weeks previously, and one week after his dismissal, another man was put in his place.

Being a conscientious type, with a high regard for the safety of human life, Farley prepared a brief about Eaton's fire prevention programme or the lack of it, and requested an interview with John David Eaton. He was seen by the president's assistant, Mr. I.W.

Unionize

DEPARTMENT STORE EMPLOYEES UNION
Local No. 1000

Vol. 2, No. 15 — April 19, 1949

EXPOSES FIRE HAZARDS

FIRE PROTECTION EXPERT FIRED DID JOB TOO WELL

G. A. T. Farley is no longer at Eaton's. Yet Farley is the kind of man both the company and the shopping public need at Eaton's.

Fully qualified in fire protection, Mr. Farley received his training on the London (Eng.) Fire Brigade. Before coming to Canada, he was in charge of the Shoreditch and Millwall stations.

Mr. Farley worked for over a year on the Eaton fire inspection staff and was responsible to Walter Smith, the Chief Engineer.

Mr. Farley, over his period of service, on many occasions drew to the attention of Mr. Smith the inadequacy of existing fire prevention measures at Eaton's. Space does not permit a full listing of these faults, but they range from lack of training of fire inspection personnel and organization of emergency brigades to defective and insufficient fire fighting equipment. Particularly shocking to a man of Farley's experience was the dangerous storing of volatile

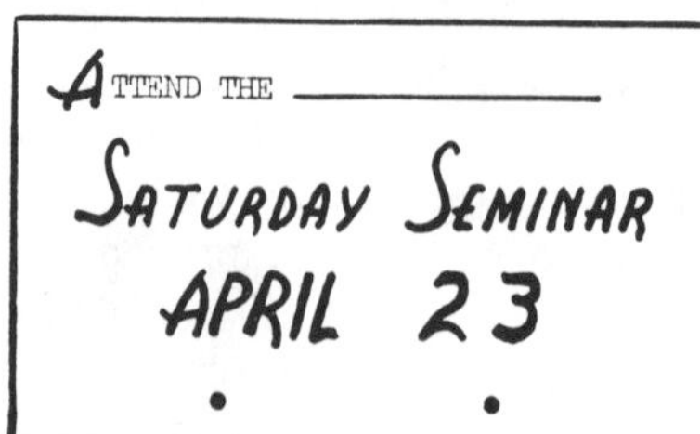
ATTEND THE
SATURDAY SEMINAR
APRIL 23

SPEED-UP IRKS EMPLOYEES' C A F. WORKERS

◆ There's work, worry, confusion and frayed nerves behind the scenes in the Employees' Cafeteria these days. The women who work in this section say it was bad enough before, but now that they are being "time-studied", their every

Ford. An immediate investigation was ordered on the basis of the contents of Farley's brief, and as a result, a special committee, responsible directly to the Board of Directors, was charged with keeping an eye on fire prevention in future. But G. A. Farley was not reinstated in his job, nor was another found for him at Eaton's. Reminding employees that without a union contract there is no such thing as "fire" protection, we commented, "It is incredible that the T. Eaton Co. should repay the sincerity and efficiency of a man of Farley's calibre with such gross ingratitude."[5]

It was equally incredible, with 10,000 copies of *Unionize* headlined:

EXPOSES FIRE HAZARDS
Fire Protection Expert Fired
Did Job Too Well

circulating around Eaton's that no newspaper reporter got wind of it. Or had advertising clout once again defused a potentially explosive news item?

Through such stories, Local 1000 was acquiring stature as the voice of employees who felt they had been wrongfully dealt with, and the stewards appreciated the talking points that our constant barrage of publicity gave them. When we discussed the ways in which they could help with members of the Stewards' Council, as the general committee had been renamed, the response was immediate and most gratifying. Up to this time, no active member had been identified by name in our leaflets or asked to take an overt stand. It now seemed that, notwithstanding all the reasons Eaton's found to rid itself of employees, union activity did not appear to be one of them, and so we proposed to the steward body a number of ways in which they could help, if they were prepared to take an open stand.

In June members began helping to hand out leaflets, and by the end of the Drive, more than half the distributors were Eaton employees. Others came to our office the night before to put leaflets through the folding machine and bundle them in the right quantity for the various entrances. Our hard-pressed office staff gained assistance in the mushrooming task of keeping membership records and department files up to date. In a direct and effective form of organizing assistance, by July some 50 stewards were devoting an evening or two a week to calling on prospective members. After a break-in period with one of our staff, they would carry on in pairs. This made for more vocal and educated unionists. It was also an eye-opener to many. Here is how Anne Stone, a Mail Order steward, recalls her canvassing experience:

> I had never belonged to a union before, and knew absolutely nothing about union activity. I think I joined because Lynn Williams convinced me I'd be a bit of a fink if I didn't... It was one of the greatest things that ever happened to me. Lynn used to call for me in his car and we'd go tooting around soliciting members. In my own family we had never been affluent and we'd lived through the Depression and everything else, but some of the places we visited were appalling, they were so poverty stricken. The poorer people were, the more they were afraid, even outside

> working hours, when we suggested that they join the union. I have crawled into cellars and climbed up to single rooms in attics. They were the people who were most reluctant... they had so little and they didn't want to lose what they had.[6]

To compensate for the stony silence of the press, we booked a 15-minute period on CKEY, one of Toronto's most popular radio stations. Our programme commenced with a dramatization of department store workers' problems, followed by C. H. Millard who pledged aid from the Steelworkers "as long as required in your efforts to build a democratic union" because (when) "men are working at Eaton's for $36 a week, the minimum of $45.76 in our industry is in constant danger.... Management points out... there are men ready to work for less than a union wage — yes — even less than a living wage. That threatens the standards we are seeking to establish." A Local 1000 steward concluded by informing listeners that there were now 4,000 union members at Eaton's and appealed to married women, part-timers and those nearing retirement to join in order to secure the required majority.

Despite a record heat wave that summer, August was an especially busy month. Plans were made at the Stewards' Council on August 8 for an all-out effort in September. To secure additional assistance for daily leaflet distributions and other demonstrations, the Toronto Labour Council arranged a meeting of local union officers. This dovetailed with an Action Banquet on August 31 at Memorial Hall, for Local 1000 activists and those from other unions.

TLC president, Murray Cotterill, always an entertaining speaker, addressed the banquet and introduced other union officials. He contrasted the relationship under a "real business partnership between employees and employer through a union" with the maudlin sentimentality of the "one big happy family" fantasy.

A surprise guest, in town on business, was A. R. Mosher. In his usual direct style, he told he gathering: "You people have done a great deal, but you haven't done enough — not one of you." Assuring them of continued CCL support, he voiced his own experience: "When you really *get* the idea of trade unionism, it becomes implanted in your very heart. And though you may get tired and have many discouragements, it stays there... and you go on and on, making your company and your nation better places to work and live." Ending with a sing-song and dancing, the evening supplied lots of adrenalin before we tackled the most strenuous month of activity so far.

When the Labour Day Parade converged on the Exhibition Grounds, Local 1000 was again represented. The theme of our float this time was

Unionize
DEPARTMENT STORE EMPLOYEES UNION
Local No. 1000
Vol. 2, No. 30
Aug. 16, 1949

LOCAL 1000 STEWARDS ANNOUNCE SEPTEMBER DRIVE

AIMED TO RAISE PRESENT 4,000 MEMBERSHIP TO CERTIFICATION PEAK

A meeting of the steward body of Local 1000 on August 8th, decided to launch an "ALL-OUT" drive for union members in the month of September.

"Our membership in Local 1000 is over the 4,000 mark now", said a spokesman for the union. "We need something like 6,500 to be safe in making application for certification. There is no reason why we can't get the 2,500 odd new members we need signed up in short order, if we all work at it."

The meeting discussed detailed arrangements for the drive. September promises to be a lively and profitable month for Local 1000.

"INTO ACTION" -- STEWARDS

The following resolution was passed by a meeting of Local 1000 Stewards on August 8:

.......WHEREAS we need about 6,500 members.....before we can safely apply for certification......AND WHEREAS we are convinced that all members of Local 1000 will be glad to do everything in their power to bring about a successful and speedy conclusion of the organizing campaign in the T. Eaton Company;

THEREFORE BE IT RESOLVED that this Local Union launch an all-out organizing drive for new members during the month of September and that every member be recruited and every effort bent to reaching our objective, namely, "CERTIFICATION FOR LOCAL 1000" and that we immediately get into action to accomplish this purpose.

WHAT CAN I DO?

"On To Certification" and was again designed to do double duty, to be driven around Eaton's during the noon hour later in the month.

Our plan for September was to concentrate one week at a time on different divisions, starting with Mail Order, nearing its majority, and the Annex Store. Daily leaflets focussed on concerns of the particular division, and advertised meetings to be held once a week from

TOMORROW
MAY BE TOO LATE
YOU NEED UNION BENEFITS NOW
COME ON STORE EMPLOYEES GET
LOCAL 1000 CERTIFIED ----
SIGN UP THE
NON-MEMBERS

5:00 to 6:00 p.m. at Rai Purdy's Auditorium, a conveniently-located hall on Queen Street, just east of Yonge. The Main Store, where about one-third of Eaton's Toronto employees worked, was the target for the second week. As anticipated, we could report that only 200 more memberships were needed to give Mail Order its majority, as well as cards from a dozen new departments in the Annex. At the end of Main Store week, gains had been made in 40 departments, of which, encouragingly, about a third were among those staffed by women salesclerks.

On Saturday, September 17, members of other unions, wearing badges lettered "Union Pay is Good Pay — I Get It!" handed out 5,000 shopping bags imprinted "Join Local 1000" to customers at all the store entrances. Apart from its utilitarian aspect, this was one of our most successful "gimmicks" during the drive, as the shopping bags were seen around for a long time afterwards.

During the third week our efforts were directed at the Delivery-Dispatch depots, already close to a majority, and the College Street Store, as well as the workshops on Hayter Street which employed a variety of tradesmen whose skills were not matched by their pay.

For instance, we drew attention to the oddity that the men who built and repaired church organs received less pay than Eaton's maintenance painters, reflecting the fact that painters in Toronto were unionized, whereas organ builders were not.[7]

Salary objectives were the subject of discussion at the weekly after-work meetings, but even three such sessions were scarcely enough to tie together points raised by such a variegated group of workers.

There was unanimous agreement that the union should seek a starting rate of $35 a week for unskilled work, to be increased by automatic increases at intervals to $45 after three years' service.

A proper job classification should be undertaken to provide differentials above the minimum of $35 for semi-skilled and skilled occupations. Equal pay for equal work, ending pay based on age, sex or marital status, should go hand in hand with classifying jobs rather than people.

Commission salespeople added their objectives, such as negotiated commission rates, no stockroom work during selling hours and no deduction of commission on goods returned 60 days or more after sale. Factory and Mail Order employees wanted piece work or bonus rates to be subject to negotiation.

David Archer, secretary of the Toronto Labour Council, and a member of the Ontario Labour Relations Board, spoke briefly at the September 20 meeting to assure those present of the confidentiality

Unionize

DEPARTMENT STORE EMPLOYEES UNION
Local No. 1000

Vol. 2, No. 38 — Oct. 11, 1949

900 NEW MEMBERS DURING SEPTEMBER

Local 1000 has just had the biggest month in its history. As a result of the stepped-up activity last month, nine hundred new applicants were admitted to membership. This gain has put the Union much closer to achieving the majority needed to make application for certification.

● LOCAL 1000's MEMBERSHIP HAS REACHED THE 4,700 MARK. It would be higher still if it were not for the fact that a good many employees who signed union cards have since left Eaton's for one reason or another (most of them to take better-paying jobs) and consequently are no longer members of the Local.

The greatest increase during the month was in the Mail Order section, which reached and passed its 51% majority. Delivery also went over the top. Both sections are steadily increasing their majorities. Stores and Factory are piling up the memberships daily. It will be interesting to see which gets over the 51% mark first.

. . . .

● OUR SLOGAN CHANGES

The recent heavy increase in membership has inspired artist Luscombe to the flight of fancy at the right - and the resulting alteration in Local 1000's well-known slogan, "EVERY MEMBER GET A MEMBER". The new version is:

"EVERY MEMBER GET half A MEMBER."

observed by the Board in certification procedures involving union membership records. "I can't understand why some people at Eaton's haven't joined the union yet," Archer declared. "Why, they aren't even asked to pay dues until the union is certain! As a Scotchman, that sounds like a wonderful bargain to me." Then he confessed a very personal reason for wanting to see Eaton's unionized: "I worked in the place myself for six years."

The final week in September was devoted to Factory departments and, while more clothing workers joined than in any previous month, the momentum from the other divisions did not seem to make any impact on Factory workers. True, they had almost the same conditions as the unions had achieved in the provincial code governing their industry, but as the secretary of the ACW's Toronto Joint Board, Irving Kalmus, warned them, "Without a contract, the company can cut you off [welfare benefits] at any time."

Toting up the results of this feverish month of activity, we found that Local 1000 had gained 900 new members, and Mail Order and Delivery were over the top with 51 percent or more. We heralded this good news in *Unionize* but didn't publish the depressing discovery, learned after a careful check of department files with stewards, that over the summer we had lost 200 members in turnover. Employees who plan to change jobs usually wait until their vacation is over. And so, as of October, 1949, we had 4,700 of the 6,000 members needed to apply for certification, and cheerily changed the slogan in our leaflets to:

HALF
EVERY MEMBER GET/A MEMBER

After our report to the annual convention of the CCL that same month in Ottawa, many speakers took the microphone to call for nation-wide support to help Local 1000 finish the Drive. The unanimously-adopted resolution was ignored by the press. A special evening session was arranged for delegates and staff, from labour councils and provincial federations, to discuss concrete measures of assisting us. It was agreed that local unions be asked to begin monthly donations, with Steel and Auto undertaking to contact all their locals in this regard. It was fortunate that this initiative started then, since some time was required to get the matter before local union meetings, and also because toward the end of 1949, we learned that our principal source of funds had dried up. The International of the ACW in New York, upon whom the jurisdiction of department store workers had been thrust a year previously, had decided that, thanks but no thanks, they did not wish to pursue this organizational responsibility. This was not publicly announced at the time. In early 1951, the CIO would set up yet another department store organizing committee along the same lines as that of the CCL in Canada. In any case, with membership now at the 5,000-mark, we felt a Micawberish optimism that funds would "turn up" from some source to enable us to complete the Eaton Drive.

More concessions were made by the Company to measures called for by the union. In October, part-timers were permitted to participate in the pension plan. The hiring rate for caretakers was raised to $35 a week, the union objective for a minimum starting rate, but applied only to men; women caretakers were hired at $26. Further salary increases of $1 or $2 a week were granted in most departments.

That fall our membership meetings centred on contract objectives, and by the end of November, a ten-point programme was adopted and published. In addition to the salary proposals already referred to, these were added:

> *Hours and Overtime:* The five-day week, with overtime at time and one-half for all work before and after scheduled hours. (The scheduling of the five-day week was to be decided later.) Double time after the first four hours of overtime and on non-scheduled days. Overtime for commission salespeople to be based on average weekly earnings. Premium of 10¢ per hour for employees working other than day shift.
>
> *Job Security:* In event of layoff, company-wide seniority (Toronto) to prevail, and rehiring in reverse order of seniority. Seniority to remain unbroken for layoff of less than one year. No discharge without one month's notice, except for theft or serious misconduct. Steward to be present when employee notified of discharge; such cases to be processed immediately under grievance procedure.
>
> *Promotions:* By departmental seniority, ability and physical fitness being sufficient. All vacancies involving a promotion to be posted in the department.
>
> *Grievance Procedure:* Step-by-step, from department to top management, to arbitration if necessary.
>
> *Union Recognition:* Union shop and checkoff.
>
> *Retention of Privileges:* No privileges in effect to be altered during the life of the agreement.
>
> *Holidays:* Two weeks' vacation between May 1 and September 30 for regular employees, after one year's service. Three weeks' vacation after five years. Nine paid statutory holidays.
>
> *Probationary Period:* Three months.
>
> *Health and Welfare:* Medical-hospital-dental plan, Company-paid, jointly administered. Cumulative paid sick leave of 1½ days for each month of service.

Pensions of $100 month minimum after 20 years' service. Retirement at 60 or after 30 years' service. Eligibility: one year's service. Company-financed, union administered.

Group Life Insurance equivalent to three years' earnings for regular employees, Company-paid.

With the exception of the health and welfare objectives, there was ample precedent in collective agreements for the others. In both the United States and Canada, the battle to have pension and welfare plans recognized as subjects for collective bargaining had not yet been won, although the victory of the United Auto Workers in bargaining a $100-a-month pension at Ford in the United States was a forerunner of many in steel and other industries.

As yet, there was no universal health plan in Canada. For Eaton employees, therefore, the need for a health plan was even more urgent than for organized industrial workers, since their pay was too low to afford adequate health care. While some Eaton employees were well-treated during illness, there was no consistency. It is not surprising, therefore, that Local 1000's programme called for measures which would represent a hefty cost to the Company, especially if salary and other improvements reduced the high turnover in staff.

On November 5, our first union dance drew a capacity crowd to the Savarin ballroom on Bay Street, indicating that employees were becoming less afraid to be seen at a union function. The 15-member Social Committee was headed by the late Mary Sutton, whose energy and enthusiasm never flagged throughout the campaign. As a Reserve Staff employee (on call for occasional work), Mary was not eligible for the bargaining unit, but she and her husband, a member of the AFL Chemical Workers, contributed more in many ways to Local 1000 than those who stood to benefit from a union.

The Committee were good planners and a hard-working group. Ernie Arnold was assigned to work with them and he developed a lasting friendship with the Suttons. Contrary to rumours that our social affairs were subsidized, they more than paid their way and added several thousands of dollars toward the Drive. To round off 1949, the drivers put on a stag, and a family Christmas Tree Party, which became an annual event, was held at the Purdy Auditorium. Early in the new year, a bowling league was organized.

In mid-November, the local sponsored another 15-minute programme on CKEY. This time ten Eaton employees, identified by name and department, told listeners why a union was needed. They were: Mrs. Enid Mould (Annex Purses); Fred Tinker and Jim Hemphill (two of the "originals," Main Store Bedding and Linens); Frank Brown (Christie

Furniture Warehouse); Terry Foley (Radio Repair); Mrs. Celia Bell (Main Store Groceries); Nick Beckwith (Delivery); Chris Graham and Sam McIlrath (Mail Order) and Mrs. Mae Coulston (College Street Cafeteria). Thanks to this courageous group, membership in November, usually a slow month, rose by 309. However, a turnover of 134 sliced into our net gain, and from then until after Christmas, with employees working a six-day week, membership petered off.

December brought more than the winter chill to test the faithfulness of our leaflet distributors. It was confirmed that the Ontario Labour Relations Board had changed their criteria for determining membership in good standing in a union. Now a minimum payment of $1 toward the union's initiation fee must accompany a signed application for membership card. We were stunned. This *couldn't* happen to us with 5,000 applications already signed. But there was no escape; we *had* to set the machinery in motion to collect $5,000. We broke the news in *Unionize*, December 13, having already discussed it with the Stewards' Council, and renewed our pledge that no dues would be collected prior to certification. The dollars would be banked in a Local 1000 account and used for expenses of the Drive. Collections would begin in January.

We were experiencing with a vengeance the "discouragements" Mosher had spoken of at our Action Banquet. But by now Local 1000 had a solid core of Eaton employees determined to do whatever had to be done to reach their goal. In the first six weeks of 1950, 2,117 of the $1 fees were collected.

CHAPTER THIRTEEN

Operation Certification

THE THIRD YEAR of the Eaton Drive began in the full realization that organization had to be completed in 1950, by spring if possible, and by September at the latest. Our staff had been meeting several times a week since November to plan "Operation Certification." At our membership meeting on January 9, after a review of the organizational situation in all divisions, I concluded by saying: "1950 will tell the tale — and we must make it tell the right tale. We must set our sights for 1,500 to 2,000 more members. The greater your majority, the better your bargaining position when you set your first contract proposals on management's desk."

Unfortunately in the first two weeks, our efforts had to be diverted to an informational mailing to all members about the change in the Labour Board policy regarding the $1 initiation fee, to sending receipt books to stewards, and to hiring another office assistant. Even so, we managed to schedule more than a hundred department meetings to discuss job classification and elect stewards. On January 25 we started a weekly series of five-minute radio programmes entitled "Eaton's Goes Union," to run to the end of March. As we did not have professional help, this was time-consuming: there were scripts to be prepared and rehearsed. The programmes were intended to inform both employees and public of the contract objectives of Local 1000. Participants were Eaton employees or guests from other unions.

Our theme was changed to "NOW is the Time." It was also the time when we needed to know where the next six months' expenses would come from. We made plans, booked radio time and ordered extra printed materials, but it was apparent to me that local union donations alone would not sustain current expenses running to about $3,000 a month. After the last CCL convention, not all provincial federations had followed Saskatchewan's example in getting affiliates to commit themselves to donate a cent or two per member monthly until Eaton's was organized. However, in February, another opportunity would come up at the Ontario Federation of Labour convention in Toronto.

The delegates from the OFL went beyond merely adopting a resolution of support, and decided that our situation warranted a special

Unionize

DEPARTMENT STORE EMPLOYEES' UNION
Local No. 1000

Vol. 3, No. 4. Jan. 24, 1950

"ON THE AIR"

TO-MORROW NITE - 9.05 C.K.E.Y.
WED. JAN. 25 (580 ON YOUR DIAL)

NEW SERIES
"EATON'S GOES UNION"

SH-H SH-SH

QUIET

"THE FIVE-DAY WEEK" IS THE FIRST IN SERIES BEGINNING WEDNESDAY NIGHT.

WINDOW CLEANERS TAKE BIG RISKS— FOR LITTLE PAY

As "UNIONIZE" has pointed out on many different occasions, there are many unfair job classifications and wage rates in Eaton's. One of the most ridiculous is the rate paid to the men doing the dangerous job of window cleaning. Window cleaners are paid only two dollars a week more than the caretakers, though they are required to wash the high outside windows of the store buildings, which is a risky and nerve-wracking job. It is reported that some inside wall washers (who also perform a dangerous job) get $2 a week more than the window cleaners.

conference of local union officers and staff to discuss ways and means of fund-raising. This took place on March 12 at Memorial Hall on College Street, and it was a measure of the importance labour attached to assisting retail workers that, as well as a good attendance from Toronto, others travelled from Windsor, St. Catharines, Hamilton, Kitchener, Oshawa and Peterboro. A. R. Mosher and members of the DSOC-CCL were there as well. George Burt, Canadian director of the UAW, terming the Eaton Drive "the top priority in organizational work in Canada," said he was sure Local 200 (Ford's in Windsor) would gladly relinquish its standing as the largest in Canada to Local 1000.

An objective of $30,000 was set to be raised by asking Ontario locals to donate monthly on a per capita basis. The following week, OFL secretary Cleve Kidd and I drafted the appeal and worked out a suggested quota for each local. To tide us over Dowling and Millard arranged short-term loans from larger Steel and Packinghouse locals.[1]

Recognizing that the need was urgent for a substantial sum, the Congress Executive meeting at the end of March decided that a delegation of Conroy, Dowling and Millard should seek a meeting with the CIO Executive Board in Washington to discuss financial aid. We prepared a brief for the delegation on the background and significance of the Eaton campaign to Canadian labour, along with a statement of receipts and expenditures in 1949. It was emphasized that in order to apply for certification in 1950, it would be necessary to double or triple the current level of expenditures.

The confidential breakdown of Local 1000 membership included in the April 1950 report signalled another compelling reason for stepping up the campaign — the constant toll of turnover. Since January 1948, of just under 6,600 members signed up, 1,822 had left Eaton's. In Mail Order, where wages and working conditions were less favourable than in Stores, turnover had exceeded 50 percent: of an estimated total of 1,900 employees, 1,408 had joined, but only 927 remained. In the "blue-collar" divisions, restaurant workers, caretakers, elevator operators, Delivery and Warehouse, majorities ranging from 53 to 76 percent had been achieved, but the rest of the Main Store, which had the largest potential, was still only 32 percent. Even the selling departments had shown more interest than the Factory where only about a quarter had joined.

The key to increasing the tempo lay in getting more and more members to take an active part, and we concentrated on this. Some were instructed how to prepare routes for canvassing, and then to arrange for canvassers to pick up their kits at the union office. Others helped to make appropriate signs for Lynn's car to be driven around the Stores on paydays to give stewards support in collecting the $1 fees. Members helped to distribute thousands of book matches imprinted: "You Can't Match a Union. Pay Your Dollar for Certification NOW." The Mugwump, symbol of the vacillating employee, materialized in the costume worn by Wally. On April 15, the Social Committee drew another capacity crowd to its second dance at the Savarin.

One of the most effective demonstrations of courage and leadership in the whole campaign took place on March 28 with the distribution of a leaflet which began with the words, "We, the undersigned One Hundred Committee Members..." and was covered on both sides of the sheet with their signatures and departments. The message was brief and to the point. Over 5,000 Eaton employees had joined Local 1000. In order to negotiate with management for the union programme which would benefit all employees, a majority must be members under the provisions of the Ontario Labour Relations Act. "Therefore...we ask you to join...without delay...and to help in signing up employees who have not yet joined." Sixty-five men and 35 women from 85 departments or work locations signed that leaflet, and they will always stand out in my memory as a gutsy roll of honour in the Eaton Drive. Looking over their signatures brings back a flood of memories of the fascinatingly diverse personalities whose interests had converged in building their union.

The April membership meeting tackled the prickly question of spelling out a proposed daily schedule of hours for the five-day week objective already part of the Local's programme. Following the industrial pattern in Toronto, only the Factory worked a five-day, 40-hour week, Monday to Friday. Stores and Mail Order employees worked 5½ days over 40 and 42½ hours respectively, while caretakers worked a 44-hour week in shifts, and drivers worked 48 before overtime. Store employees were required to work 30 minutes over scheduled hours before extra pay began. There was a larger than usual turnout for this meeting, and a long, free-ranging debate took place before members settled on a 37½ hour, five-day week as the objective for all divisions.

Apart from the cost factor, which would be part of the monetary package negotiated, a schedule of 8:00 a.m. to 4:30 p.m., Monday to Friday, posed no operational problems except in the Stores. These members recognized the complexity and decided to hold a special meeting for Store employees only on Saturday work. Thus May 30, Store employees called for a Monday-to-Friday schedule of 8:45 to 5:15 p.m., with four Saturday mornings prior to Christmas, at time and one-half.

The Stewards' Council was now meeting regularly on the second and fourth Tuesdays of every month. In April, elections were conducted for three co-chairmen and three co-secretaries to share the experience and alternate at stewards' meetings. To complete the Stewards' Executive (almost a trial run for the election of Local Union officers which would come later) 14 others were elected to represent their divisions. Co-chairmen elected were: Fred Tinker, a Main Store salesman; Terry Foley, a radio technician; and Sam McIlrath from Mail Order, a recent immigrant from Ballymena, Ireland, Timothy Eaton's birthplace. The co-secretaries were Charlie Norman, later to become president of the local, Rita LeGard who worked in the Louisa Street Employees' Cafeteria, and Mary Sutton, also chairwoman of the Social Committee. Capable and steadfast, these six gave unstintingly of their own time and, through daily contact, were soon closely integrated with our staff. Soon after their election, their leadership reached a wider audience on Local 1000's radio series.

Mary Sutton voiced her motivation: "I'm so interested because I think we can make Eaton's a better place for the younger generation. We can leave them nothing better, or more necessary, than a union." The issue of equal pay was raised by Rita LeGard: "I'd like to see women paid the same as men when they do the same jobs — in *every* department." Sam McIlrath's convictions arose from his experience in Ireland: "I was a union man before I came to Eaton's, for six years, in the Amalgamated Engineering Union. I *know* [it] provides protection. Everybody has a protective society these days. Back home there was even a Donkey Protection Society. Employers have theirs."

Terry Foley, a cheerful and competent radio repairman serving Eaton's customers for 15 years, with time out in the Air Force, told what Local 1000 meant to him: "It has made me realize... how democratic the union movement is, how necessary it is to our Canadian way of life. Our members make the decisions at meetings. They all have a chance to speak and many of them do. We'll never have real democracy until working people have a say in their conditions, until they can sit at the same table with management and bargain as equals."

At the end of April we suffered a real setback when Marjorie Gow, whose arthritis and other health problems had worsened, felt she had to lead a less stressful existence and returned to British Columbia.

Despite extra initiatives, membership did not reach the required strength that spring. Around this time there were long discussions at staff meetings on the pros and cons of applying for certification for Mail Order which had a majority signed. The idea was finally rejected for a number of reasons.

As soon as an application is filed a "wait and see" attitude sets in. This might make it difficult to keep on trying to sign a majority in the Stores. And if Mail Order were certified and, following protracted

Unionize

DEPARTMENT STORE EMPLOYEES UNION
Local No. 1000

Vol.3, No. 21 — May 30, 1950

Steelworkers DONATE $25,000

NEGOTIABLE WITHOUT CHARGE AT ANY BRANCH OF THE BANK IN CANADA — A4435

THE CANADIAN CONGRESS OF LABOUR
OTTAWA, ONT.

Pay To the order of Department Store Organizing Committee, C.C.L. — May 11, 1950

Contribution to T. Eaton Fund from United Steelworkers of America

$25000 AND 00 CTS — $25,000.00

BANK OF NOVA SCOTIA

TO HELP EATON EMPLOYEES in Local 1000 finish their organizing drive in high gear, The International headquarters of the United Steelworkers of America have made a grant of $25,000 toward the Eaton Drive.

This is the largest single donation made by any union toward the drive to date. It was arranged following a conference between Philip Murray, president of the Steelworkers, and also of the C.I.O., Allan Haywood, C.I.O. organizational director and three members of the Department Store Organizing Committee of the Canadian Congress of La-

contract negotiations, gains were passed on to the rest of Eaton employees, it would be even harder to complete organization. We felt a responsibility not to dash the hopes of the several thousand members in divisions other than Mail Order by leaving them behind in the first application.

As a matter of fact, this was exactly what happened to Local 468, RWDSU, which was certified in 1948 for the restaurant, delivery, maintenance, warehouse and two other now non-existent units of the Hudson's Bay Company in Winnipeg. In talking with Mr. J. G. Ritchie, RWDSU representative for Manitoba and Alberta, I ascertained that as of early 1981, whereas the certified groups still have a collective agreement, relatively the same wage increases and other improvements obtained in negotiations are passed along to the non-union employees. To this time, efforts to unionize the rest of The Bay's Winnipeg operations have not been successful.

May brought a change in our fortunes. We decided to try a different organizing technique, based on Lynn's experience in group work at the Hamilton YMCA. The idea, in a nutshell, was to set attainable goals for individuals and provide group recognition for achievement. The most active stewards would be asked to be team captains for a number of departments; a realistic weekly quota for memberships would be assigned to each captain; success would be rewarded in some non-material way.

One wall in our largest office was fitted with blackboards, with a vertical list of team captains and their quotas and a horizontal date for each week. If the quota was met, a large gold star would be placed in the column beside the name of the team captain. We were all soon convinced of the powerful incentive provided by the approbation of one's peers as the 44 team captains dropped in to the office every Monday to see the results of the week's work — and those gold stars!

In the meantime, the DSOC-CCL delegation had met with Philip Murray, CIO president, and Allan Haywood, director of organization, who advised it would take some time to have the Eaton Drive considered by their executive board. Then the trio from the CCL appealed to Murray wearing his other hat, as president of the United Steelworkers of America, and were successful in getting a loan of $25,000 from his International. Together with the increasing flow of monthly local union donations, we were at last able to hire more staff and step up the pace of the campaign.

The timing was ideal. The university year was ending, and we immediately recruited three students: Harvey Hay, Walter Parker and John Gilbert, for the summer months. Olive Richardson was promoted from office manager to organizer, to assume a large part of my work in the Main Store. Others including Ron Monkman and Patricia Ford worked for short periods, and the office staff was augmented by several temporary employees. In addition, we were fortunate to add two women organizers on a part-time basis. Mrs. Mae Coulston had just retired after many years as cashier in the College Street Employees' Cafeteria. She had been an outspoken supporter of Local 1000 from the outset, and her ability and integrity carried much weight. Mrs. Enid Sampson was a Reserve Staff saleswoman, usually in women's apparel. During that summer, when she wasn't working for Eaton's, she devoted her talents to "selling" unionism.

We arranged a repeat of the shopping bag demonstration which had been so successful in 1949. On Saturday, May 20, Toronto unionists gathered with placards identifying their union and announcing support for Local 1000. Others handed out 5,000 shopping bags to customers along with a thousand balloons to their kiddies, both with the message, "Join Local 1000." Balloons had been filled with helium and shopping bags stuffed with leaflets by our members who arrived at the union office at 7:00 a.m. There was lots of fun all round. Except for management. Predictably, when a child let go of a balloon, it floated up to the ceiling. The sight of a manager in the Main Store climbing a ladder to retrieve this novel form of union propaganda caused considerable comment.

By mid-June the team approach was in high gear, bringing us new life. A banquet at Purdy's Auditorium was attended by 200 team members and captains to learn the results of the first five weeks' effort. They were seated by teams so as to become better acquainted. During dinner they jotted down names of prospects, applauded captains with five gold stars for signing up their quota every week, joined in a union sing-song, and laughed at skits on how *not* to approach a prospective member. The evening ended on a note of determination to achieve a majority by August. The following week 207 more joined, and the Annex became the first store to go over the top. Interestingly it was another shoe salesman, Gerry Sandford, who fired up his team members to sign seven weeks' quota in three.

Eaton's reaction to this spurt was another round of $1 or $2 a week increases in most departments. For some employees, it was the third or fourth raise since the Drive began. The trend to simplify commission arrangements continued; quotas were eliminated and instead commissions of 1 or 1½ percent were paid on all sales. Straight commission salesmen had one of their grievances settled by changing the calculation for overtime pay to average earnings, rather than their draw (advance on commission). However, there was still no consistency as one member testified in a letter to *Unionize* (August 1, 1950):

> I am a union member, and was wondering if you would answer this question in your paper. I am in my 29th year with Eaton's. My pay is $28 a week. By the time I get my pay with so much taken out I get $25. I have asked for an increase since the middle of March... three different bosses and they all say the same — "You will get it." We are now in the middle of July and I am still waiting.... When the union gets in, how long will we have to wait for our increases?

> We are all just about going crazy with the price of food and rents, trying to make ends meet. (name withheld by request)

Organizational effort was concentrated on the Main Store in the next weeks. George Luscombe drew one of his best illustrated leaflets, "Come on Main Store/We're Waiting for You!" a bird's-eye view looking south on Bay Street, with arms waving from Mail Order and Annex. A little man waved from City Hall, "We're Organized," while another leaning out of Simpsons' window on Queen Street signalled they were waiting too. Main Store employees were told that Local 1000 could apply for certification as soon as 12 percent more joined.

This was followed up by "An Open Letter to Store Employees" signed by 126 members in Mail Order:

> We have had our majority in the Mail Order and have been waiting for you for the past eight months. Let's remember that every week, every month of delay is costing ALL of us money — the salary increases and other gains we want in a union contract.

To assist the teams we made up "conversation starters." One of these involved 10,000 little bags, each stuffed with five peanuts and the message, "Don't Work for Peanuts." For Store employees, we distributed white collars, cut by a special die from white card, cautioning, "Don't Let it be a Yoke."

Combined with such stunts, our bulletins carried factual information about unions: a comparison of time lost in strikes compared with illness and industrial accidents; a breakdown of how CIO unions spent their share of dues; how the union shop worked and why it was essential in an industry with high turnover. In every issue of *Unionize* we included a message from an active member telling why they joined. Speaking for Annex teams, Gerry Sandford, who like other young veterans at Eaton's was finding world news and the Korean War unsettling, spoke of the "far-reaching conflict for the preservation of democracy" and told his co-workers "right here and now we have a job to establish our own democracy... to be free from the fear of poverty and insecurity."

Women outnumbered men among the 230 at the second team banquet on July 4. To show team members how the scoreboards were changed every week, they were moved to Purdy's for the occasion, and as captains handed in memberships for that week, Lynn changed the boards and affixed more gold stars. A wire of encouragement was received, signed by all the members of the CCL Executive who were meeting in Ottawa that day. Guest speaker Murray Cotterill, TLC president, commended the local for developing decision-making from the

Vol. 3, No. 29

DEPARTMENT STORE EMPLOYEES' UNION
Local No. 1000

Aug. 1, 1950

6000-MARK REACHED

OVER 5000 PAID

MEMBERSHIP

LOCAL 1000

Local 1000 passed another milestone in its organizing history this week when membership went over the 6,000-mark.

Credit for this achievement is due the Team Captains and Team Members, who are putting every ounce of effort they have into this final membership campaign.

In preparation for the "last lap" of the drive, before applying for certification, many Teams, particularly in the Stores, are being enlarged so that the active organizing group of Local 1000 will be at a maximum.

Over 5,000 of the 6,000 who have signed application cards have also paid their $1.00 special initiation fee, the minimum required by the Labour Board. Stewards do not anticipate much difficulty in collecting from the rest, now that the drive is reaching its final stages.

bottom up, and predicted that, "A union will make Eaton's a better company, a better place to work, a place management will be more proud of — but it is something you must do yourselves."

On the way in to work on a sweltering August 1, 1950, employees received *Unionize* announcing that Local 1000 had reached the 6,000-mark and more than 5,000 had paid the $1 fee. (This figure did not include the 2,056 who had left.) Our team members and stewards reported a new high of interest. Now, if we could just survive a few more weeks of 16-hour days, there was the exhilarating prospect of reaching our goal.

The announcement touched off another round of anti-union rumours, a tactic familiar in industrial plants, but confusing to store employees with no union background. The story was spread that stewards were receiving $5 for every membership. We were able to reply truthfully that not one Local 1000 member or volunteer from another union had received one cent for their help. Over the "grapevine" by which news travels as fast or faster in department stores as elsewhere, the Main Store Millinery supervisor let it be known that, in his opinion, if the union got in, Store employees would be working all day Saturday *and* two nights a week. We had to remind him in a special leaflet, "Is Your Bonus Bothering You, Mr. Beal?" that when a union is certified, conditions of work are decided by negotiations, and members have as much to say as managers.

Then *Justice*, the purveyor of yellow journalism dependent on street sales to department store workers, got into the act. The previous December, *Justice* knocked down the strawman they set up and told readers they had learned that Local 1000 wasn't planning a strike after all. Now, after I refused to tell their editor when we would apply for certification, their July 15 issue came out with a long story under the head: "Has Eaton Drive Met with Reverse?" To support this speculation, they printed a letter from an Eaton employee, identified only as "MG," to the effect that those who had joined Local 1000 were now sorry.

In a second letter in *Justice* M.G. inferred that Local 1000 organizers were Communists and racketeers, but seemed to be confusing us with some people he had had a disagreement with in the Amalgamated Clothing Workers 20 years previously!

I mention M.G.'s reasons for opposing Local 1000 because, by an interesting coincidence, they reappeared in Eaton's propaganda during the vote campaign, dressed up in much more professional style.

Anne Stone, who chaired our Publicity Committee, recalled later "what a great fear there was of being called a Communist. It's always been a strange thing to me that anyone who speaks for social reform is considered to be either a Communist or a bleeding heart... .It's a sad reflection on society that people will still readily label you as a Communist."

As far as our staff were concerned, we never tried to conceal the fact that we belonged to the CCF, predecessor of the NDP, which had a philosophy of democratic socialism, in consistent opposition to Communist Party ideology. However, we were not so foolish as to press our political views upon the Local or on individual members. Politics came up, however, as they must in any discussion of current affairs. For example, on the merits of pressing for better health care and pensions by collective bargaining or by legislative action, we pointed out that organized labour and CCF parliamentarians had long advocated a universal health plan and adequate public, rather than private, pensions through legislation. The fact that the two older parties failed to introduce such measures forced unions to negotiate for them. The result was a patchwork, reflecting the strength of the adversaries, which established inequitable treatment between organized and unorganized workers.

Certainly, when David Lewis was chosen as our legal counsel, he was as well or better known as former national secretary of the CCF than as a labour lawyer with the firm of Jolliffe, Lewis & Osler. A Rhodes scholar and brilliant debater, Lewis brought more dedication to his work than is found in the usual lawyer-client relationship. Those who heard him at our third team banquet on August 15, which drew 340 team members, sensed this from his stirring address. After a brief outline of certification procedures, he dwelt on the social significance of their undertaking:

> The people in the labour movement are the true heirs of those pioneers who hewed this vast country of ours out of the forests and the rock. They are the true heirs of those who fought for and won liberty. They are the true heirs of the Fathers of Confederation...of MacKenzie and the rebellion of 1837.
>
> Surely not all this was done that a few may have all they want while the rest have very little. Surely they built Canada so that all may have as much as Canada may provide, in fairness and justice. We in the labour movement are the ones who want to complete that job.
>
> Unionism... means increased pay... but it [also] means establishing the dignity of every worker. In my experience, from coast to coast, you simply cannot compare the sense of self-respect of the organized worker with the sense of helplessness of the unorganized.

Sid Moffat, a recent immigrant from Northern Ireland, understood all too well what Lewis was talking about. Laid off from construction work, he took a job as a dispatcher at Hayter Street depot for $32 a week, which he found was more than single men were getting for the same job. His wife was pregnant — no medicare to pay doctor's bills in those days — and they were living in rooms. Even more important to him was dignity, however, and later he related an illustration:

> There was an old fellow working with me . . . I was young then, only 29 . . . he was in his 60s. He knew the Eatons personally, John did. He'd been a manager at one time . . . and then as it usually is, if you're not within a certain clique . . . if that clique goes out, you go out along with it. So he ended up where I worked. The abuse that old fellow stood from foremen made me sick . . . and I thought, "My God, I'd never like to see the day that I was having to take that."

Sid, a fellow countryman of Timothy Eaton, also recalls the calling down he got one morning when he handed *Unionize* to another Irishman who accused him of "going against Timothy."

The flurry of activity continued. A general meeting in August forwarded a resolution to Eaton's asking them to institute a minimum wage of $35 immediately to help employees with the rise in cost of living, and partially to close the increasing gap between wages in retail and other industries. On August 15, a special leaflet called for a Family Health Plan. Benefits recently negotiated by the UAW for General Motors in Canada were cited, including shared-cost hospitalization and medical care plans, life insurance and up to 26 weeks of sick pay.

Perhaps it was the stifling August heat that brought forth the idea of using thermometers to indicate the membership in the seven divisions. In any case, a canvass sign painted with seven large thermometers appeared across the second-storey windows at 572 Bay Street. The top of the thermometers represented 51 percent, with the lettering, "Put Local 1000 Over The Top." Those for Annex, Mail Order, Delivery and Maintenance were filled and overflowing, whereas Main Store, College-Hayter and Factory showed a level of 45, 43 and 35 percent respectively. The score was there for all to see as buses and street cars passed by. But still not one inch of coverage appeared in the daily papers.

Lynn and I spent many evenings at David Lewis's home, as he prepared our case. Department by department, Lewis meticulously noted the number of employees, names of management personnel who should be excluded from the bargaining unit, and whether or not the function of the department made it logical for inclusion. With September coming up, it was agreed to delay filing an application for the month, usually our best for gaining new memberships.

Two of our summer staff, Harvey Hay and John Gilbert,[2] left in September, but Walt Parker carried on a few more weeks, chasing up $1 initiation fees which were still outstanding. Unfortunately, pressure of work kept me from becoming better acquainted with these young men who pitched in and worked hard with our regular staff. Mae Coulston, Alex Gilbert and Hugh Webster stayed on until after the vote.

Unionize

Vol. 3, No. 34 DEPARTMENT STORE EMPLOYEES' UNION Local No. 1000 Sept.5,1950

LOCAL 1000 INSTRUCTS LAWYER

BE READY TO APPLY BY SEPTEMBER 30

Have you seen the new front of our Union Office at 572 Bay St.? You will be able to follow the final stages of the drive from the thermometers which indicate how far we have to go yet in each division. Watch for the changes week by week - and FILL 'EM UP!

Daily consultations are being held with Local 1000's legal advisors in preparation for making our application for certification to the Ontario Labor Relations Board.

A great volume of detail in connection with our records must be checked before we are ready to apply. We are anticipating that this can be completed on or before September 30. By this time we must have all members paid up, as it necessary to submit proof to the Board that all applicants have paid a minimum of $1.00.

Changes in the Ontario labour law, passed last spring by parliament, will go into effect shortly. Our lawyer will want to study the new law to make sure our application conforms to the new regulations.

We understand one new feature of the law is that a union with a 55% majority can be certified without a vote. Local 1000 should certainly try for this percentage in order to avoid the further delay of a vote following the cross-check of our cards with the payroll.

Local 1000 had a float as usual in the Labour Day Parade. The issue of *Unionize* that week carried the upbeat headline:

Local 1000 Instructs Lawyer
BE READY TO APPLY BY SEPTEMBER 30

Statue of Timothy Eaton, founder of the company, now located in the Eaton Centre. Courtesy of Sandy Gage.

Eaton employees leave work Saturday morning on James Street 1910. Courtesy of the James Collection City of Toronto Archives.

T. Eaton Co. Terauley Street Factory, 1910. Courtesy of the James Collection, City of Toronto Archives.

Wakunda Community Centre, Toronto. A committee of Eaton employees met here January 12, 1948, and decided to form Local 1000. Department Store Employees Union. Author's collection.

A.R. Mosher presides at the 1951 convention of the CCL in the Hotel Vancouver, as Eileen Tallman reports on the Eaton Drive. Author's collection.

Local 1000 Labour Day Parade float and CCL convention display, 1948. Author's collection.

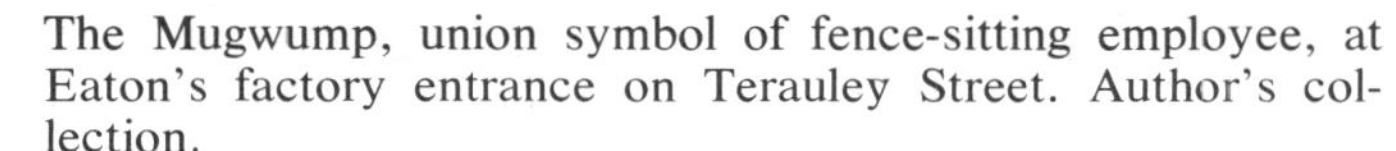
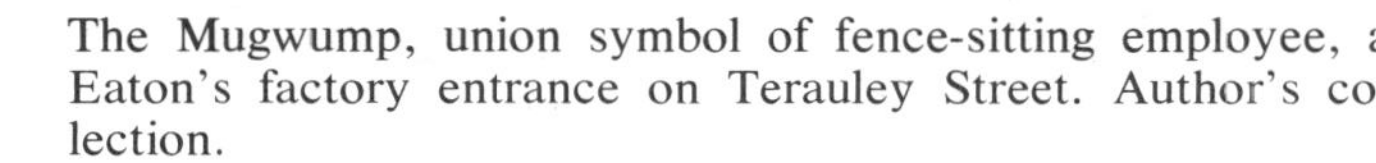

The Mugwump, union symbol of fence-sitting employee, at Eaton's factory entrance on Terauley Street. Author's collection.

Jack Jolly, Henry Weisbach and unidentified supporter urge Eaton employees to get off the fence. Author's collection.

Banquet of Local 1000 team drive members, Purdy's Auditorium, June 1950. Author's collection.

Union Shopping Day at Eaton's, September 1949. Wally Ross, Marjorie Gow, Lynn Williams and Ernie Arnold on return to Local 1000 office. Author's collection.

Toronto unionists demonstrate support for Eaton workers, September 1950. Author's collection.

Lady Eaton and Amelius Jarvis at Eaton Hall Farm (King). Courtesy of James Collection, City of Toronto Archives.

Eaton's College Street store opening, 1930. Lady Eaton and John Eaton. Courtesy of the James Collection, City of Toronto Archives.

Thermometers at union headquarters, 572 Bay Street, show membership percentage by divisions of Eaton's, September 1950. Author's collection.

Local 1000 unionists with ballons for the kiddies. Author's collection.

Department Store Organizing Committee, CCL, approves Local 1000 application for certification, October 1950 l. to r. C.H. Millard, Eileen Tallman, T.B. Maclachlan, Fred Dowling, David Lewis, George Burt and Pat Conroy. Author's collection.

"Quit Stalling Eaton's" Labour Day Parade float, 1951. Author's collection.

Marian Malanuck, Miss Local 1000 (centre) and other beauty queens in the 1951 Labour Day Parade. Author's collection .

Local 1000 first educational seminar, Dagmar, Ontario, 1951. Author's collection.

Local 1000 Bowling League. Jim and Mary Sutton centre front. Author's collection.

UAW rally for Walter Reuther, Toronto, June 17, 1951. l. to r. C.H. Millard, Fred Dowling, George Burt, Eileen Tallman Walter Reuther. Author's collection.

CAPTER FOURTEEN

Application Filed

SEPTEMBER 1950 was the most strenuous month of Local 1000's campaign thus far. It was also the most rewarding in membership gains. The new Ontario labour legislation, which became effective September 1 (Chapter 6), raised the possibility of certification without a vote, provided the applicant could show more than 55 percent membership in the bargaining unit. This was a powerful incentive to exert every last ounce of energy to reach that percentage as it would accelerate proceedings, and therefore, hasten the day on which collective bargaining could commence. The advantages were discussed with the team captains, who were now holding weekly dinner meetings, the best way to ensure maximum attendance.

Plans for the month's activities included: daily leafleting; another demonstration downtown with Toronto unionists participating; radio spot announcements at 7:00 a.m. three times a week to report on progress; as well as a number of meetings. Drivers from all depots met on September 11 to formulate their objectives for wages and hours of work, and voted to ask for a minimum of $50 a week to bring them more in line with union truckers in the city. At the monthly general meeting on September 19, members had two opportunities to hear David Lewis explain certification procedures, at 5:15 and 8:00 p.m. The By-Laws Committee, chaired by Charlie Norman, met weekly to draft by-laws in preparation for the election of officers for Local 1000.

Appeals in *Unionize* for volunteer help met with immediate response. One Mail Order member alone lined up 17 clerical workers to assist our hard-pressed office staff to keep abreast of the inflow of memberships. Several evenings a week work parties met in various parts of the city to make home calls, converging later on 572 Bay Street for refreshments prepared by the ever-present Social Committee. Another crew came every evening to fold and bundle the leaflets for the next morning's distribution. In six weeks, more than 300,000 pastel-coloured sheets of paper rolled off Thistle Printing presses, and thousands more were cranked off on our mimeograph machine.

Fifty Toronto unionists turned out on September 9 to stage another demonstration at Eaton's stores. Some carried placards drawing attention to their union's gains, particularly the five-day week, then enjoyed by about 85 percent of Toronto's industrial workers, while others handed out hats to customers' kiddies, imprinted "Join Local 1000 Now."

The main emphasis was, as always, higher salaries to meet the rapidly rising cost of living. It is interesting to look back on some prices which were then considered to be getting out of sight. An article in *Unionize* (September 12, 1950) entitled "$2 Wage Increase won't Cover These" cited these prices: steak, $1.05 lb.; coffee, 89¢ lb.; bread 16¢ a loaf; telephone $4.35 a month. It reprinted two ads of small apartments for rent at $100 and $115 a month. There is less cause for nostalgia if one considers that Local 1000 was aiming for a modest minimum of $35 per week, whereas the average weekly wage in Toronto over the next 30 years rose by almost nine times that amount.[1] It may also have a familiar ring that we claimed record corporation profits were the villain in the piece, and gave as an example a 3¢ rise in the price of beer, the working-man's beverage, "because the poor, destitute breweries can't afford to absorb the new government tax," the three largest having only cleared $11.7 million net profit in 1949.

In mid-September employees in many departments received another round of weekly salary increases, in Eaton's usual fashion: $3 to men, $2 to women and $1 to part-timers. We inquired: Does a landlord charge less rent to a woman? Does the butcher charge less for a pound of beef to a female customer? When it was learned that these increases were to be general, but paid to the rest on the next payday two weeks later, we called for retroactive pay. Another precedent was set when the remainder of the employees received the increase on October 4, *retroactive* to the previous pay period.

That month Mail Order workers were granted a small concession toward their objective of a reduction in hours to bring them in line with Stores. One hour was chopped off the Saturday morning schedule, now to end at 12:00 instead of 1:00 p.m., thus reducing their work week to 41½ hours.

The supervisory staff in some departments were becoming more vocal in spreading rumours such as, "If the union gets in," employees might lose welfare, shopping discounts — even statutory holidays with pay. In the Factory, the word was passed around that Eaton's would move it to Montreal rather than deal with Local 1000. Weekly reports of membership gains helped to counteract the fears and doubts raised by such rumours.

September 15, we could announce a record week: 327 had joined; 130 in the Main Store. This was topped the following week with 407 new members, including 164 from the Main Store. It now appeared certain that we would have at least the minimum 45 percent required for a certification application by September 30.

However, we decided to keep the Drive rolling as long as possible. We could not be sure how many employees would end up in the bargaining unit to be determined by the OLRB. The search was continuing for several hundred members who had not paid the $1 fee; they might well have left Eaton's. Extra help had been hired for the Trans-Canada Sale and some would stay on until after Christmas. In the event that Eaton's had hired them as regular rather than casual employees, we urged the teams to approach all newcomers.

Finally, to offset turnover while the Board was hearing our case, it was best to have the largest cushion attainable. I don't recall that our staff were ever optimistic about obtaining certification without a vote, regardless of whether we could show 55 percent membership. Eaton's, the third largest employer in Canada, had too much power.

Before month end, we were able once again to "scoop" the Company by announcing that a voluntary, employee-paid health protection plan would be unveiled early in October. Welcoming the plan as a step in the direction of Local 1000's programme, we pointed out that employees could not afford another deduction from present salaries and that Eaton's could well afford to pay the full cost: $2 for single employees and $5 for families to cover combined medical-hospitalization protection. It was also pointed out that through collective bargaining, employees would have a say in selecting a plan, rather than having to accept the Company's choice. And should anyone doubt that this latest improvement was due to union pressure, there it was in fine print: the plan was open to regular employees *in Toronto only*.

Interspersed with our criticism, the positive role of unions in improving employer-employee relations and hence the general welfare of the enterprise was not neglected. For instance, one leaflet featured the evaluation of Mr. Bishop Brown, director of the Research Bureau for Retailing at the University of Pittsburgh, made during visits to department stores in Sweden in 1947. He had found Swedish salespeople to be "courteous, well-trained, intelligent, helpful and dignified.... They have a respect for their job and a respect for themselves.... Yet the stores are absolutely unionized." The owner of one of the largest stores in Stockholm was quoted by Mr. Brown: "...the stores couldn't live without the unions. If our store has a problem, management calls the union stewards together and in an hour we settle the whole thing." He might have added that in Sweden co-operation rather than conflict is a way of life. It is hard to say if Eaton employees were impressed but obviously John David Eaton was not.

On September 27, the Company distributed "An Open Letter to Eaton Employees" their first statement about the union. The tone was fairly restrained, compared with those to follow. It assured employees that the Company did not intend to interfere with their right to join or not to join the union, and then proceeded to berate Local 1000 for failing to give equal prominence to the fact that employees were free *not* to join. Our reply was that employees knew this to be the case and, by the same logic, why did Eaton's advertisements not tell their customers:

BUY A NEW THINGUMMYJIG — ONLY $1.98
BUT
PLEASE FEEL FREE NOT TO BUY A THINGUMMYJIG

The Company devoted most of their letter to their own interpretation of the objectives in the local's programme. On promotions, for example, they said: "It is the Company's policy to promote from within rather than to bring in new persons from outside for senior positions." Mail Order Catalogue employees were quick to respond that a young university graduate had just been hired as assistant manager in their department.[2] The union programme called for departmental seniority in promotions, ability and physical fitness being sufficient. Employees were warned that if the union got in, they would have to join or lose their jobs. Eaton's did not suggest, however, that only union members should receive the benefit of gains made in negotiations.

The main thrust of the attack was reserved for the five-day week. In the unionized stores in New York, they pointed out that "[it is] a five-day employee week, with any day but Saturday being the day off." It was inferred, as in most subsequent Company leaflets, that the Monday-to-Friday work week for Store employees was Local 1000's No. 1 objective.

As already noted, I personally thought this goal unrealistic, and should have said so more emphatically at meetings. Union organizers are frequently accused, and sometimes rightly so, of raising false expectations among workers as to the improvements they will achieve by forming a union. With us, the opposite was true. In my opinion, we did not do enough to deflate the hopes of the militant core of sales-clerk unionists for a Monday-to-Friday work week.

It must be remembered that in 1950 Eaton's stores were open 5½ days a week, 5 in July and August, compared with 6 days worked by employees of Simpson's and most other downtown merchants. Night openings and shopping centres in suburbia had not yet appeared. However, as we repeatedly stressed in *Unionize,* hours of work like other conditions were negotiable and in the final analysis, the union membership would sort out the priorities.

In a special leaflet, "Let's Set The Record Straight," distributed October 2, we asked Eaton's why they had not informed employees of all the facts about Macy's. They could have reported that about half the employees, in office and non-selling departments, did not work on Saturdays, whereas the sales staff had rotating days off, which included some Saturdays. On Thursday evenings when Macy's was open until 9:15, most employees worked their regular day shift; others started at noon and worked till closing. Overtime, which was voluntary, was paid after eight hours in a day. To get the ball back in our court, we inquired why the Company's "Open Letter" avoided any mention of Local 1000's primary objective — more pay. Why stop at the hours of work in New York stores? Why not report that the union at Macy's had established a minimum of $35.50 a week, automatically raised in four steps to $42.50 after 18 months' service? And that a maximum of $49 was possible through a union-management review on the lowest-rated jobs, while higher salaries applied to those requiring more skill and responsibility? We asked rhetorically, "How many women at Eaton's earn $42.50 after 18 months' service?" As a matter of fact, most male employees did not earn that much either.

The day prior to the Company's salvo, Lynn and I were in Winnipeg to report to the annual convention of the CCL. Our announcement that Local 1000 would apply for certification shortly was met with rounds of applause and a standing ovation. Due to the pressure of writing leaflets for daily distributions, I returned to Toronto the next day while Lynn stayed on to talk with delegates, many of whom were hoping to see organization started in stores in their communities. He reported on the Eaton campaign during a CBC network programme of convention highlights, September 28.

That same week the first full account of the Eaton Drive appeared in print when the October 1 issue of *Maclean's* magazine went on the newsstands. It contained an article by June Callwood, "She's Organizing Eaton's," a lively account of our organizing techniques and stunts, as well as the improvements Eaton employees were seeking. There was a picture of leaflet distribution at the Main Store entrance on Yonge Street, and another of our staff, still inflated by summer help, with the team scoreboard as background. Sympathetic, if belated, the story had obviously been held until it was almost certain that an application for certification would be made.

September 30, the target date for obtaining a majority, was a Saturday. In the previous three weeks, 1,079 new memberships had come in. Our leaflet heralded the long-awaited news:

> We've made it, folks! Local 1000's organizing drive is right up to schedule today — September 30th! Sufficient memberships have now been received to permit us to apply for certification for Eaton's Toronto retail and mail order operations. We are instructing our legal counsel, Mr. David Lewis, to forward our application to the Ontario Labour Relations Board just as soon as possible.

It was a red-letter day. The "bouquets" printed in red ink "to all our members who have given so much of their time and energy to make this campaign successful" were accompanied by a real red rose, handed to employees as they went in to work. We could do things with panache in those days when the cost of roses was not prohibitive. Those who had not yet joined were invited to celebrate too, and take advantage of the special $1 initiation fee, which would remain in effect until the Labour Board had dealt with our case.

The news of Local 1000's majority was broadcast over CKEY on the evening of October 2. C. H. Millard and David Lewis were guests. Offering congratulations, Millard told them:

> I only wish (you) could have been out there in Winnipeg last week to gain encouragement from the tremendous enthusiasm with which delegates from all over Canada greeted the report on the Eaton Drive. Although very little appeared in the press, it was an outstanding part of our convention.

He then continued with the warning:

> ...Until the Labour Board has finished its hearings on your application, these will be critical weeks for your union. Eaton employees should be forewarned to withstand any attempts to confuse the situation... .At this stage in affairs, rumour-mongers usually make hay while the sun shines for the boss. Check the facts with your union office... I assure you that the support you have had from the Canadian Congress of Labour and its affiliates will continue now and in the future... .

Lewis reported that preparation of our case was proceeding well and offered this advice:

> .... the safest position in which your union can be before the Board is to have a sufficiently large majority that, regardless of any technicalities... your claim to represent a majority... will be indisputable. It would be good sense, therefore to continue signing up as many as possible.

At their dinner meeting the next evening, all 44 team captains took his advice to heart.

"HERE WE GO"—
APPLICATION FILED TO-DAY.

Local 1000's application for certification is being forwarded today to the Ontario Labour Relations Board. They will advise us of the first hearing, and we will in turn report to you. Meantime, keep up the good work! Cards received today with the $1 initiation paid can still be counted.

DEPARTMENT STORE EMPLOYEES' UNION
Local No. 1000
Affiliated Retail, Wholesale & Department Store Union, C.I.O. - C.C.L.

I hereby request and accept membership in the DEPARTMENT STORE EMPLOYEES' UNION, LOCAL 1000, affiliated with the Retail, Wholesale & Department Store Union, C.I.O. - C.C.L. and promise to abide by the by-laws and constitution of the Union. I hereby authorize the Union to represent me in any negotiations concerning salaries, hours and working conditions with my employer.

Date accepted .... Signature

Address .... Phone ....

Employed by T. Eaton Co. Ltd. Building .... Floor ....

Department Name and No. ....

Issued by: LOCAL 1000, DEPARTMENT STORE EMPLOYEES' UNION, 572 BAY STREET AD. 8581

On October 3, we took a full-page advertisement in the *Toronto Daily Star* to acknowledge moral and financial support received from labour and to advise that Local 1000 was ready to file. Greetings from union headquarters, locals, labour councils and federations in nine provinces made it a unique and impressive display of labour solidarity.

There is no doubt that the additional financial assistance in 1950, particularly the $25,000 from the Steelworkers' International headquarters, enabled us to bring the organizational part of the campaign to completion. Donations of almost $7,200 came in from 105 locals and councils, plus those in Saskatchewan who contributed through a central fund. This was matched by the initiation fees for Local 1000, $7,301 for the year 1950, which was also used for the campaign.

While all expense items showed an increase, the two largest were publicity, which more than doubled compared with 1949, and salaries for the extra temporary staff, $10,000. Although I do not have the record of the amount spent during the first 18 months when RWDSU was still in the picture, the *Financial Post's* estimate of the cost to October 1950, of $100,000 would not be far out.[3] Through monthly financial statements, the members of the DSOC-CCL were able to assess how funds were being used.

To place their stamp of approval on our application, the DSOC-CCL met in Toronto that week, with David Lewis in attendance, and reviewed the membership figures. Fred Dowling, chairman of the Committee, stated, "While it is extremely difficult to determine the exact number of employees in a firm as large and diversified as Eaton's, we feel that the staff and stewards have made as accurate an estimate as... possible... and are satisfied that Local 1000 has the required percentage." It was agreed that the application should be for the retail and mail order operations of Eaton's, excluding the Factory departments and the general administrative offices, which we felt could be legitimately viewed as separate bargaining units, and in which we did not claim to represent a majority.

On October 5, some 60 artists and photographers in the Advertising Department, who had joined Local 24515 of the Commercial Artists and Photographers, AFL, were certified without a vote by the OLRB. It was another opportunity for us to urge employees to join Local 1000 and "make it 55%."

The Social Committee added to the air of jubilation by a celebration which drew 600 to dance to the music of Bert Niosi at Columbus Hall on October 13.

Five days later, on October 18, 1950, Bill Newcombe's illustration of a little man loaded with bags of membership cards, running up a path to the "Certification Board," needed only a few lines to tell Eaton employees that our application was being forwarded to the OLRB that day.

CHAPTER FIFTEEN

The Battle of the Bargaining Unit

AS SOON AS it became apparent that Local 1000 was actually near filing for certification, Eaton's retained J. C. Adams, then without doubt the best-known consultant in Ontario on how to beat unions. Their strategy changed from non-interference to open hostility.

On October 23, five days after our application, a second and more serious broadside was mailed to all employees. "An Important Personal Message to You from Eaton's" told how to withdraw from the union and prevent it from being certified.

To understand the deception of the leaflet, one has to know something of the certification procedures of the Ontario Labour Relations Board at the time. Regulations[1] under the Labour Relations Act prescribed printed forms for use in informing interested parties of the application.

On the form to be used by the applicant, the union was to name the employer, describe the proposed bargaining unit, estimate the number of employees, give the name of any other union(s) that might be interested, and supply information as to existing or recently-expired agreements held by any unions covering some or all of the employees affected by the application.

When notified, the employer was to file another form within a specified time, giving the general nature of the business, total employees, number in the unit applied for, the employer version of the appropriate unit, and information as to other unions who might be interested.

Yet other forms were to be used to notify employees and these, in sufficient number, had to be posted on company premises for not less than five days.

Any unions mentioned by either applicant or employer were to be advised of the application, and given seven days to state their interest, so as to receive notice of the Board hearings.

This brings us to the Intervention Form itself (Form 7). It was short and straightforward and is reproduced here in full:

Form 7

The Labour Relations Act

INTERVENTION

Before the Ontario Labour Relations Board

Between: Applicant

— and —

Respondent

.... intervenes
(name of intervener)

in this proceeding.

*1. The intervener is

(a) an employee,
(b) a group of employees,
(c) a trade union claiming
  (i) to represent employees, or
  (ii) to be the bargaining agent of employees, or
(d) the employer of employees,

who may be affected by the application.

2. The intervener claims to be interested in the proceeding upon the following grounds:

DATED at ....this ....day of ,19

....
(signature of intervener)

* strike out clauses not applicable.

Eaton's tried to scuttle these procedures by printing their own "intervention" forms with an added statement which did not appear as part of the Board's Form 7, to the effect that, if the employee did not desire to be represented by the applicant union, he or she could so indicate. The Company intervention forms were in triplicate, accompanied by a stamped, addressed envelope to the OLRB, and their "Important Personal Message" which read in part:

> Employees *who do not wish* the Union to be certified as their sole and exclusive bargaining agent have the right *at this time* to make their wishes known to the Board.
>
> The Labour Relations Board of Ontario invites every member of the staff, whether or not he belongs to Local 1000, who does not wish Local 1000 to be certified as his sole and exclusive bargaining agent, to so advise the Board by using the enclosed Intervention Form.

The rest of the leaflet was in question and answer form.

> Q. *If the Union is certified, how soon can we get rid of the Union if we choose?*
>
> A. You cannot get rid of the Union once it is certified until at least a year after any Agreement is signed between the Company and the Union... [which] may not take place until several months after certification, so that you cannot oust the Union... until between a year and two years after the Union is certified. The procedure in having a Union voted out is complicated. First, a petition, signed by *more than 50% of the staff*, must be presented to the...Board requesting a vote. Then *if* a vote is granted a majority vote of more than 50% of the staff against the Union is required in order to get rid of the Union.
>
> Q. *Can I withdraw from the Union now, even though I've paid my Initiation Fee?*
>
> A. Yes. You can withdraw from the Union at this time even though etc.
>
> Q. *How do I go about it?*
>
> A. If you wish to withdraw from the Union you may write it a letter, but this is not important. What is important is that the Board wants to know *now* whether you wish the Union to represent you as your exclusive bargaining agent. You can indicate your wish not to be represented by the Union by simply filling in all three copies of the attached Intervention Form, signing all copies, and mailing all copies in the attached stamped addressed envelope to the Ontario Labour Relations Board.
>
> Q. *If I have not joined the Union, should I fill out one of these Forms?*
>
> A. If you object to having the Union act as your exclusive agent, this Form is your means of advising the Labour Board that you do not wish the Union to be certified.

It is easy to imagine the confusion this sheaf of papers created among members and non-members. How were they to know the intricacies of labour law forms and procedures, or to detect their misuse? To add to the chaos, the Company mailed their forms to thousands not covered

MR. BIG BIG AND ALL THE LITTLE BIGS....

"MANAGEMENT TALKS IT OVER."

by Local 1000's application: Saturday-only casuals, employees in order offices outside Toronto, even to a man who had not worked at Eaton's for five years!

A rumour was started that the reason the "intervention" forms were in triplicate was that the Board would send one copy to the union and *one to the Company*. The Board was flooded with these phoney forms. After all, unless you mailed it, wouldn't the Company know for *sure* that you were in the union? The rumour, like the forms, was false. In fact, all three copies of the Board's Form 7 were for its exclusive use.

Our phones at 572 Bay Street rang steadily as members called to say they figured it best to mail the forms, but "didn't really mean it" and were still all for the union. A meeting of stewards was called immediately. They were furious. However, hearings set for November 13 and 14 were postponed, no doubt to give Board members time to decide what to do about Eaton's "interveners."

While our stewards fought back inside as best they could, we used the only weapon we had on the outside, the support of organized labour. On Saturday, October 28, Eaton's customers in five provinces heard of these tactics, as all their major stores were leafleted by CIO-CCL unionists. Labour councils were alerted to send protests to the Company. In Toronto, we distributed "An Open Letter to John David Eaton" regretting the change in policy and urging him to recognize that "this is 1950."

Some department officials, previously given to more subtle forms of combatting unionism, perceived the "Personal Message" as the green light to try more openly to intimidate our stewards. Rumours of how many had "withdrawn" from Local 1000 by mailing "interventions," ranging anywhere from 500 to 5,000, were widespread. Some of our most active members began to be asked by management — just out of curiosity, of course — why it was they had got so involved. Those we heard about stood their ground well, and we were very proud of them. Anne Stone recalls:

> I remember being called into the boss's office — not my immediate boss or his boss, but the next higher one — I didn't know whether it was to be promoted or fired, I didn't know for what reason.... He said, "I understand you are involved in the union," and I said, "Yes, I am." I hadn't expected this so I spoke quite spontaneously. I said I felt it was the only way I was going to make any progress. I felt I could become stagnant, and the only thing I had in common with Timothy Eaton was that he didn't want to be stagnant either; otherwise we would still have a little store at Queen and Yonge. And I said, "I'd like to show a bigger profit this year than last, and I don't think Eaton's are going to make that possible.... I'm sure he wanted to ask me about memberships.... I think he said something about "on company time"... So I said, "Oh, I know better than to do that.... If I were to do that, you'd fire me, wouldn't you?"... He didn't answer....

We continued working with David Lewis almost daily. The bargaining unit, estimated at 11,500, was described as follows:

> All permanent, regular full-time and part-time employees of the respondent in their Toronto retail and mail order operations, save and except the staffs in the Executive and General Offices, those who are members of a craft by reason of which they enjoy collective bargaining through a craft union, supervisors, managers, heads of departments, first assistants and others who exercise managerial functions.

In its reply, the Company stated that the unit they considered appropriate totalled 16,365 employees. This would have to be their entire Toronto staff in the midst of the Christmas rush! Our 6,629 cards obviously would be far short of the 45 percent needed, if the Company figure could be made to stick. Clearly, the argument over the size of the bargaining unit was going to be crucial.

The Board hearings were rescheduled for December 5 and 6 and the war of words continued.

Eaton's reprinted and distributed an article from the *Financial Post*, October 14, entitled, "Here's Why CIO-CCL Spent $100,000 on Drive to Organize T. Eaton Co.,'' and began by relating why the CCL, looking for unorganized fields in 1947, decided retail had the potential to become the largest union in Canada. The Eaton Drive was regarded as the stepping stone, and while its success would probably have the significance to labour of the auto campaign in 1937, the *Financial Post* writer noted: ''Organizing white-collar workers is regarded as the toughest in the union field... [with] sales people it's worse... turnover is usually high.... This broke the back of the AFL attempt to organize the Robert Simpson Co. in Toronto a few years ago. They spent close to $40,000 before calling it off.''

In the article, Eaton's attributed the length of time taken to sign up about half their employees to wages and benefits second to none in the retail field, and proceeded to list these in considerable detail. Naturally, they had not told the *Financial Post* about the improvements, particularly in wages, which had been made since Local 1000 appeared on the scene. The latest occurred October 20, when Eaton's announced increased welfare pay rates, and for the first time placed on record an employee's entitlement to sick pay, based on length of service. Like the Health Protection Plan, to become effective December 1, the Company bulletin advised that the welfare pay schedule applied to *Toronto employees.*

Shortly thereafter Simpsons announced that, while its store would continue to be open six days, employee hours would be cut to 37½ over a five-day week. ''Jitter generosity'' we called it. Simpson workers were showing renewed interest in organizing, and we assigned Alex Gilbert to keep in touch with contacts and gather information about both Simpsons' store and mail order.

The Ontario Labour Relations Board commenced hearings on the Eaton case at 10:00 a.m. on December 5. This was the largest unit to come before the Board to date, and the first in a new field, department stores. Predictably, the Board would exercise the utmost care and caution, so as not to allow any opportunity for the case to be thrown into the courts over procedural defects.

The chairman of the Board was Mr. P.M. (Paddy) Draper. He was well-versed in Canadian labour history. His father, a Toronto Typographical unionist, had a distinguished career beginning in 1900 as secretary-treasurer of the Trades and Labour Congress of Canada, an office he held until 1935 when he was elected TLC president. The four other members were David Archer and Russell Harvey, labour nominees, and E.N. Davis and H.F. Irwin representing employers. (Russell Harvey had led the AFL campaign at Simpsons, 1943-46).

At the very outset, J.C. Adams, appearing for Eaton's, challenged the validity of the hearings on the grounds that the Board had failed to notify all (Eaton's) "interveners" individually in writing, and further had not advised the Company of their names. In the meantime, the Board had made a new ruling that "mass" interveners could be notified by having the Company post the notice of hearings on the premises. Several hundred notices had been sent to Eaton's for this purpose and had been posted. But Mr. Adams objected that the new ruling could not be made retroactive. Mr. Draper pointed out that had previous practice not been amended, the Board would have been obliged to notify each (Eaton) intervener of the names of all the other thousands of interveners. This would surely have posed a problem even in today's computer age!

X David Lewis attacked Eaton's "intervention" campaign as a "piece of colossal, arrogant impudence." The "Personal Message" misled employees by stating that the Board "invited" them to return the forms. Purporting to be a form required by the Board, the added line for the employee to indicate he did not wish to be represented by the union was "fraud and intimidation," showing contempt for the Board's authority and the legislation it administered. He called for Local 1000 to be certified without a vote, even if lacking the 55% membership, under a provision of the Act permitting this if more than 50% were members and (if) "the true wishes of the employees are not likely to be disclosed by a representation vote."[2]

In reply, Adams maintained, "We attempted to decipher the official language of the Board... we translated and explained it [Form 7] and made your original invitation, shall we say, a little more cordial." The thousands who mailed in forms opposing the union could not be ignored, he contended. Asked why not a single one of the "interveners" was on hand to make his objections known, he blamed it on lack of written notice of the hearings.

The Board reserved judgment on this matter, and the discussion on the bargaining unit commenced.

Eaton's proposed one all-inclusive unit embracing 16,365 employees in Toronto. The gist of the argument was that functions of all employees were so interrelated that it was impossible to separate from the unit such groups as Factory, craft unions, administration offices or non-regulars. To substantiate this charade, a long list of witnesses were called, led off by Mr. I.W. Ford, staff superintendent, who had been designated by the Board of Directors to carry the ball for Eaton's.

Managers of selling departments testified how one and indivisible their link was with the manufacturing counterpart in the Factory.

Unionize

Vol. 3, No. 47 | DEPARTMENT STORE EMPLOYEES' UNION Local No. 1000 | Dec. 19, 1950

EATON'S PLEA- We can't tell.

Lashing out at the refusal of company representatives before the Labour Board to assist the Board by defining its various divisions, David Lewis, union counsel, charged, "This is piling confusion upon confusion - it is like a landscape blotted out by layer after layer of mist."

The four large units not included in Local 1000's application are: Executive and general office staff, non-regular employees, the Factory, and crafts in other unions. Mr. J.C.Adams, company lawyer, and his parade of "top brass" witnesses, including Messrs. H.B.Halliday, I. W. Ford and W.G.Upshall, kept right on maintaining ad infinitum that it was impossible to segregate any group of Eaton employees from another.

They were unable to tell the Board any difference between an Invoice Section clerk in the General Office and a Mail Order clerical worker or an Exchange clerk in a sales department in the Stores.

(cont'd page 4)

For example, the manager of Department 248, Fur Salon, told how his buyers consulted with the production manager of Department 1609, Fur Manufacturing, as to what was required. Adams summed up: "In the real sense of the word there is no Factory at all... because there is no production for sale except for retail in the Store and Mail Order business."

He went on to say he did not know if the employees in Eaton's large Printing Department belonged to other unions or not.... There were no existing collective agreements. This was quite true, of course, since the Printing Trades Council's difficulties with Eaton's dated back to the turn of the century. Under questioning, it was admitted that the Company passed along to their staff the gains won by union printers.[3]

Mr. H.B. Halliday, in charge of the General Offices, which among other responsibilities handled the Company's overall accounting, was called to testify. He was unable to differentiate between a clerk doing accounting in his office, a clerical worker in Mail Order or an exchange clerk in a Store selling department.

As to Eaton's large contingent of some 2,000 occasional and reserve staff, as well as seasonal help, Mr. W.G. Upshall, head of the Employment Office, proved equally unhelpful. He told the Board that employment application forms were "all in a pile," and although some were stamped "Temporary," the applicant could use whichever one he or she pleased. Under questioning by Lewis, he did admit there was a separate record of Christmas help. And he did supply the key to the figure of 16,365 employees. According to Mr. Upshall, his office held Unemployment Insurance books for 16,365 people. He did concede that some had not worked at Eaton's for weeks or months at the time of our application.

Lewis accused Adams of "piling confusion upon confusion... like a landscape blotted out by layer after layer of mist" and proceeded by means of a copy of Eaton's management signature book to show the structure of the organization in its distinct parts and possible separate units for bargaining purposes.

There was the odd lighter moment such as:

> Company Counsel: I understand Santa Claus [who was presiding in Toyland at the time] wants to belong to the union.
>
> Board Chairman: He would certainly be a seasonal employee.
>
> Union Counsel: We're taking his place.

The December 6 session lasted all day and until midnight. The Board adjourned to consider the evidence before reconvening.

A case of this importance, with public hearings, could scarcely be ignored by the squeamish editors of the Toronto dailies. The first day's hearings and crossfire about the "interventions" were reported.[4] Then the whole case was put under wraps until the following year when the Board made its final decision.

Members of Local 1000 heard a report at its meeting on December 12, and voted to notify CCL locals and labour councils of the Company's "deliberate policy of obstruction and confusion before the... Board" and to ask them to express their indignation to John David Eaton.

During these weeks it had been business as usual at 572 Bay Street: leaflets to be written and handed out; stewards and committee meetings held; arrangements for the nomination and election of the Local's first Executive made; plans for the annual Christmas Tree party for members and families drawn up.

The Christmas holidays provided much too brief a respite for our staff to spend time with family and friends. Jack and I always enjoyed this season, photographing the water-sculptured ice and snow along the lakefront, listening to our collection of jazz classics, entertaining our friends. But by now I was finding every effort required a constant fight with weariness. Even between Christmas and New Year's we must have worked: Volume IV, Number 1, of *Unionize* appeared on January 3, 1951. Two days later we distributed our first leaflet to Simpsons employees, promising help in organizing as soon as possible, and inviting inquiries.

On January 9, the Board asked its examiners, A. M. Brunskill and J. M. Flannery, to obtain more information on the disputed categories of employees, and a week later inquiries began on Company premises. Present, as well as the examiners, were: Company counsel, J. C. Adams and J. T. Weir; I. W. Ford and others; union counsel David Lewis and John Osler; with Lynn and myself for the Local. Even though we met almost daily, these sessions dragged on most of February. Tedious and time-consuming (not to mention costly), but unavoidable to reinforce our case for the bargaining unit.

The poor examiners could not be selective and refuse to hear the staggering volume of trivia heaped upon them. I must say they and their staff must have worked extremely long hours to process that unpalatable mess in time to serve it up for the Board to read before the next hearings.

Meantime we were able to trumpet a victory. On March 6, 1951, we received a wire from the Board that "In view of the evidence before the Board... [it] is not prepared to accord the purported interveners the status of interveners in the proceeding."[5] In high spirits, we quickly got out a leaflet commending the Board. Looking back, I think we took too lightly the fear engendered by the Company leaflet, repeatedly urging employees to withdraw from the union. However, I am not sure what else could have been done. After all, our members were not miners or construction workers, ready to protest by downing tools at the drop of an employer's anti-union hat.

When Board hearings resumed on March 20, J. C. Adams held forth hour after hour on the merits of the Company's proposed all-inclusive unit. It was almost too much when he straight-facedly told the Board there should be only *one unit for all*, so that *every* employee might enjoy the benefits of collective bargaining!

Board decisions concerning bargaining units had developed on the basis of precedent rather than stated policy, and each case was considered individually. However, a frequent test for determining an appropriate unit was "community of interest." That is, was there sufficient community of interest among employees in the unit proposed to facilitate the conclusion of a collective agreement? For instance, there are many precedents in Board decisions for establishing separate units for factory and office workers of a company. Differences in methods of pay, hours and other working conditions for the two groups suggested that two collective agreements might be simpler to negotiate and administer — or so the Board appeared to think.

Relying on such precedents, Lewis maintained that logically there might be three bargaining units in Toronto: the retail operations for which Local 1000 had applied; the General Offices which served the Company as a whole across Canada; and the Factory, where other unions, such as the printing trades, had an interest. As for including seasonal or casual help, it made no sense whatsoever, Lewis argued, since they would be in the unit today and gone tomorrow.

Another session had to be scheduled to hear the legal argument over General Offices. Leading off on March 29, J.T. Weir took seven and one-half hours to state the Company position, Lewis, one hour and a half. The Board had no alternative but to schedule yet another session to hear summation by counsel. In their discretion, they decided that this hearing should commence at 7:00 p.m. on April 4. No doubt they were hopeful that they might get home by midnight.

On April 4 the stage was set for the final and most dramatic act of the battle of the bargaining unit. It was more exciting than a play because its ending would affect the livelihood of real people — and the people were there. Every available seat in the visitors' section was occupied by Local 1000 members.

Both counsel cited Labour Board decisions in Canada and the United States to make a case for all-inclusive versus smaller retail bargaining units. When J.C. Adams named three employers where the unit covered "all employees," Lewis was able to quash this evidence by revealing that in all three stores, the staff consisted of *only one employee*! This was typical of his meticulous preparation: Lewis must have searched every last department store case on record.

Finally, Lewis argued, the Act itself contemplated flexibility by defining a bargaining unit as "a unit of employees appropriate for collective bargaining, whether it is an employer unit or a plant unit or any subdivision of either of them."[6]

And then at last it was over. In the wordiest case in its experience, the Board had to come up with a decision; it took them eight weeks less two days.

On May 28, almost seven months after the application was filed on October 18, 1950, we were advised that the Board had upheld the unit requested by Local 1000 in all but minor respects.[7]

In fairness to the chairman, it must be said that, throughout, Mr. Draper exercised great caution not to give Eaton's lawyers any excuse to seek a motion for *certiorari* and *mandamus* from a court,[8] which would have caused longer delays. In allowing them unlimited latitude in presenting their case, the Board had had to listen to their prattle ad nauseam. It was all a part of the Company's deliberate tactic of delay.

As for David Lewis' superb preparation and eloquent presentation, Wally Ross had this to say:

> In 14 years with the Steelworkers (1952-1966) I heard a lot of cases argued before Boards in Ontario, British Columbia and Saskatchewan — probably 50 in all — by some very competent labour lawyers. But David was not the brightest star in that firmament — he was a whole goddam galaxy. I have never more admired anything than David's mastery of every aspect of that case. And a further pat on the back to you and Lynn would be in order for your tremendous job of marshalling all the departmental evidence — and to David for absorbing it.

But the bargaining unit was only the first hurdle. The next was a crosscheck by the Board examiners of our membership cards against the payroll for the unit as it was now established. Then, if a vote were ordered, there would be the complex preparations to hold it in such a large, physically-dispersed organization.

Timing was of the essence. Summer vacations were under way, making it impossible to have a full complement of stewards on hand for a vote campaign. However, supposing that the card check took two or three weeks and vote preparations another month, this could put the date into September, an ideal time for the union. We wore out calendars marking off the possibilities.

CHAPTER SIXTEEN

The Insiders

EATON'S ALWAYS refused to admit publicly that Local 1000 could not have reached the Board stage without the active support of thousands of their employees. Instead they made it a point to refer to the union as "those outsiders." In this chapter, I want to mention a few "insiders": employees who helped to build their local more than 6,600 strong, many of whom subsequently accepted the responsibilities of office.

While waiting for our certification hearing, it was agreed that we should strengthen the local by electing officers.

For some months a 16-member committee, headed by Charlie Norman and Alex MacMillan as chairman and secretary, had been drafting by-laws. As distinct from the constitution, which governs every national or international union, by-laws establish rules for local unions. They cover duties of officers, election procedures, standing committees, rules of order and the like.

Local 1000 by-laws provided for a large Executive Board, consisting of ten officers elected by the membership at large, and 27 others to be elected at division meetings, to ensure representation to all Company operations. Authority for major decisions was vested in the membership. Between general meetings, business was to be carried on by the Executive Board, to meet at least monthly. A smaller Executive Committee acted between board meetings.

The Executive Committee were nominated at the November 1950 membership meeting, with voting to take place in December; the rest of the board was to be elected at division meetings during January.

By this time, everyone realized that the Drive had moved into a stage of open hostility, and that the outcome was still in doubt. It was therefore a measure of their commitment that 17 candidates accepted nomination for the ten executive committee offices: president, vice-president, assistant vice-president, recording secretary, corresponding secretary, financial secretary, treasurer and three trustees.

Two salesmen were contenders for president: Charlie Norman from Main Store Linens, co-secretary of the Stewards' Council and chairman of the Education and By-Laws committees, and Gerry Sandford of

Annex Shoes, co-chairman of the Stewards' Council, whose leadership during the Team Drive earlier in the year had brought his store to 60 percent membership.

Three contestants for vice-president had been active stewards from the start, as well as serving on comittees: Len Horrocks of Main Store Women's Shoes; Phil Murphy from Merchandise Returns; and Larry Nielsen, an upholsterer and chief steward for the Hayter Street workshops.

Five positions were filled by acclamation: assistant vice-president, Fred Tinker, M.S. Bedding; recording secretary, Margaret (Littlejohn) Morton, M.O. Coats; corresponding secretary, Doris Griffiths, M.O. Billing; financial secretary, Bill Edwards, Branch Stores Distributing; and treasurer, Maude Fisher, M.O. Dresses.

The seven nominees for the three trustees reflected the widespread interest in being chosen for the first executive. They were: Margaret Brown, M.O. Circulation; John Carroll, Delivery; George Cotton, M.S. Shoes; David Hughes, M.S. Men's Clothing Alterations; Ella Lindley, College Street Dresses; Andrew McDonald, Elevators; and Harriet Wood, Factory Shirts and Pyjamas.

After two days of voting, Charlie Norman and Larry Nielsen were declared president and vice-president. Margaret Brown, George Cotton and Andy McDonald were elected as trustees.

This group, and particularly the three presiding officers, provided the sinews that held the local together during those endless months of delay. After a day's work at Eaton's, they grappled with the demands of their positions, an entirely new experience for most, and attended weekend seminars. Watching them develop new skills and gain self-confidence was a source of great satisfaction.

To those unfamiliar with the labour movement, a union leader is often pictured as an aggressive, bombastic spell-binder, ordering workers out onto picket lines. Few fit this image. Like generals, most learn fairly quickly not to get too far ahead of the troops.

To see Charlie Norman behind the counter, in the white-collar-and-tie-suit uniform of Eaton salesmen, one might have been surprised to learn that he was the union president. His manner was reserved, yet courteous; this quiet exterior masked a strong character. Before coming to Canada from London, England, in 1946, Charlie had worked for 11 years in the British Merchant Marine, and was a member of the Radio Officers' Union. Lynn Williams, who probably worked more closely with Charlie in Local 1000 than any of us, pays him this tribute:

> Charlie had all the essential elements of "character" in the traditional sense: integrity, poise, intelligence, competence, thoughtfulness and courage. His above-average talents might well have been recognized by the Company had he determined to pursue a career at Eaton's, but his understanding and concern propelled him in the direction of the union, and once he made that decision there was no turning back. He was not one to waste time or effort — he felt keenly his full range of responsibilities to family, community and job as well as to the union — but he was always available and willing to do whatever his responsibilities in the union required, and carried them out superbly. Charlie gave the union an image of decency and responsibility, and inspired a great deal of confidence among the other activists and the membership in general.

Interviewed on our radio programme Charlie gave his views on the future of the local. After touching on major contract objectives, he stated,

> Right now the top priority is getting our union contract proposals in final form. Later on, with so many thousands of members, the possibilities of what we can achieve by co-operation are unlimited. Eventually, we hope to have a complete counselling service like many CIO-CCL unions, so that our members can secure advice on matters affecting them. Personally, I'd like to see our local establish a credit union. Many Eaton employees find it necessary to borrow and are in debt to the Company . . . (that) isn't good for their independence. Of course, higher salaries would help here too.

For example, Local 1000 had set up a blood donor service for members which was much appreciated, as hospitals charged $25 a pint for a blood transfusion. Before her death, Mrs. Kay Hunt had some 40 donors among members.

Larry Nielsen, elected vice-president, would not have been taken for a white-collar worker. He was a huge man with the physique of a logger. No doubt his Swedish origin accounted for his strong union and Democratic Socialist convictions, which had brought him into many an argument with the leaders of the Communist-controlled Boilermakers' Union in Vancouver during the war years.

Perhaps because his wife was still in Vancouver, 572 Bay Street became a second home for Larry. There one could find him almost nightly, working on the framework of signs for demonstrations, showing others what was to be done in preparing for one of our stunts, or helping a group make ornaments for the tree at our Christmas party. As well as his manual skills, Larry was a fount of ideas — usually one a day — presented in his low-key, smiling but insistent way. He made union education fun through games such as "baseball" in which the players scored runs or struck out by their answers to questions. And he took particular delight in handing *Unionize* to Lady Eaton, whose office was in the College Street Store.

I got to know Larry better than some others on the executive as he would come out to our house, and regale us with stories from his colourful past.

The assistant vice-president, Fred Tinker, was a salesman in Main Store Bedding and Linens, and he fitted the "image" well: tall, suave, greying hair, and dress a little on the flashy side (he sported a "skimmer" in the summer). The approach of a customer brought forth an instant and engaging smile. With this difference. Unlike many who perfected a great sales pitch, but in fact sold their own personality to the employer, Fred did not allow himself to be manipulated. He was a realist with a devastatingly satirical sense of humour. With his friend, Jim Hemphill, from the same department, Fred was among the first to become active in Local 1000. His reply to my recent query as to why he became involved was typical:

> Unionizing was the second item on the list for Jim and me. Our first was to get a numbers racket going so we could retire at 50 and become, as the papers say, prominent sportsmen, with horses and baseball teams and yachts. Unfortunately, Toronto was still The Good, and our dreams did not materialize. Then we got interested in organizing the place — for *our* union — but you were already doing that, so we joined forces.

Lynn remembers the Hemphill-Tinker duo very well and describes their interest in another way: "They were really outraged about the entire situation — the money, the conditions, the childishness of the way in which employees were treated, the incompetence of the management, and often too, the foolishness of the customers." (On the last point, a customer who kept insisting on a "thicker" towel, just might end up with a bath mat.) "Fred was one of those people who felt that in one way or another he would find his way through life, and survive, and have a few laughs."

Fred and Jim spent a lot of evenings canvassing for new members, and Fred contributed this anecdote:

> One place we called at looked like Skid Row Blvd. The occupant earned less than I, but would he join? Not him. Ordered us out of the hovel. Loved that company, and wouldn't have any truck with "comrades." Our next call was at a veritable mansion . . . not much hope here, I thought. But to our surprise we were welcomed in by a stately white-haired gentleman who insisted on us having cake and tea with him. Told us his daughter had left Eaton's a few months back. But why hadn't we

organized the faculty (his profession) at the U. of T.? Sometimes people are hard to figure out.

All four women on the executive committee worked in Mail Order. They were among those responsible for putting that division over the top a year earlier than the Stores. I have placed such emphasis on the difficulty of interesting women, especially marrieds and part-timers, in unions that it may well have overshadowed the fact that, once convinced, women can be quite as strong and committed, if not more so, as men, despite their double workload of job and home. Dozens of such women made the extra effort to help to overcome fear and apathy among their co-workers and bring the number of women members in Local 1000 to about half.

Of those elected, Margaret Littlejohn, recording secretary, was the youngest. Her interest had been sparked by her father, a Railroad Telegraphers' union official, who took her along with him to labour schools. As soon as Local 1000 started, she came to the union office and joined. One morning as she was dusting off the desk of her boss in M. O. Coats, she found a transcript had already been placed there of everything she had said on our radio programme the previous evening. Indicative of her spirit, Margaret recalls this incident as "hilarious!" And relates that during a job interview after leaving Eaton's, when asked about past interests, she volunteered: "Well, I was secretary of the union when it was organizing Eaton's." She got the job; later her manager confided that "we figured you must be honest." Twenty years later, as part of the firm's personnel management, Margaret views her Local 1000 experience as giving her "a better understanding of the employee's point of view when a grievance comes up."

At a stewards' meeting, Margaret met Ray Morton who worked in the Toy Stockroom. They married in 1951, and have shared the same interests ever since. As enthusiastic as ever, she told me at a small gathering of former Local 1000 members in April, 1980: "You taught me how to keep minutes, and I've ended up doing that for every organization I've been in since" which includes the Kingston NDP, where the Mortons now reside.

Doris Griffiths was not only one of the most articulate members of the executive, but also endowed with a down-to-earth approach to problems. An avid reader, her interest in the union stemmed from a social conscience acquired as a student of working-class history. Her ability to express herself well and to the point came from participation in many organizations, such as the Ontario Federation for the Cerebral Palsied, of which she was secretary. To these duties were added those of corresponding secretary of Local 1000. With six years' service at Eaton's, Doris was well respected by co-workers in Mail Order Billing, and remained a steadfast activist, before and after the vote. In one of her contributions to union leaflets, she reminded women employees:

> Fifty years ago there was grave doubt as to whether a woman could properly be considered a person.... Denied the privilege of voting or running for office, she was considered incapable of running her own affairs. In industry, untrained and unappreciated, except as a source of cheap and abundant labour, women worked 12 or 14 hours a day under inhuman and unsanitary conditions.

Urging women at Eaton's to "move forward over the road to social progress on which so many have travelled and sacrificed," Doris credited unions and the legislation they had fought for with alleviating the worst exploitation of working women, but emphasized there was much still to be done, as: "Nothing like equality of pay for comparable work has yet been achieved."

By contrast, the office of treasurer was the first that Maude Fisher had held in any organization. This might have been lack of opportunity rather than by choice for Maude was a very able person. Although her looks belied it, she had the longest service of any on the executive Committee — twenty years, twelve spent in Mail Order Dresses as an adjuster. Ernie Arnold remembers her as a "gentle yet absolutely fearless person, solid as a rock, who had a profound effect on all those who worked with her." She was one of the first stewards to hand out union leaflets at her building. Even in poor health, Maude remained very active. She still used to phone the union office when her voice was a mere whisper from the throat cancer that finally took her life.

Elected as one of the trustees, Margaret Brown's interest in uionism also stemmed from her father's influence. He was an official of the AFL Photo Engravers in Youngstown, Ohio. When he transferred to Toronto, he build up his union, serving several times as president. Once a member, Margaret took on the job of steward in Mail Order Circulation, in which she had eight years' service. Her common sense and pleasant personality made her a persuasive advocate of industrial unionism. "One employee can't battle a company like Eaton's but one union can," she told them. "In such a large organization, the individual loses importance and needs a union to bargain for rights and protect privileges."

Bill Edwards started at Eaton's during the Depression, and returned from the War with eleven years' service credit, to resume his job in the warehouse supplying Canadian Department Stores, subsidiaries of Eaton's in Ontario. Bill was typical of young veterans who were incensed on their return to find salaries totally inadequate to begin raising a family. As no dues were to be collected until after certification, Bill's duties as financial secretary were not onerous, but he was otherwise very active, and on one radio programme expressed the concern of many of his age:

> I believe a union contract will end a promotion system [that has] no rhyme or reason. Lots of young men start at Eaton's, ambitious to get ahead, but they become pretty discouraged when they see that favouritism and "knowing the right person" govern promotions.
>
> We want seniority in our contract, so that promotions go to those with the most service who also have the ability to do the job.... This would give some incentive to younger fellows.

The other two trustees worked in the Main Store. George Cotton was one of the active group of "shoe boys" and served on the Social and other committees. He replaced Margaret Morton as recording secretary when she left Eaton's.

Andy McDonald was an elevator operator, and along with Jennie McKenzie and others, helped to organize this group solidly behind Local 1000. His job brought him into contact with a great many Main Store employees.

I hope these capsules will provide a glimpse of the calibre of leadership which came to the fore. It could be expanded many times over with vignettes of others on the Executive Board and Stewards' Council, a colourful blend of personalities woven into the fabric of the union's heart. I still vividly recall many of them, as I am sure other staff members would. At least, the remainder of the board elected by their divisions should be named; their departments will give the reader some indication of the depth of union penetration into Eaton's Toronto operations.

Executive Board of Local 1000

MAIN STORE		
Selling:	Len Horrocks	Women's Hygrade Shoes
	Alex Mowat	Men's Clothing
	Shirley Allen	Foundation Garments
	Celia Bell	Groceries
Non-selling:	Dave Hughes	Men's Clothing Alterations
	Evelyn McRae	Women's Clothing Alterations
	Bill Lewin	Georgian Room Bake Shop
COLLEGE STREET STORE		
Selling:	Wilma Johnston	Curtains
	Lilian Gadd	Paints

Non-selling:	Mary McGregor	Budget Plan Office
	Mark Robbins	Round Room Kitchen
ANNEX STORE		
Selling:	Dick Russell	Linoleum
Non-selling:	Jack Edwards	China Packing
MAIL ORDER		
Merchandising:	Ellen McDonald	Dresses
	George Whyte	Showrooms
Operating:	Chris Graham	Shipping
	Bob Woods	C.O.D.s
DELIVERY DISPATCH	Harry Neelands	Hayter Delivery
	Jim Cook	Hayter Dispatch
WAREHOUSES	E. Bradley	Christie St.
MAINTENANCE	J. Bentley	Elevators
	Jerry Douglas	Caretakers
FACTORY		
Men's Clothing:	Harriet Wood	Shirts and Pyjamas
Other Manufacturing:	Sid Byers	Universal Thread

To ensure close liaison between the Executive and Stewards' Council, the chairman, vice-chairman and secretary of the latter were also Board members; these three were Bill Young, another stalwart from Main Store Shoes, Bob Woods of Grocery Packing, and Rita LeGard, Louisa Street Employees' Cafeteria.

Turnover and transfers made the job of keeping the network of stewards intact a never-ending chore. Up to this point, the main function of the stewards had been organizing, but now the structure was reviewed from the standpoint of efficient processing of grievances under a union contract. To carry out step-by-step grievance procedure, there must be a union member to parallel each level of managerial authority. At the first step, the grievance is usually handled orally between the steward, the employee and the first level supervisor. If not settled, it is then put in writing with the supervisor's reply on the form. Next it goes to the chief steward responsible for an area, to be taken up with the appropriate management official. And so on up the line, if necessary, to be considered by top union officials including outside representatives and the company's industrial relations spokesmen. Labour legislation generally requires that, while a collective agreement is in effect, the final step in grievance procedure is binding arbitration.

In a company with only a few hundred employees in one location, it is quite simple to devise a steward system. At Eaton's, it was very complex and required a good knowledge of the chain of management authority in order to devise a workable steward structure, to serve at least until practical application could indicate necessary changes. With our help, the By-Laws Committee wrestled with this problem for some time, and finally came up with a grouping of departments into 40 sections, by division, physical location and/or occupational classification. The stewards in each section would meet to choose a chief steward.

The icing on this democratic cake was provided by an event which brought quite a different group of Eaton employees into the limelight. A highlight of the Spring Frolic planned for May 3 1951, by the Social Committee, was to be a Miss Local 1000 Beauty Contest. The Royal York Hotel had been engaged for the occasion, with Mart Kenney, a leading band of the day, providing the music. A trio of Toronto union notables, Murray Cotterill, Jim Perna and Eamon Park, were to judge the lovelies.

Shirley Allen, Executive Board member, saleslady, mother of three, and herself a beautiful person, was active in encouraging the 14 contestants to enter, including the winner, Marion Malanuck, 19, a Main Store elevator operator. The picture of Miss Local 1000 in her formal gown, with sash, crown and an armful of roses, appeared — you guessed it, not in the daily press — in the next *Unionize*, a pleasant memento of the local's most successful social event.

And so, inadequate and truncated as it is, this is my salute to the Insiders. Without them, neither Local 1000 nor any other union would ever get off the ground.

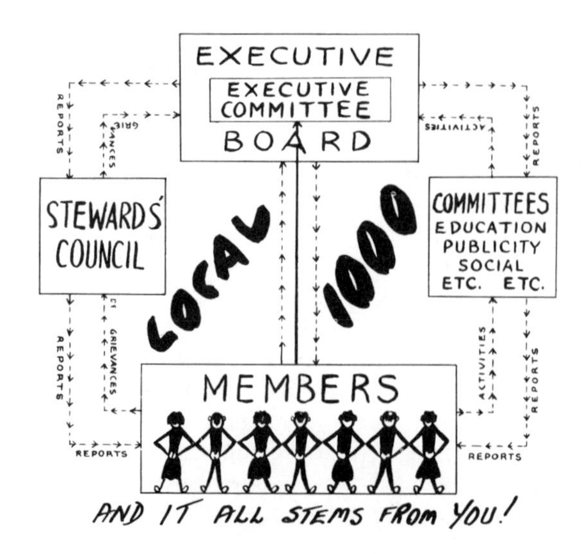

CHAPTER SEVENTEEN

The Macy Model

BY 1950 MOST LARGE CIO-CCL unions in Canada were able to point to at least one model collective agreement. In the department store field, however, there was no such model. For examples of how such employees had benefited from unionism, one had to turn to the United States, and particularly, to New York City.

For comparisons which would appeal to Eaton workers we chose Local 1-S, United Retail Workers, representing Macy's in New York. It was the largest department store local in that city, with about 8,500 members in the main Herald Square store and four others. The problems of contract negotiations and union administration would therefore be similar to those of Local 1000.

Even the early history of Local 1-S, which we reprinted,[1] was reminiscent of conditions at Eaton's, past and present, such as:

> Before we had a union we were under the constant threat of a wage cut or of being fired. We had no security.
>
> Everyone worked a basic 6-day, 54-hour week. Nobody got overtime pay.
>
> There was no such thing as a minimum wage or automatic increase.... By the Macy wage rate, women were considered inferior to men.
>
> And if we didn't like it we could leave it! After 20 years on the job, they would coolly tell us that we were "not the Macy type."

That had all changed from 1938, when Local 1-S had only 600 members, over 12 years of collective bargaining. We publicized the impressive gains they had won in salaries, elimination of job inequities, reduction in hours to the five-day, 40-hour week, job security, severance pay, and a comprehensive family health plan fully-paid by Macy's.

Eaton's selected just one part of the contract, hours of work, to try to persuade employees that they were better off on a 5½-day week, with a half-day off on Saturday, than the Macy schedule which included Saturday work on a seniority-rotation basis, except during July and August, when, like Eaton's, the store was not open on Saturdays[2].

Convinced that we had not heard the last of this from Eaton's, Lynn and I decided it would be desirable to obtain first-hand information, and accordingly we arranged to visit Local 1-S on July 5 and 6, 1951.

The chaotic situation which prevailed in New York department store unions in the late Forties has already been briefly noted (Chapter 11). When the split in RWDSU occurred in 1948, Sam Kovenetsky, president of Local 1-S, and his executive persuaded the membership to remain independent of affiliation rather than join the pro-Communist leaders whose locals formed the Distributive Workers' Union.

In 1950, one year after the Amalgamated Clothing Workers had been handed the jurisdiction to organize department stores by the CIO, they decided it wasn't for them and returned the responsibility to the CIO. Still concerned to bring more than a million unorganized department store employees into the fold, the CIO set up, early in 1951, another Department Store Organizing Committee.[3] They appointed R. J. Thomas, former UAW leader and CIO assistant director of organization, as chairman, with David J. McDonald of the Steelworkers as secretary-treasurer. The key position of the Macy local was recognized by wooing back Sam Kovenetsky as vice-chairman in charge of organization for the new DSOC. RWDSU's interest was represented by their secretary, Al Heaps.

Lynn and I received excellent co-operation from Kovenetsky and other officers of Local 1-S, who spent the first day and evening with us supplying the answers to our questions about their bargaining and administrative practices. Over the noon-hour it was obvious that the union's headquarters was well-frequented by members, either on business or just to chat. This was partly due to the fact that the local administered the company-paid health plan. The union also sponsored health clinics in which some of the finest New York specialists participated. One evening a week members could come to the office for free legal advice. They even sold fresh eggs! We noticed a large stack of cartons and were told that when egg prices rose very sharply, the local arranged with a co-op to provide eggs at a much lower price. A credit union of 1,200 Macy employees provided members with low-interest loans.

Members also came to the office to pay their dues. Although Macy's was a union shop, that is, all regular employees had to be union members, Local 1-S preferred to have dues paid at their office rather than by checkoff. The officers felt it enabled them to keep their finger on the pulse of the membership, since membership meetings were only held three or four times a year.

Lynn was intrigued with the way these meetings were handled. They were obligatory (that is, a fine was assessed for non-attendance) unless a member had a valid excuse. According to Kovenetsky, every dentist and doctor in Manhattan must have been fully occupied on the evenings of membership meetings by the number of signed "excuse slips" turned in! Even so, more than half the members, in excess of 4,000 people, usually attended and the executive put much effort into a well-prepared, exciting programme. Ideas and proposals accumulated from departmental and sectional meetings held in intervening months were placed before the members as a whole.[4]

Local 1-*S* officers provided us with valuable insights into the workings of the job security and promotion clauses in their agreement, which were reported in *Unionize* on our return.

In a layoff due to work shortage, an employee with one year of service had the right to "bump" an employee in a comparable and equally-paid job, with lesser service, in any department. Those who could not so transfer were subject to recall in inverse order of seniority. Severance pay of one week's salary for one to three years' service, two weeks' pay up to five years, plus an additional week for every year of service after five, was another feature of job protection for long-service employees.

Added job protection clauses prohibited supervisors from doing the work of any employee in the bargaining unit. Macy's was not allowed to use reserve staff to fill the job of an employee on layoff who had reinstatement rights.

Over the years, management and union had developed a novel approach to promotions. An employee could file an application with the union, stating the type of work desired and his or her seniority standing. At the end of each day, management would inform the union of all job openings, company-wide. Within 48 hours, the union could submit a list of interested employees by order of seniority. All applicants had to be interviewed, and the names of those not selected, with reasons, returned to the union. An employee who was not satisfied with reasons given could file a grievance. This enlightened, joint administrative approach was rare, but it worked: morale was high.

The second day of our visit was spent in Macy's main store, visiting departments with which we were familiar from our experience at Eaton's. Employees talked freely and without hesitation of their salaries, commission arrangements and working conditions. In general, the sales-clerks we talked with were earning $15 to $25 a week more than their counterparts at Eaton's. They were very much aware of the existence and value of their union.

Greatly encouraged by seeing a department store union in action, we returned with a wealth of information, and a picture of a photogenic Macy saleslady which appeared shortly in a special leaflet.[5] A relatively new employee, Marguerite Galvin, earned more than $60 a week and told Eaton employees: "We'd do absolutely anything to keep our union strong, because we know that the company, given a free hand, would like to take away much of what our unity has compelled them to give."

Vol. 5, No. 4 | DEPARTMENT STORE EMPLOYEES' UNION Local No. 1000 | Feb. 28, 1952

EMPLOYMENT CUTS GIVE BOSS A BIGGER SLICE

This month the supervisors and department heads at Eaton's got their big slice of the profit cake - their annual bonus.

Employees usually receiving a two-week Christmas bonus (including section heads who carry a good bit of the load for department managers) got the go-by this year at bonus time. Yet the bonus some department heads get, on top of already substantial salaries, would nicely provide a bonus for ALL their employees - and then some.

The way Eaton's decide on how much bonus a manager gets is a pretty sound reason for organizing a union. Keynote of their calculations is how much they can keep expenses down and how much profit they can show for the year's operations. The lower the expenses, the bigger the bonus. (cont'd p.4)

CHAPTER EIGHTEEN

Eaton's Weapon: Delay

ONCE LOCAL 1000's bargaining unit was established by the Ontario Labour Relations Board on May 28, 1951, the next step would be a request to Eaton's for their payroll, so that the union's percentage could be determined by a crosscheck with membership cards. To forestall this, Company counsel advised the Board that a new proposal was being placed before the union's legal advisors. Their proposition was to: 1) dispense with the card-payroll check as too "time-consuming"; 2) hold a vote in the third week in July with all arrangements to be made by the two parties; 3) include employees in the overall unit, with minor changes, as sought by the Company before the Board. If accepted, J. C. Adams promised that a voters' list could be ready *in two weeks.* On June 22 Adams put this in writing, and it was immediately conveyed to us by David Lewis.

Our initial reactions revealed a contrast between optimism and pessimism. Lynn and Wally favoured the idea. It would bring a speedy conclusion to a situation already too long delayed. Should we win a majority in the overall unit, it would bring in divisions not fully organized, such as the Factory and General Offices. I was as strongly opposed. I had misgivings about how the vote would go in the unit we had just established, let alone in one with thousands more employees of unknown sympathy. Ernie, as I recall, was neutral, since Mail Order already had a good majority. Olive had left on June 1 to spend a year abroad. For two days, we went over our prospects, department by department, marking on the blackboard the total employees, union members and estimated pro-union votes. After this exercise, it was agreed that Adams' proposal was too risky, especially in July when many stewards would be on vacation.

More compelling than this speculation about winning such a vote, there were serious drawbacks under the Ontario Labour Relations Act to be considered. Without a certification issued by the OLRB, Eaton's would be under no *legal* compulsion to bargain with Local 1000. Nor would the Act's prohibition against changes in wages or working conditions during negotiations be applicable. Moreover, should negotiations reach an impasse, an almost foregone conclusion, the union would not be entitled to the assistance of Labour Department conciliators, nor to the appointment of a conciliation board, which was a prerequisite for a legal strike.

When these pitfalls were drawn to the attention of the executive board and chief stewards on June 24, they voted to reject the Company trap. Eaton's counsel was so advised on June 26, with a counter-proposal. Why not proceed under Board auspices with a vote in the unit established, and concurrently hold "voluntary" votes among groups of employees such as the General Offices and parts of the Factory? If the union won a "voluntary" vote in any such group, we would agree to bargain for these employees. Predictably, the Company was not at all interested in our counter-proposal.

On July 4, I wrote to John David Eaton urging that there be no further obstruction to Board procedures. The Company's reply blamed the union for the delay as we had rejected their proposal for a vote in July. The position of both sides was distributed in leaflets to the employees. Eaton's began to receive wires and letters from unions across the country echoing our protest. No doubt convinced that there was to be no "deal" between the parties, the Board on July 11 requested Eaton's to supply the necessary payroll list. By July 30 there was no sign of the lists. I again wrote to the president expressing our concern, "in view of the speed with which your solicitors indicated lists could be prepared for a vote under circumstances more favourable to the Company." Copies of this letter were distributed to employees and mailed to all CCL locals.

Although our energies were increasingly diverted to pursuing every avenue of protest over the delay in certification proceedings, June and July saw a great deal of constructive activity in the local union.

When Charlie Norman became president, Otto Klingbeil took over as chairman of the Contract Committee. Otto was a specialist in repairs to Mail Order farm equipment, and an employee of 25 years' standing. By the end of May, after research into the content of other collective agreements, the Committee had finished drafting contract clauses based on Local 1000's ten-point programme, except for salaries. It was obvious that the minimum $35 a week objective set in September 1949 needed upward revision to bring it in line with the rise in the cost of living and the level of wage gains in the community since that time.

From 1946 to the end of 1951, the cost-of-living index had risen by 46.6 percent. The sharpest rise occurred in the first two years of this period during which time the index shot up 25 percent and then levelled off until the start of the Korean War. Between July 1950 and December

31, 1951, the overall index had climbed another 15 percent, with food prices accounting for the largest increase at 20 percent.[1]

Unionize had been publicizing each rise in the cost-of-living index as it occurred. It must have impressed Eaton's as well as their employees. In February 1951, employees were notified in writing that all salaries were being increased by five percent in view of the higher cost of living. We pointed out that a percentage increase created wider inequities in wages paid to women as compared with men, and that five percent or roughly $2 a week was entirely inadequate for lower-paid employees to meet the pressure of higher prices. For the remainder of 1951, salaries were raised quarterly, but the Company reverted to a flat $2 a week for full-time and $1 for part-time employees.

The Contract Committee decided that a salary survey should be undertaken to assess the effect of the many general and departmental increases since our campaign began, and to provide up-to-date information for collective bargaining. Employees were asked to fill out printed questionaries giving their department, job title, sex, length of service and present salary, but not their name. More than 500 survey forms were returned, and the information amply confirmed the existence of salary inequities. Numerous examples were cited in subsequent issues of *Unionize*. Male elevator operators were receiving $44 a week, females, $31. Warehousemen were earning $43 a week after six months and the same after 20 years on the job. Hosiery salesclerks in the Annex Budget Store were paid $2 a week less than those selling hosiery at College Street. For the same office job, a man with five years' service was paid $47.50 while a woman with 28 years' experience received $34 a week. It took three news items in *Unionize* to have Eaton's outside painters brought up to the painters' union scale of $1.70 an hour.

The results of the survey showed that employees were from $8 to $15 a week better off than when the union started in 1948. More increases had been granted than for any comparable period in the Company's history. Inequities brought to light showed clearly, however, that the information Eaton's fed to the *Financial Post* (October 14, 1950) about their uniform wage rates and automatic increases was just so much eyewash.

Our Drive received a welcome morale booster on Sunday, June 17, when Walter Reuther came to Toronto to address a rally of the United Automobile Workers, the million-strong union of which he was international president. Through the kindness of Moses McKay, president of Local 439, UAW (Massey Harris), Jim Perna and others, Local 1000 was the only other union to be invited to attend. A block of 300 seats was reserved for our members in the Uptown Theatre on Yonge Street where the meeting was held. Charlie Norman and I were accorded the privilege of making a brief report on the Eaton Drive and thanking UAW members for their support.

An apprentice tool and die maker at 15, Reuther had become a leader in the CIO Auto Workers' organizing campaign at 28, and now at 43, put the full weight of his union and his own powerful social conscience behind the international free trade union movement. Speaking at the height of the Korean War, Reuther declared at the rally:

> ...to those people in your country and our country and in others in the free world who fight against every effort to make social progress, whose selfish interest blocks every attempt to get a better life for working people, whether consciously or unconsciously, I say they are playing the game of the Kremlin, because their road leads to strengthening the forces of communism in the world... In Asia, the Communists have made great progress because the western world has made the tragic mistake of believing that freedom's fight could be won on the battlefields alone... All the time we should have known that it had to be fought also in the rice fields... When a person is hungry and his kids are starving, you can't fill an empty belly with pious slogans about democracy's virtues...

For us, he had the encouraging words:

> ...I say to the Eaton workers, "Carry on!" You are laying the foundation, and just as surely as you get that finished, you will build brick by brick just the same as the UAW did. And not far down the road, the workers in Eaton's stores and warehouses all over Canada will be in the ranks of the labour movement with all the other unions.

UAW Canadian Director George Burt had arranged for Fred Dowling, Charlie Millard and myself to meet with Reuther following the meeting to discuss possible financial assistance. We came away with his pledge that the UAW International would match donations of their Canadian locals, dollar for dollar, to a maximum of $10,000. It had been an exhilarating day. The world labour movement and the United States suffered an irreparable loss when Reuther's career was cut short by a plane crash in 1970.

By July, our funds were at a new low. A. R. Mosher, CCL President, wrote to all locals explaining the obstacles we were encountering from Eaton's and urging them to make a substantial donation to keep the Drive going. Lynn was assigned to work with the Ontario Federation of Labour to follow up on the appeal, another drain on our already over-extended staff.

Early in July, Lynn and I paid a two-day visit to Local 1-S, Macy's in New York (Chapter 17) and reported our findings to the

July 10 membership meeting. Ernie worked with the Social Committee to put on another successful dance at the Club Top Hat on July 13. The local's first weekend seminar was organized by Wally and the Education Committee at Skyloft Lodge, Dagmar, near Toronto. Alex was kept more than busy arranging extra leaflet distributions in our efforts to get Eaton's to move on filing their payroll list. Although our hopes for a September vote were fading, preparations were started at the July 24 meeting of the Stewards' Council. Every steward was asked to appoint a "vote steward" for every six or eight employees in the department.

A special meeting of the executive board and stewards was called on August 7 to consider the reply to my letter of July 30 to John David Eaton. It was another Adamesque insult to our intelligence, contending that the bargaining unit defined by the Board was so hard to interpret that it would require a check of *every single employee* to decide who was eligible for the unit and should appear on the payroll list. Lewis's suggestion to Adams that they jointly approach the Board for any necessary clarification was ignored. And to really make it "time-consuming," as Adams had predicted, he had advised the Company to prepare two lists, one of the payroll on October 18, 1950, the date of application, and the second as of December 5, the date of the Board's first hearing. (A significant change in the union percentage of membership between the two dates might provide the lawyers something to argue about.) Lewis had already advised that the union was prepared to have the crosscheck made on one payroll only, that nearest to October 18. It was apparent that we would have to find ways to escalate the pressure on Eaton's.

Through the Labour Council, a luncheon meeting of all full-time union representatives in Toronto was arranged, at which ways of widening the protest were discussed, as well as what assistance we could count on during a vote campaign. The kick-off came on August 10 when our faithful friends appeared again at Company entrances, carrying placards "Stop Stalling, Mr. Eaton / File the Lists" with their union's name below. A leaflet in the same vein, signed by Murray Cotterill, president of the Toronto & Lakeshore Labour Council, was handed to employees and customers.

Our regular reports to CCL locals were beginning to pay off with a mounting number of letters and wires of protest to Eaton's, such as this from Division 5, Canadian Brotherhood of Railway Employees, which read in part:

> ...At a recent meeting of this Division of more than 6000 members, the majority of whom are customers of your store in Moncton, N.B.,

> Local 1000's case was discussed at great length... Eaton's has always enjoyed a good reputation in this... highly organized railway city... However, your clearly anti-labour stand toward your Toronto employees has done much to destroy the well-being... between your company and working people in this area.

The "Quit Stalling, Eaton's" theme was repeated on our main float in the Labour Day Parade, which saw the largest turnout of Local 1000 marchers, especially women, to date. A 1909 Buick symbolized Eaton's labour relations. Wally drove an open car carrying Miss Local 1000 and other beauty contest queens. It was our fourth year in the parade, still waiting to be recognized as a union!

The same week, the Department Store Organizing Committee met in Toronto. Pat Conroy was asked to visit the Board chairman to express the Committee's concern about the delay. It was agreed that Eaton's tactics receive a full airing at the CCL Convention opening in Vancouver on September 17. Further, 20,000 postcards addressed to Eaton's would be distributed to delegates for use as a customer protest. My organizational report to the Committee revealed that while 776 new members had been enrolled since our application was filed, 1,098 had been lost in turnover. Plans for a fall membership drive were under way.

On the agenda of the CCL Convention were the perennial problems: layoffs, low-cost housing, government refusal to act on price controls with corporate profits at record highs, the need for a universal health care plan and many others. Nevertheless, after my report for Local 1000, an emergency resolution was introduced calling on all affiliates "to make it known to the T. Eaton Company that we resent their obvious attempts to delay and obstruct Local 1000's certification proceedings and urge [them] to discard this policy and co-operate in a speedy settlement of this case."

Delegate after delegate rose to condemn Eaton's tactics and pledge continued support to Local 1000. Stewart Alsbury, district president of B.C.'s largest union, the International Woodworkers of America, promised "to make it known to the heads of Eaton's stores in the West... that we're going to get a contract [in Toronto] or there are other places we can shop."

"This story has never got into the press, and the answer is easily found, on the back page of most Canadian newspapers," declared Larry Sefton, veteran of the Stelco strike in Hamilton. "We should carry on a sustained public relations programme, with pickets outside every Eaton store in this country, till we get this story across."

Ever practical, Pat Conroy suggested money would help. "We've

been taking on the heavyweight champion of department stores in this nation,'' he told delegates. ''Heavyweights . . . are not easy to knock over; they are big and husky and have lots of resources. We cannot defeat the heavyweight . . . by condemning him. We must arm ourselves with the same sinews that he is using. . . . If we are going to defeat this company, and get down to do a job of collective bargaining . . . the only way that can be done is for every union in the Congress to dig up the money. This fight will be a milestone in the future of the Congress.'' Debate on the resolution was recorded, and played at the October membership meeting of Local 1000.

The following week, the pressure was turned on the Ontario government. A delegation comprising Charlie Norman, Fred Tinker, Margaret Morton, George Cotton, Lynn Williams and myself secured a meeting with Ontario Labour Minister Charles Daley. We presented him with a four-page brief detailing, month by month, the techniques used by Eaton's to prolong the certification proceedings, and later distributed copies to all members of the provincial legislature. Summing up, the brief stated:

> Only one conclusion is possible from this story of delay and obstruction. Fully aware of their employment turnover and of the frustration which these delays engender among the employees, the T. Eaton Co. hope

> that time will render the union weak and ineffective. Such an attitude violates every principle of fairness on which our Canadian system of law and justice is based.
>
> To carry out its functions effectively, the Board should receive the full backing of the Labour and Attorney-General's Departments, and the Act should give it greater powers to deal with recalcitrant parties.

Charlie Norman told the Hon. Mr. Daley that the faith of Eaton employees in Ontario labour law had been severely shaken. It was tragic, he said, for thousands of our union members, having adhered strictly to the law themselves, to see how it could be circumvented. While sympathetic, Mr. Daley didn't see why we should lose faith.

The members of the Ontario legislature were now aware of Local 1000's frustration, but not the general public. Our press release about the interviews was ignored as usual.

Leaders of the CCF and Liberal opposition parties were visited and promised support. In the debate on the Speech from the Throne, E. B. Jolliffe, opposition leader, condemned the length of time permitted under the Act for certification proceedings, citing the Eaton case as an outstanding example.

That same week the chairman of the OLRB conferred with both company and union counsel. At a second interview with Mr. Daley, we were informed that the payroll lists should be finished "within two weeks." Three months after requested to do so by the Board, Eaton's filed the lists on October 9.

Next day a Company report to employees disclaimed responsibility for the delay: "It was a big job... the biggest tabulating and sorting machines were pressed into service.... The Company has done its level best to get this matter settled as quickly as possible." Granted, it was a big job. Eaton's was a big company. According to our informants, much of the work was pushed through after the CCL Convention and our visit to Queen's Park. The leaflet again made reference to the Company's offer of a July vote in the overall unit, ending on a holier-than-thou note: "Our only concern then and now is to give every last Eaton employee a chance to exercise his or her democratic right to say Yes or No on a matter that can have a vital bearing on the future of us all." It conjured up a crocodile, jaws wide open!

On October 13, *Hush* was selling its scandal tabloid outside Eaton's with the front page given over to announcing in huge type:

JOHN DAVID EATON'S KNOCK-OUT PUNCH
BLOCKS UNION DRIVE

DOING THEIR "LEVEL BEST"...

"IT HAS TAKEN A LONG TIME BUT THE COMPANY HAS DONE ITS LEVEL BEST TO GET THIS MATTER SETTLED AS QUICKLY AS POSSIBLE."

-'A Report' from Eaton's, October 10, 1951.

EATONIAN DEMOCRACY

In its last leaflet the company said it had offered the union a democratic vote of all the employees in the Eaton organization. This offer, it said, was turned down by the union. This is not so. The kind of vote the company offered was one where everyone on the list who does not vote at all is counted as having voted against the union. This may be the practice under the labor law but it is not a democratic one.

The leaflet omitted to inform employees that when Mr. David Lewis, union lawyer, suggested that the vote be a democratic one, the company counsel did not even take his suggestion seriously.

HIGH QUOTAS CUT EARNINGS

The quota has been raised so high in Annex Men's Furnishings, Dept. 928, that these salary-plus-commission employees find it almost impossible to make their quotas, let alone exceed them and thus make any commission. Basic salaries are totally inadequate. The manager was approached by employees but said he had no control over setting quotas. This situation should be rectified by top management, as Annex employees resent discrimination in salary compared to Main Store selling sections.

Dept. 928 employees feel the best solution would be a straight salary at an adequate rate.

To supply the sex appeal, two smaller headlines referred to stories inside: "Off-the-Beam Lover Hounds Pretty Girls" and "War Bride Charges Hubby's 'Friend' Attacked Her." It turned out that the "knock-out punch" had been delivered in January 1948 when John David brought forth "a modern Magna Carta." Garbled inaccuracies spread over four pages were devoted to the editor's view of union leaders "drunk with a sense of power... money-mad and dictatorial..."

by order of men sitting comfortably and well-paid in their own offices, employees could be pulled out from behind counters to parade in picket lines'' and so on.

Meanwhile, back in the shop, employees were continuing to benefit from the ''Magna Carta'' or the union, depending on one's point of view. On September 10, Mail Order employees at last had their hours reduced to 40, Monday to Friday, and Saturday work became a thing of the past. All employees received another round of $2 a week increases as the cost-of-living index continued to move upward. Local 1000 members and friends celebrated on September 22 with a Fall Dance at the Royal York Hotel.

The Board's examiners took just over two weeks to complete the card-payroll check. The exact number of valid union cards is considered confidential by the Board, and we were advised that, being satisfied that Local 1000 had not less than 45 percent membership, a vote was ordered. The total eligible voters turned out to be closer to 10,000 than the 11,500 estimated in our original application. Therefore, the 6,629 cards filed with the Board should have represented more than 50 percent. It meant that turnover had been much greater than we knew, a sobering indication of the margin of our voting strength.

Eaton's response to the Board order was to sow more confusion. They advised employees that the only way to ascertain if they could vote or not would be to check the voters' lists when they were posted in due course. They still moaned that ''*4,000 Can't Vote.*''

Art Brunskill, Chief Returning Officer for the OLRB, got the parties together to decide on dates, polling places and preparation of voters' lists. We pressed for November 19 and 20 as voting days, but the Company insisted that voters' lists could not be ready until December 3 and 4.

From our point of view it was the worst possible time. In the middle of the Christmas rush, it was the busiest time of year. With all the extra seasonal help, stewards would have the task of figuring out who was eligible to vote. Everyone in the Stores was working all day on Saturdays and had to get their own shopping done on noon-hours or relief periods. Add the bone-chilling Toronto winter for our leaflet distributors, while Eaton's handed out theirs on the inside!

CHAPTER NINETEEN

Paper War: The Vote Campaign

AFTER FOUR YEARS of intense and sustained effort it was almost too much for us to grasp that the dates for the vote had actually been set. But there was no time to catch our breath. Nineteen working days remained before the 72-hour publicity cutoff, required under Ontario labour law, prior to the vote on December 3 and 4, 1951.

The first thing I did was to contact the Department Store Organizing Committee to ask for the loan of staff from other unions and all the funds they could muster. I reported great enthusiasm among our members over news of the vote, and that "depending on the degree of opposition in Company propaganda during the campaign, we feel fairly optimistic."

A week earlier we learned that there would be an additional adversary. A group calling themselves the "Loyal Eatonians" had been formed, led by Alfredo Bassonesi, a furniture salesman in the College Street Store, assisted by a Mrs. Temple, secretary to the Furniture department manager, and her husband, a supervisor in the Electrical department in the same store.

It was brought to our attention by one of Eaton's veterans that Mr. Bassonesi had been interned during the War for expounding fascist views. When we publicized this, the Company sprang to his defence, regretting "any embarrassment . . . as a result of the cowardly attack to which the professional outside organizers stooped . . . ," although admitting his internment for six months commencing June 1940.[1]

Through an inquiry made by Alistair Stewart, M.P., to Hon. Stuart Carson, Minister of Defence, we eventually reprinted a copy of the Minister's reply, dated November 17, 1951, which stated: "I understand that Mr. Bassonesi was actively associated with Italian fascism in Canada, and that it was considered necessary to detain him . . . ."[2] Curiously enough, this diversion may have done the union more harm than good, for some employees agreed with Eaton's that we had "stooped" to say nasty things — however true — about Mr. Bassonesi!

The deluge of pro- and anti-union propaganda began on November 8. On most days thereafter Eaton employees were handed three leaflets, one each by Local 1000 and the Loyal Eatonians outside the entrances, and another by the Company inside. Close to half a million pieces of paper. How many were read? Was there a saturation point? With the Christmas rush on, it would have been incredible if employees took time to digest it all.

Alex Gilbert recalls the first day the Loyal Eatonians put leaflets out:

> They started with the part-time workers at the Mail Order. I came by around four o'clock and found young girls at the doors with a bundle of leaflets. I took one and read it and realized what was up. So I told the girls I'd take over and they could go home, which they did. Then I hurried around to the garbage in the lane and got rid of the leaflets. I did that at two doors and then came back to the office with the first Loyal Eatonian leaflet.

Their one-page leaflets were marked by an almost studied amateurism, badly written, full of typing errors and dull in appearance. The theme was "love that Company." But what they lacked in content was compensated for in effect by the number of employee distributors. Apparently, it was quite permissible for Loyal Eatonians to be late for work or get off early for their distributions. Toward the end they were mobbing the bus stops. Alex Gilbert recalls his amusement early one morning at the College Street Store: "There I was, surrounded by about 50 Loyal Eatonians, all females, when a big limousine pulled up and Lady Eaton stepped out to inspect her troops, giving me a dirty look at the same time."

Lady Eaton's version of those days is related in her autobiography:

> A few years ago our Stores in Toronto were picketed (sic) by some labour union people who were attempting to organize the employees into Local 1000. No sooner had the union representatives' ambitions become known than a group of our employees banded together, without any word to Company management, to form themselves into an organization called "Loyal Eatonians." Through a levy of 10 cents per member they financed a weekly paper in which they forcefully answered the unionists' arguments, and stated in no uncertain manner that they did not want to see Eaton's changed. They wanted *their* Company to be kept a family affair.[3]

It was remarkable that Lady Eaton failed to recall that Local 1000 had been distributing leaflets for four *years*, whereas the Loyal Eatonians came into existence four *weeks* prior to the union vote:

> During those weeks of union activity and strike talk, I went down to the College Street Store one morning, arriving before 8:30. It happened to be the day when the "Loyal Eatonian" paper was being handed out at

> the doors. I walked around the building, spoke to the girls who were on duty, and they were glad to see me.... Next I went down to the Main Store and did the same thing there.... If those people who worked all day for us could stand at the Store doors from 7:00 a.m. until 8:30 to prove their loyalty to the Company, then I felt I could very well get up and go down among them to give them a nod of encouragement.[4]

As for "strike talk," Lady Eaton was being disingenuous, for it was raised solely in the Company leaflets, and not by any group or at meetings of Local 1000. Undoubtedly, a successful work stoppage would have expedited matters at several junctures along the way. But it would have been folly to contemplate such action, which would have lacked majority support, and by its illegality would have jeopardized our case before the Board.

In contrast to the feeble efforts of their allies, the Loyal Eatonians, Eaton's propaganda had obviously been prepared well ahead of time by professionals. A recurring theme was set out in their first leaflet:

> On December 3rd, you will be called on to make an important choice: between the Company for which you now work, the benefits and rights you now enjoy — and the promises of outside organizers... You are entitled to know something of the motives, methods and purposes behind these intruders and the powerful groups who control and direct them; for what you decide in the next two or three weeks can affect your whole future and that of your family.[5]

Later, the tone became more strident:

> ...a group of professional organizers are asking you to put yourself and your family in their hands... the CIO-CCL is master-minding the drive to get control of the Eaton staff and eventually all retail employees everywhere.[6]

> ...The choice is clear. You can turn your future over to those professional organizers whose main interest in you is what you mean in terms of dues and power — or you can retain your future in your own hands...[7]

> ...consider how little these organizers in New York and their counterparts in Canada know about you, this Company, or the retail business. Compare them and their knowledge with the people directing this Company. Most of THEM started right at the bottom and worked their way up. Your future is safer in the hands of people like these than it could ever be in the hands of outsiders whose main concern is building union power and collecting union dues.[8]

Eaton's leaflets agonized more about the dues money the union would acquire than the power. No doubt power could be taken for granted by a family concern which had amassed an estimated $400 million in assets. But for Local 1000 to have any financial muscle was another matter. It was inferred that the local wouldn't see much of their dues: the CIO or the "professional organizers" would grab it. As they pointed out in their first leaflet:

> At the recent [CCL] convention in Vancouver, Eaton's was named the No. 1 target. In response to this directive, CIO unions have poured men, money and propaganda into the campaign... from $100,000 to $150,000... there is a lot more to all this than warm, brotherly love.[9]

Eaton employees must have been amazed at the allegation that $150,000 had been "poured" into the campaign since the CCL convention two months previous. The Company knew full well, of course, that this was an estimate of the amount contributed by organized labour over a four-year period, and that Local 1000 expense for the last year or more was directly attributable to their deliberate policy of delay. Ironically, when I appealed to the DSOC-CCL for funds on November 8, we had less than $100 in the bank!

At the current RWDSU dues of $1.50 per month, Eaton's calculated that if on checkoff, Local 1000 would receive about $200,000 a year in dues. They carried their argument further. If dues doubled "as they have in many unions," they said, the "take" for the CIO "out of your pockets" would be "in the neighbourhood of... $400,000 A YEAR! Multiply that by the scores of department stores and thousands of retail outlets in Canada and you begin to get a glimpse of the rich prize the CIO is grasping for. You are the first step."[10]

Later, the Company returned to the same theme to inject more misinformation:

> ...how could you possibly get $200,000 worth of service a year? Local 1000 already has a staff of seven. If they average about $75 a week, the annual salary bill is running around $25,000. Let's double it, to be on the safe side. And toss in another $25,000 for other costs. That's $75,000 a year. What do *they* propose doing with the rest of the potential $200,000...? [*our emphasis*][11]

What indeed? Not being one of the Eaton family, it had never crossed our minds. We did publish the fact that none of our five full-time organizers, including myself, earned $75 a week. However, truth never seems to catch up with lies — at least, not in time to erase first impressions.

Not content with smearing the motives of the CIO-CCL and its organizers, the red herring of communism and the spectre of strikes were very much a part of the anti-union campaign.

Under a capitalized subhead of "COMMUNISM," one Company leaflet was devoted to the split in RWDSU in 1948 when New York locals under Communist leadership broke away. There followed a list of members of the CIO's Department Store Organizing Committee formed in the spring of 1951, with their organizations. The reader was left to wonder if these latter were also of a "crimson hue." [12]

As for the RWDSU in Canada, it was "pitifully weak" with "no more than 3,500 dues-paying members from one end of Canada to the other," not enough to pay the Canadian staff. [13]

Even the credibility of the OLRB was cast in doubt:

> ...it [RWDSU] claims and has persuaded the Ontario Labour Relations Board, that it has at least 45% of the Eaton staff in the bargaining unit — something over 5,000 people...
>
> But there's a lot of difference between signing a card, paying $1.00 under pressure, and being a full-fledged dues-paying member.
>
> On Monday, December 3rd... you will be able to make your choice freely and secretly. There will be no union pusher at your elbow needling you... [14]

Strikes were deplored in three of the Company broadsides, always with the inference that union members did not have any say in deciding if or when one was to be called:

> ...strikes don't bother union bosses too much, anymore. After a while, you can get used to anything especially if it doesn't hurt your pocketbook. If they are really desperate, strikers may get $10 a week relief vouchers from the union. But union leaders go on collecting anywhere from $75-$100 a week, plus expenses. [15]

After Eaton's obstructionism during the Board proceedings, we had anticipated all-out opposition in the vote campaign. To defeat Local 1000, the Company would have to persuade enough union members to vote against it. What we were not prepared for was the virulent invective turned on the CIO and ourselves as organizers. What had happened to the Methodist ethics which Timothy Eaton had espoused? Was this the same Company that had built a retail empire on its reputation for honest and fair dealing with its customers? Where was their much-vaunted pride in truthful advertising? How naïve we were. We should have known from Eaton's past history: the customer was "always right" but the employees had always been expendable.

We debated how best to deal with the verbal assaults the Company was delivering almost daily. Even with Thistle Printing's unfailing co-operation, it required one or two days to have 10,000 leaflets printed. Eaton's had their own print shop. Given the limited time, we decided not to be sidetracked from putting Local 1000's case forward. Rebuttal of company attacks would have to take second place.

Under the theme, "Vote Yes / Get a Contract," we reiterated the Local 1000 programme, explaining the union's stand on issues which would be the subject of collective bargaining. The question of better pay received the most attention, as it had throughout the Drive. A number of leaflets featured a message from and photo of members of other unions in Toronto to tell Eaton employees what they had achieved.

John Muir, who started as a machine operator at Massey Harris in 1947, calculated that increases won by Local 439, UAW, had raised his hourly pay by 58¢, whereas his union dues cost him less than 1½¢ per hour. "My pay is now $1,206.40 a year more than when I entered the plant.... Add all the rest of the gains we've won through the UAW, and you can see why I say union dues are the best investment a working man — or woman — can make," he declared. "We don't begrudge a cent of our dues that go toward helping store employees to get a union contract too.... You'll get lots of phoney propaganda between now and your vote, but don't be sidetracked. Local 1000 is the chance of a lifetime to win your rights."[16]

We reproduced the pay slip of G. Brooks, a woman employed in the sewing department of Swift Canadian, and a member of Local 208, United Packinghouse Workers, and compared it with that of a Main Store salesclerk at Eaton's. The take-home pay of the Swift employee was $41.71 for a 35-hour week. Even after increases amounting to $16 a week since Local 1000 appeared in 1948, the salesclerk's take-home pay for two weeks was only $63.74, or about $10 a week less, for five hours' more work.[17]

Understandably, the key issue of wages was ignored by the Company except for a single reference which compared their benefits with Macy's and inferred that Eaton's had been more generous:[18]

MACY'S With A Contract	EATON'S Without A Contract
General wage increases 1950-51, $4.25 (Feb./50, $1, Nov./50, $3.25)	For the 2-year period 1950-51 general increases based on the cost of living were given to staff across Canada ranging from $8 to $12 per week.

We pointed out the facts that they did not tell employees, as for example:

> ...[women] at Macy's were earning $10 to $15 a week on average more than Eaton's paid for the same job... the differential for [men] would be

> even higher. Today, the average of all salaries at Macy's is $56 per week [not including management].
>
> ...in negotiations last year Local 1-S won an extra $100,000 fund to be used in adjusting inequalities... 1,400 such adjustments were made.
>
> ...automatic increases... after 60 days, 6 months, 12 months and 18 months on the job.[19]

The focal point of the Company attack on the union's objectives was the Monday-to-Friday five-day week. They claimed to be "the only store in North America" to give employees Saturday afternoon off most of the year. Again, the criticism was directed at:

> ...the professional organizers who... talk so glibly about closing all day Saturday are either woefully ignorant of or indifferent to what this would mean to you and the benefits you now enjoy, or they are *deliberately deceiving you* in order to get your vote and your money.[20]

On this issue, we were on the defensive. After replying that hours and daily work schedules were a matter for collective bargaining, we once more quoted Timothy's expressed hopes for weekends off, and cited the numerous meetings at which Eaton employees themselves had decided to seek Saturdays off. Had not Mail Order, also a retail operation, already ended Saturday work just two months earlier?

Loyal Eatonians busied themselves on this issue, circulating petitions among store employees asking the Company to keep store hours unchanged.

Local 1000's programme for job security was set out in another leaflet. Contract clauses to be sought would: make seniority count in event of layoffs; require warning before discharge, except for theft or serious misconduct; cushion layoffs with severance pay on a scale increasing with length of service.[21]

On this subject, Eaton's invented a demand which was not even part of Local 1000's programme, which they lifted out of the Macy agreement:

> Everyone employed at Eaton's even Quarter Century Club members, would be outranked by short-service stewards if these self-appointed "representatives" on Bay St. had their way. *In case of lay-offs the stewards would be the last to go regardless of ability or seniority.*[22]

In view of the enormous turnover at Eaton's, superseniority for union stewards, so vital to both union and management in the administration of a collective agreement, would have been an entirely reasonable proposition.

Job security was misinterpreted and equated with guaranteed employment:

> Eaton employees have it [job security] now and will continue to have it to the same extent... as Eaton's itself... But not even the biggest richest union in the world can *guarantee* it.... Ask some of the auto workers laid off...[23]

Local 1000's programme on welfare called for company-paid pensions with a minimum of $100 a month, and eligibility to join reduced from five to one year's service. Similarly, we asked that health plan premiums be paid for by Eaton's, with cumulative paid sick leave.

Under the heading of "welfare and pensions," Eaton's told their employees:

> These outsiders are trying to sell you something inferior to what you have owned for a long time and which cost you nothing. Eaton's extra benefits, rights and privileges rate among the most generous in the country. It must be obvious too, that if Local 1000 takes over, all these "extras" you now enjoy would be placed in jeopardy. Everything would be subject to collective bargaining. Unless they were written into a contract, they would not exist any more.[24]

The Company's statement amounted to illegal threats under the Labour Relations Act, but with a week to go before the vote, nothing would have been gained by initiating legal proceedings. It was also one of their more brazen distortions of the facts, since employees paid the *full cost* of Blue Cross and Associated Medical Services coverage, and had *five percent of earnings* deducted for the pension plan over which they had no say.

Despite the account thus far, the vote campaign was by no means conducted solely on paper. It just seemed that way to Hugh Webster and myself, churning out leaflets as the days went by in a kaleidoscopic blur.

To lend a hand with many other activities, seven organizers were assigned to us. This competent group included: from the Steelworkers staff, "Scotty" Reid of Sudbury and Don Montgomery, Toronto; Orville Kerr from Local 1005 (Stelco) in Hamilton; Bob McLeod, CCL organizer, London; Moses McKay, president of Local 439, UAW; Dick Hynds, Textile Workers' organizer; and Hugh Buchanan from RWDSU, later to become Canadian director of that union.

Preparations for the vote were proceeding under the direction of Art Brunskill, chief returning officer for the OLRB. At the monthly membership meeting on November 13, David Lewis and Dave Archer spoke about procedures under Board-conducted votes. Social activities were not neglected: both Mail Order and Delivery sections held dances. Local 1000 had a weekly radio programme with Charlie Norman, Doris Griffiths and Bill Edwards speaking for the executive.

The union office was filled every evening with members to help with whatever was needed. Each of the extra organizers was assigned to work with one of our staff to make sure the network of vote stewards was in place.

Under the pressure of time and work, it became more difficult to keep track of what was happening throughout the dispersed operations of the Company. Some department managers were calling in staff, one by one, to talk about hours of work, or to inquire why anyone should be discontented. Loyal Eatonians were circulating letters, purporting to have been written by union malcontents, unidentified by name. But Local 1000 stewards were also aggressive in defending their rights. For example, Len Horrocks from Main Store Shoes recalls:

> When our boss started passing out the Loyal Eatonian leaflets, I walked up to him and said, ''You know I have the same right to pass out union pamphlets if you're going to do that on the floor.'' So he runs over to the manager's office to see, and comes back empty-handed. We thought he might even go round and collect those he'd handed out!

The totally unexpected adverse reaction of Eaton employees to our leaflet in the Bassonesi incident has already been mentioned.

Equally surprising was the aftermath of a "spoof" leaflet we mimeographed, entitled, "We Stand For Eaton's," ostensibly distributed by "More Loyal Eatonians." Its tenor was summed up in the final paragraph:

> Leave your fate COMPLETELY in the hands of the Company and stop thinking, as we have done. Then we can all stand and stand and stand until we all go down together. Wouldn't that be wonderful?

As Lynn recalls, "We — the staff at least — thoroughly enjoyed this effort with much hilarity. But a rather sinking feeling set in when it was over. The 'Lily Whiters,' as we called them, reacted with much indignation, and I remember being involved with many of our store people in defending what we had done. To them it seemed a 'low blow,' of the kind we often attributed to the Company... [it] made me aware in the many campaigns since, that before using a 'gimmick' or whatever to liven things up, it's important to be sure of the response of one's supporters."

I feel sure that somewhere in these two incidents lies a key as to why white-collar workers are so difficult to unionize. Perhaps we could learn from sociologists what to avoid.

The best answer to the Loyal Eatonians was given in an open letter, composed and signed by Lilian Gadd, Local 1000's Executive Board member representing the College Street Store, where she had worked 27 years as a saleswoman in the Paint Department.

Born and educated in England, Lilian Gadd was a person with unusual capabilities which should have been used at a much higher level in Eaton's. They were recognized during the War when she served four and one-half years with the Canadian Women's Army Corps, in charge of army stores across Canada. Shortly after her election to union office, she addressed her fellow employees through *Unionize*:

> Eaton's is a company with big ideals, but it will be even bigger when the union is in. Such a vast organization cannot afford to remain small-minded. Once we're unionized, not only will employees benefit, the Company will too.[26]

She said she had studied trade unionism for some time, and discussed it with friends in and out of Eaton's, before joining Local 1000. Once a member, she was active, steadfast and fearless in support of the union. Her "Open Letter to Eaton Employees" on November 16, 1951, said in part:

> We have heard much lately of the words "family" and "loyalty." We all know that a family... pertains to home life rather than to the business world.

> Does a mother or father discriminate against their children? Do they give one child all the good things in life and deprive another of the self-same things? Yet our Eaton "family" does this. There are many instances of discrimination.... If we are the happy family some people would have us believe, then these things could not exist.
>
> ...if John David Eaton is to become cognizant of the wide and varied discrepancies that exist in the Eaton organization today, he should know of conditions at first hand, from those best able to speak for employees without fear of reprisals — their union.
>
> Building Local 1000 has been a long and arduous task. The election of the Executive... the Stewards Council, various Committees, contract preparations, and much other work has been the result of hours of patient labour by Eaton employees, not of "outsiders." We have had the help of an experienced organizing staff, financial and moral support from the Canadian Congress of Labour.... But the major work... has been done by us, your fellow employees.
>
> ...We are seeking higher wages, seniority rights, elimination of favouritism.... By working together, members of Local 1000 believe we can be builders of individual and social peace.
>
> Are these the words of a "disloyal" person? I think not. They are the words of an employee who has given loyal service to the T. Eaton Co. for nearly thirty years.
>
> (signed) Lilian Gadd
> Department 275,
> College St. Paints

The Congress sent Jack Williams, their public relations director, to prepare the publicity for our final distribution on November 29. A former journalist, Jack was so unobtrusively professional that I recall only one or two sessions to discuss contents of the excellent four-page tabloid which he wrote and guided through the printers. Under the head, "We're Voting YES," the entire back page was given over to photos of Local 1000 members from a cross-section of Eaton divisions.

The final rally on November 27 was the largest meeting Local 1000 had ever had. More than 500 stewards and vote stewards packed Memorial Hall on College Street after work to hear A.R. Mosher, president of the CCL, wish them well. "All members of the Congress are looking forward to the day when Eaton employees in Toronto will enjoy the benefits of a union contract," Mosher concluded.

It was an enthusiastic, confident and determined gathering. Not one steward rose to report that Eaton's propaganda had created disaffection among union members.

CHAPTER TWENTY

Opportunity Lost

THE UNION REPRESENTATION VOTE at Eaton's was the largest held in Ontario up to that time. The onerous preparations were supervised by A.M. Brunskill, chief returning officer for the Ontario Labour Relations Board.

Once the location of the polls, and departments covered by each, was settled to the satisfaction of the parties, a voters' list had to be prepared for posting in each department, stating the poll location and voting times. These arrangements were completed without incident. When there was no advantage in delay, Eaton's could move with despatch. On November 20 the Company distributed a leaflet giving a list of the departments covered by each of the 43 polls which were to be open on December 3, and the 12 which would remain open the following day. Grasping every opportunity for anti-union propaganda, Eaton's pointed out:

> You are not obliged to choose a union at all. The question is whether or not a new form of internal government in this business is to be instituted and therefore the legislation provides that the union does not win the vote unless it receives a "yes" vote from a majority of all those who are eligible to vote... all ballots marked "no" and all ballots that are spoiled, all ballots that are not used by persons who do not vote, have the same effect. They are all votes against the union.

They went on to say, however, that it would be more "emphatic" to defeat the union by voting "no" than simply by not voting.

To supervise the vote, Art Brunskill had to supply 43 deputy returning officers; each party was entitled to one scrutineer per poll. Local 1000 scrutineers were all employees who had to arrange with supervisors for time off.

To check on the turnout of voters, Wally Ross and Moses McKay were assigned to arrange an outside scrutineering system. Six extra phones were installed in our office, so that our inside scrutineers could report from time to time on the turnout. As the reports came in, it became clear that voting was very heavy. Indeed, 94 percent of the eligible voters did cast ballots — a very high proportion in any type of election.

By 6:00 p.m. on December 4, all polls had closed. The count was to take place that evening in the Fifth Floor Cafeteria of the Main Store. When David Lewis, Lynn Williams and I arrived, we found a solid line of management officials stationed along one side of the cafeteria.

At the time the voters' lists had been prepared, there was disagreement over the eligibility of some supervisory employees, and their ballots had been segregated. Seated at a table with Staff Superintendent Ford, Lynn and I were still arguing over these disputed cases, but without much vigour, so tense were we about the outcome of the vote. The count was taking place at long tables arranged to accommodate the deputy returning officers and scrutineers with their ballot boxes.

Unable to contain his curiosity, Lynn got up and walked along the tables as the count was being tallied. Before he got very far, I saw him turn pale and went over to join him. Far too many "no" votes were being tallied. When Lynn saw "no" votes in the warehouse poll where we had almost 100 percent membership, he knew we were in trouble. By the time the count had ended, earlier indications were confirmed, and the union had lost.

Despite our shock, we had to remain until the ballots were double-checked, bundled in fifties, and recorded by Brunskill on a statement for both parties. As we waited for the official return, along with Ford and other Company officials, it seemed incumbent on me to say something. With as jaunty a smile as I could muster, I told the assembled management, "We'll be back!"

David, Lynn and I were the last of the union people to leave the building. Lynn still has vivid memories of our departure:

> We had to take the elevator down to the main floor, and then walk to the north exit on James Street. Again the Company had their lineup of supervision, this time on both sides of the aisle, so that we had to walk the gauntlet through this row of people until we finally got out of the place. I still remember that as one of the longest walks of my life, and how I felt like kicking the shins of every one of them as I walked by, feeling so disappointed and angry, and unable to bear their arrogant witness to our pain.

Once outside in the cold darkness came the walk which I dreaded, to our headquarters three blocks away, full of members and supporters waiting for the news. How to tell them that their years of effort had failed? How to cushion the shock of learning that enough of their own fellow members had voted against them to defeat the union?

Only a few hours before, Lynn and I had dropped into a tavern on Yonge Street to pass a half hour before we were due for the count. We spent the time talking about getting ready for negotiations. As Lynn recollects:

> That was the striking measure of our confidence — or maybe just of my naïveté. But it seemed inconceivable after all we had been through that there would not be an outpouring of support from the workers at Eaton's. I don't think I've ever been confident about a vote again. There have been some great victories in the years since, and some shattering defeats, but never another like Eaton's.

At headquarters, disbelief turned to disappointment on the faces of our members and friends. It was already late and many drifted off home. The chagrin felt by our staff must have been exceeded in the feelings of these men and women having to go in to work at Eaton's the next day and the days after.

Among the supporters gathered, Ken Bryden, then provincial secretary of the Ontario CCF, and a frequent leaflet distributor for us, predicted to Fred Dowling and me that "It will take another 20 years to organize Eaton's again." As Fred and I sat down around midnight to prepare a news release for *Canadian Press*, we probably shared the unspoken gut reaction that Ken might well be right. Nonetheless, in the release we sounded a note of optimism not only for Local 1000 members but for the thousands of unionists across Canada who would also be shocked to learn that the vote had been lost.

In my statement, I said the results "reflected the tremendous amount of pressure exerted by the Company on employees" ever since Local 1000 applied for certification in October 1950, and continued, "We are proud of the number of union members who stood up under it... with the spirit they are showing... it is only a matter of time until we can re-apply." Fred Dowling, speaking as chairman of the Department Store Organizing Committee, CCL, and Canadian director of the United Packinghouse Workers, related, "We lost our first vote at the Toronto plant of Canada Packers, but within a year we had a second vote and won it."

As we were leaving Eaton's, David Lewis had told me he was proud that I had not shed any tears. When all those who had come to our offices to celebrate and remained to commiserate had left except for Alex Gilbert and Don Montgomery, I let my hair down and wept. Eaton employees heard the results of the vote on the radio before leaving for work next morning, and no doubt some of them cried too.

Now that it was quite safe to mention the attempt to unionize Eaton's, all three Toronto dailies ran news stories on the outcome of the vote.

As for the Company, they made no comment. They didn't have to. *The Globe & Mail* did it for them in a lengthy editorial on December 5 which attributed the vote results to:

> ...the fine relationship which exists between the staff and management at Eaton's... [and] the interest which Mr. John David Eaton has shown in the welfare of his employees.... Sick benefits, pension funds and the like, which are provided by such firms as Eaton's, may not be appreciated by new or transient employees. But older workers set great value on them, and quite naturally resent seeing them belittled by outsiders.

Then, the editor offered his opinions, without offering one shred of evidence, on the conduct of the union campaign which his newspaper had avoided mentioning for over four years:

> The biggest deciding factor was the revulsion most Eaton employees felt at the tactics used by the union. In its four-year drive to organize them... it sank to vituperation of the meanest sort. On the radio, in leaflets and pamphlets, the union conducted a campaign so scurrilous and vehement that loyal, long-term members of the Eaton staff formed their own organizations to defeat it.
>
> It may be hard for Miss Tallman, and people of that type, to realize... that there can be such a thing as pride of employment... what it means is that unionism based on the principles of class warfare is gone.... By trying to peddle that moth-eaten notion among intelligent workers of an up-to-date company, the Department Store Employees' Union simply succeeded in slitting its own throat.

The editor neglected to mention that the "revulsion" of the Loyal Eatonians did not manifest itself until *four weeks* prior to the vote. Had the propriety of our radio scripts been questionable, we would hardly have been able to broadcast more than 30 programmes during the campaign. As for the "class war" approach of our leaflets, it raised the question of whether the G & M editor ever set eyes on them, or simply took the word of some third party.

Still feeling rather numb, our staff spent the day after the vote talking to members who dropped in the office or phoned. At noon, when a dozen red roses arrived for me from Larry Nielsen, the union vice-president, the tears started again, and I hid for a while in a back office.

However, on December 6 we began to pick up the pieces and plan the next moves. We discussed the contents of a leaflet calling a general membership meeting for December 11, and arrangements to hold a meeting of the Executive Board and Stewards' Council over the weekend.

An analysis of the final vote tabulation showed that while Local 1000's defeat was unequivocal, it was by no means overwhelming, even under the Ontario labour legislation of the time, which required a union to obtain a majority of those *eligible to vote* rather than *of ballots cast.* On this basis, all who did not vote, together with the spoiled and segregated ballots, were counted as "no" votes. As can be seen from the figures, the employees who voted "no" also did not constitute a majority of those eligible:

Number of eligible voters:			9,914
Majority of eligible voters:			4,958
Number of ballots cast:			
"Yes" votes	4,020		
"No" votes	4,880		
Spoiled ballots	295		
Segregated ballots	141	9,300	
Number of non-voters:		614	9,914

Not until twenty years later was the Ontario Labour Relations Act amended to change the requirement for certification to a majority of those who actually cast ballots.[1] Had this been in effect in 1951, Local 1000's showing would have improved by five percent, but would still have fallen short of a majority, as the following comparison indicates:

	Results of Eaton vote as a percentage of:		
	Eligible voters (9,914) %		Valid ballots cast (8,900) %
"Yes" votes		40.5	45.1
"No" votes	49.3		54.9
Non-voters	6.1		n/a
Spoiled ballots	2.6		n/a
Segregated ballots	1.4	59.4	n/a
		99.9	100.0

Had the vote at Eaton's been conducted, as political contests are, on the basis of valid votes cast, it would have taken a swing of only 431 votes for Local 1000 to have attained a majority of the 8,900 valid votes cast.

Even under the 1951 rules, our actual margin of loss was less than the figures suggested. Our scrutineers claimed that practically all of the 259 spoiled ballots were intended for "yes" votes. Although in union votes it was usual to count ballots where the intent was fairly clear, Eaton's scrutineers had been instructed to challenge every ballot on which there was the least irregularity in the marking.

In any case, with 4,020 members who had withstood all efforts  to change their minds, Local 1000 had not suffered a drastic rout and could not be expected to fold its tents and silently steal away. However, Eaton's began immediately to foster that course of action.

On December 7, the Company's secretary-treasurer, J. Elliott, sent a letter to all department heads, with instructions that employees be asked to read and initial it. The contents read:

> The Directors of the Company are anxious that the traditional spirit of harmony which has always prevailed in the Eaton establishment should be restored as soon as possible.
>
> We are particularly anxious that no person with supervisory authority should do anything which could be interpreted as retaliation against those employees who were supporters of the union.
>
> If, in spite of the verdict of those employees who were allowed to vote, the union persists in its attempts to inflict itself on this organization, we may find it necessary to take some measures to protect our employees from such activities on Company premises, bearing in mind, of course, that the law gives employees complete freedom to belong to a union or to organize a union.
>
> You can be assured that the whole matter is receiving a careful study, and employees may be assured by you that any improper influence to which they may be subjected at the hands of union organizers will be stopped in due course, although we expect that it will not be necessary for us to take any action, as it is likely that the promoters of the union movement will very soon realize that the will of the majority of Eaton employees is not to be lightly flouted.

Meanwhile, Santa Claus was again ensconced in Toyland personifying the commercialized spirit of Christmas, but Eaton's had decided there were to be no gifts for the 43 "bad children" who had scrutineered for Local 1000. They declined to pay for their lost time, amounting in most cases to one day, and deducted it from their last pay before the holiday season. Some scrutineers figured they had donated much more than a day's pay to the Company in "free" overtime over the years. Local 1000 paid for the lost time, not all of which was claimed, for a total of $495. It was the one and only time that members were paid for working for the union.

Considering the season, the general meeting on December 11 at Purdy's was well attended. It was spent in a full discussion of factors contributing to the setback. There were no inflammatory speeches, no accusations levied against individuals or departments. The consensus was that the most important factor had been the members' lack of knowledge of the democratic nature of their own union, and of the aims and objectives of the local and of organized labour in general. Consequently, the Company's misrepresentation of the union's programme was often not perceived as such. The threat of losing benefits and privileges, conveyed in leaflets and by word of mouth by management and Loyal Eatonians, created an atmosphere of fear that inhibited calm reasoning.

The members concluded that the only way to prevent the recurrence of this was to place more emphasis on education and on ways to secure greater participation in union affairs. In other words, they recognized the dilemma of every organization aspiring to achieve its objectives in a democratic manner.

No one suggested that we should accede to Eaton's and just go away. None of the union executive had resigned. There were the more than 4,000 members who had voted "yes" to be considered. It was the unanimous decision of the meeting to carry on with a view to making a second application for certification in 1952. To do this, it would be necessary to re-sign and collect the $1 fee from at least 45 percent of the bargaining unit. Under the labour law, a period of six months had to elapse before a second application could be made after certification was denied.

Perhaps because it was too recent and painful a subject, there was no discussion as to why not one of the 500 stewards at the final, enthusiastic rally a week prior to the vote reported any decline in support arising from Company opposition. Very likely, members who were influenced to change their minds kept quiet about it and did not discuss their doubts with the stewards. It must be remembered too that there was little or no time to discuss anything with the Christmas rush on.

At a reunion in April 1980, a number of former stewards who gathered for the occasion admitted that they were quite as shocked and surprised by the results as our staff had been. During the social activity of the evening, which drew about 75 greying but still spirited supporters among former Local 1000 members and other unions, some of their recollections, were recorded.

Sid Moffat formerly of Hayter Dispatch, echoed memories expressed by all who attended the reunion: "We thought right up to the last moment it was going in.... I guess it was the increases they were getting, or the way the whole tone of management changed, telling them not to get involved and pay union dues... this is the way they started thinking. I was amazed when it was turned down."

Olive Boxall, former steward in Main Store Books and Stationery: "I was just dumbfounded. People complained so much about needing a union. At one point I felt it was going to go in with a swing. But then Eaton's started printing pamphlets and when [the Loyal Eatonians] started, you could feel the change in people. They were getting scared... some of the members I signed up didn't vote for it." Her husband, Art, from the restaurant section, agreed: "So many people were ready to vote for it, but when they got $10 a week or more in raises, they wanted no part of the union."

Len Horrocks, a salesman in Women's Shoes who was a former union executive board member, gave his views: "... the married women and part-timers killed us. Then there were old maids, Loyal Eatonians, who had been at Eaton's since they were 14. There was no way people like them were going to change.... We don't have to apologize for not getting in. People worked hard to organize, but the turnover still got you. We did one helluva job. We figured we had signed up over 10,000 members." Len was correct. At the end of four years, there were that many membership applications in our files. A few years after the vote, he left Eaton's to sell shoes for a manufacturer.

Another significant factor was mentioned by Ruth Savage, a former steward in Main Store Housewares: "If the vote had only been held a couple of months after we applied, instead of over a year later.... The Company literature was terrible... it accused us of doing things but they were the ones doing them. We didn't realize that people were getting scared."

The women Mary Stanko had worked with at Eaton's, the elevator operators, were solidly behind Local 1000. During the War, Mary had been in the TTC (Toronto Transit Commission) union, was laid off when "the boys came back from overseas," and took a whopping pay reduction when she started at Eaton's for $16 a week. Her husband was "a strong union man" and Mary found being active in Local 1000 "a challenge — besides there was unemployment insurance, so I really didn't have much to lose. We were so sure it was going in, but people got discouraged waiting. And then there was such high turnover."

At the reunion, Mary (Gilchrist) Eady interviewed one group of former members for us. She had been one of our most faithful distributors and now is director of the CLC Women's Bureau. She recalled being told by her mother, at the time a steward in Infantswear: "Some managers went around saying, 'We'll know if you don't vote that you didn't vote for the union.' That must have discouraged some women from going to vote."

Another former shoe salesman, still employed by Eaton's, recollected: "We were a little overconfident. When I heard the radio next morning I was shocked. The union wouldn't have solved all our problems but it would have been a big step in the right direction. It was one of the disappointments of my life when we lost that vote."

And then there was the anecdote told after the vote by Shirley Allen, Lingerie steward, about a member who confessed to her that she had not voted for the union. Pressed for an explanation, she offered: "Well, you know, except for the wages and working conditions, Eaton's isn't such a bad place to work."

On December 18, 1951, the Department Store Organizing Committee of the Congress met in Toronto. As anticipated, there was deep disappointment. But there were no recriminations. All of these men had come through hard and bitter struggles before their unions became established, and they never expected the Eaton Drive to be easy. When we related the decision of the membership meeting to make another try for certification, the Committee promised to assist Local 1000 in every way possible.

THE SUGAR'S OFF THE PILL

COMPANY LAYS OFF EMPLOYEES...EATON'S "ASKS" EMPLOYEES TO TAKE TIME OFF...

These are the news flashes coming out of a great many departments as this is written. Most selling departments have put employees on a two-days-off-a-week schedule, workrooms such as the Drapery Workroom are on a 3-day week, and so it goes.

As usual, employees are taking the beating. Managers and directors still have their salaries rolling in. This multi-million-dollar company can't take a few slack weeks without penalizing its employees.

What's happened to the T. Eaton Company we read so much about last November? You know, the one that looks after you..gives you job security...the one you can trust?

Let's face it. The "cure-all" on the label of that medicine bottle turned out to be a fake. The company's concern for your welfare can now be analyzed as colored water.

Total years of service don't count if you're a "junior" in your present department. If a layoff comes along, out you go. An important point in Local 1000's program is that, in case of a layoff, seniority with the company not just a department should count.

CHAPTER TWENTY-ONE

Second Round

There is a destiny that makes us brothers; none goes his way alone.
All that we send into the lives of others comes back into our own.

— *Edwin Markham*

THE INK WAS HARDLY DRY on John David Eaton's message to his "friends and associates," promising a square deal for all as they marched forward together, when hundreds of the big, happy family found themselves marching out the door. Again in 1952, post-Christmas layoffs cut deeper than seasonal help. In many departments, regular employees were laid off or asked to take time off without pay.

With sales estimated at $500 million, 1951 had been another good year for Eaton's.[1] Department managers received their usual annual bonuses, but supervisory staff did not fare as well. The previous year's bonus of two weeks' pay to those earning $50.60 a week or more was not repeated. As for the rest of the employees, their so-called "cost of living" bonuses were discontinued.

For Local 1000, the year began in a familiar state of penury. The Department Store Organizing Committee had undertaken to assist Eaton employees in a second try, but the source of funding had not been identified. From the outset, the committee had seen its role as temporary until department store employees could establish a foothold. The extent of the support, almost $200,000 over a four-year period, has already been noted. In 1950-51, local union donations, many on a monthly basis, were of great assistance. However, without the large lump sums contributed at various times by the Steelworkers, Railway Brotherhood, Clothing and Auto Workers' unions, the Eaton Drive could not have been maintained.

Once Local 1000 applied for certification, the Retail Wholesale and Department Store Union evinced renewed interest in department store jurisdiction. After the vote, this quickly evaporated as RWDSU were still lacking the resources for another prolonged organizational effort.[2]

The Ontario Federation of Labour convention opened in Hamilton on February 2, and afforded an opportunity to see what grass roots support Local 1000 might expect for a second round.

$500,000,000—AND YOU

How often do you stop and think about the fact that Eaton's do more business than all other Canadian department stores put together?

Eaton's sales volume for 1951 has been estimated at $500,000,000 by the Financial Post. Take a good, long look at those "zeros".

Profit on this sales volume can only be estimated, since Eaton's keep their financial affairs a dark secret from everyone but the income tax department. But an analysis of stores in the highest sales volume range in the U.S., made by the Harvard Business School, shows that net profits (before taxes) amounted in 1950 to 7.4% of sales volume. ("Operating Results of Department & Specialty Stores, 1950")

If you apply this to Eaton's half billion dollar sales volume, the net profit for 1951 would approximate $37,000,000.

And if you take it a step further, on a country-wide payroll of 35,000 this estimate would mean an annual profit of $1,057 per employee!

When Eaton's fight unions, it is because their enormous profits are at stake. Remember how they tried to divert your attention by placing exaggerated emphasis on the $1.50 monthly dues that you would be paying to your union? Actually, their real concern was to "protect" you from getting a larger share of the profits you help to create.

Collective bargaining through a union is the only effective way for you as an employee to protect and advance your interests.

WATCH IT!.. HE'S ONLY AFTER YOUR MONEY.

T. EATON Co PROFITS

LOCAL 1000

Lynn and I both gave reports on the vote, salted with quotations from Eaton's anti-union barrage. The 300 delegates were so angry at Eaton's falsification of labour's aims and behaviour that in a standing vote they resolved to continue support for Local 1000. Later, a meeting of Labour Council officers decided to follow the lead of the Hamilton Council which had already set the wheels in motion to build up monthly donations from affiliates. Not a word of this appeared in the press. After front-paging Local 1000's loss on December 5, the conspiracy of silence resumed.

By the end of June, contributions were coming in from 196 local unions in 25 centres. To my knowledge, this kind of labour solidarity was unique. It also attested to the value of good communication which we endeavoured to maintain through correspondence and in person.

With a reduced budget, it was essential to cut back on salaries and publicity, the major expenses. In our closely-knit group, it was a real wrench to have to part with Alex Gilbert, Hugh Webster and Mrs. Coulston in March and, two months later, with Wally Ross. Leaflet distributions were maintained, averaging one a week, stepped up at times, as in September.

Organizing effort was directed at reviving and rebuilding the steward system. Although a substantial nucleus of stewards remained active, a number of younger ones left the Company. With others, it would take time before their resentment over employees who had voted "no" died down and they could be induced to be active again. Lynn and I were responsible for Stores, Delivery and Warehouses, and Ernie for Mail Order. Noon-hours were spent lunching with key people, and evenings contacting them by phone or at meetings. Much of our effort and publicity was directed to assuring employees of their right to organize *on company premises*, in the coffee shops and lunchrooms, so long as it was on their own time.

As well as donating their services, members began monthly voluntary contributions to a Local 1000 Organizing Fund, usually 50¢ or $1. It was not an auspicious time to start collecting dues. However, the local did discuss the question, and adopted a by-law which would later provide a sliding scale of dues based on salary levels to ensure equitable treatment of part-time workers.

Membership meetings were now held at Woodsworth House at 565 Jarvis Street, which had kitchen as well as meeting facilities. On meeting nights, a group supervised by Gus Parsons, a cook in the Georgian Room restaurant, would prepare supper at cost for those who wished to stay downtown. There were usually 30 or 40 for the meal, and a good camaraderie as the dishes were washed. These were the staunch supporters who would have turned out whether they numbered six or 60.

Occasionally Gus Parsons was called out to cook for one of the Eaton family but he was as proud of his union membership as his skill in the kitchen. At the April 1980 reunion of Local 1000, which he attended even though he was getting married (again) the next day, he told us:

> I joined the union because I wanted more money. I'd go in and ask for a raise from Mrs. Ryley and she'd give me a dollar a week. She thought that was pretty good, $52 a year. But I got more afterwards. When I left Eaton's in 1967, I was getting $88 a week. The company was good to me in lots of ways . . . when I was sick.
>
> I signed members up in my lunch hours. I didn't do it in working hours.

> They knew I was a steward but they never bothered me. They never got tough after the union folded up.

Mary Sutton and her Social Committee continued to play an important role in a wider circle. Local 1000 dances had such a good reputation that they always drew 300 to 400 and added to the local's organizing fund. The bowling league ran another full season.

Early in 1952, two developments in Eaton's retailing practices signalled the shape of things to come. The first was the introduction of self-service in Main Store Smallwares and Toy departments resulting in layoffs in both.[3] This trend spread widely throughout the store in coming years, reducing not only the numbers but the skills of salesclerks, as the cashier and wrapper in a central enclosure left the customers to fend for themselves.

The second innovation was Friday night openings in Eaton's Hamilton store. This appeared to be "kite-flying," as hours of work on Fridays were shifted to 1:00 to 9:00 p.m., thus not requiring additional staff.[4]

During the vote campaign, the Company had warned that competition might force them to adopt all-day Saturday openings in Toronto, and pointed to the Bay-Bloor shopping area where stores were already open on Friday nights.[5] In 1952, the trend in urban centres in the United States had moved to a second night for shopping, Thursdays.[6]

Local 1000 continued to remind employees that as individuals they were helpless before the retail giants. Exerting any influence on patterns of hours of work, salaries and other conditions, would require a strong union organization.

After the vote the Company distributed questionnaires soliciting employees' ideas on how best to deal with "You and Your Problems" ("grievances" was a nasty, union word). In the meantime, we publicized an example of how *not* to deal with an employee. It was based on the experience of an Eaton employee in Vancouver,[7] who passed his exchange of correspondence with the Company along to the Retail Wholesale & Department Store Union office in that city, and authorized its publication. On November 3, 1951, Harold F. Harford addressed this letter to John David Eaton, at the same time returning his Veteran's Button:

> At the time of the change from David Spencer to Eaton's, [1948] the veterans on the staff... were assured to have no fears as to the future of their jobs.
>
> Upon returning from... vacation... on September 25, I was told to report to the Employment Office where I was informed that an open transfer had been put through for me. Five weeks of promises have gone

> by without employment or a satisfactory explanation as to why my being laid off was necessary...
>
> Finally on November 2, I was again asked to report to the Employment Office, given two weeks' wages and my outright release. Is this a general policy of Eaton's personnel relationship or merely the method adopted... subsequent to the amalgamation of two famous merchandising families?
>
> Having served fifteen and one-half years' combined service with these two companies in their furniture warehouse departments, I am unable to believe there is no place for me or that I have ceased to be of use to the company at this time.

The president's reply through a secretary advised Mr. Harford that, "as matters concerning employment... are dealt with locally," his letter had been referred to the manager in Vancouver. Nor did he get any more satisfaction from the reply of J. R. Rutledge, dated November 27, who still offered no reason for his discharge, but concluded: "While you feel badly about the loss of your position, we hope that you will adjust yourself to the change and will soon find other employment."[8]

On May 14, 1952, in a message from the president to "friends and associates," the Staff Counsellor Plan was unveiled.[9] The role of these "specially-trained" counsellors was to assist employees with problems, personal or otherwise, right up to top management if necessary. Toronto operations were divided into six sections, with a male and female counsellor for each, who could represent the employee in turn before the department manager, personnel supervisor, staff superintendent, and finally, the general manager. At least it was an admission that grievances existed, and that the "family" was now too large for paternal (or matriarchal) attention alone.

Two days later, we distributed a comparison of the Counsellor Plan with grievance procedure in a union contract. Referring to them as an enlarged Personnel Department, we pointed out that one company-paid counsellor per thousand employees was a far cry from an elected union steward per department.

So long as the Company retained the sole right to dispense with an employee's services, despite the assistance of a counsellor, he or she could not afford to be overly aggressive in pursuing a complaint. Management's right to dismiss an employee was curbed in union agreements by provisions requiring warning before discharge except in case of serious misdemeanour, seniority protection in case of layoff, with outside arbitration as the final step in the grievance process.

Eaton's Plan promised employees answers to their problems "as soon as possible." However, unlike union grievance clauses, no time limits were specified for management's reply at any level. Finally, and most important, counsellors could not change Company policy; union negotiations could.

There was no way of knowing, of course, how widely the services of counsellors were used, but it was not long before stewards began to report a growing disillusionment with their effectiveness. A case in point was the handling of an employee's complaint in the Customer Accounts Office.

Employees alleged that G. Leyland, manager of Customer Accounts, ran his large office like a schoolroom taskmaster, and a hard one at that. Conditions had deteriorated to the point that over a period of three or four months, there had been almost a complete turnover in staff, including long-service employees. The grievor in the case had been hired as a ledgerkeeper. Supposedly as a temporary measure, counter work with customers and then switchboard relief were added to her bookkeeping. When she complained to the manager that the combination of these duties was not compatible, nothing happened, and she decided to see a counsellor. The advice she eventually received was that, although nothing could be done to change her work load, she was not to worry. Mr. Leyland considered her work to be very satisfactory! She too left the Company.[10]

Low salaries were still the most prevalent source of discontent, and were stressed most frequently in our publicity. As six months, and then nine, went by with no wage increase, even some Loyal Eatonians were grumbling.

Our steward in Main Store Infantswear reported being urged: "You should start up the union again. We might get more increases." Then, as she said: "I'd get so mad. I'd tell them: 'If you'd voted for it when you had the chance, you'd have more increases by now. Why should all those other workers spend their money to help you organize when you didn't vote for it.'"

In May, on the recommendation of the Programme Committee, Local 1000 members revised their salary objectives to seek an $8 per week general increase, with a minimum starting rate of $40 or about $1 an hour for most employees. Equal pay, job classification and negotiated commission rates remained as part of the programme.

Gains made by the Newspaper Guild and other Toronto unions were reported in *Unionize*. Government statistics confirmed that the gap between average weekly wages in manufacturing and retail trade was widening, and by June 1952 had reached 22 percent ($59.27 for manufacturing, $48.53 for retail).[11]

If wages were low at Eaton's, they were even lower at Dupuis

Frères, the Montreal department store catering to east-end French-speaking customers. In 1951, employees in its store and mail order organized a *"syndicat"* or local union, affiliated with the Canadian and Catholic Confederation of Labour.[12] Union demands were even more modest than those of Local 1000: a $25 weekly minimum, general raise of $5 per week, five-day work week with overtime for Friday night work. After protracted negotiations, a conciliation board recommended a 16 percent wage increase.

Dupuis Frères refused to implement the board's recommendation, and in late May 1952, more than 1,000 of their employees struck. Regardless of central affiliation, all Montreal labour rallied behind the strikers with assistance in funds and on picket lines.[13]

For two months, Dupuis Frères tried to operate on a self-service basis with supervisory help, offering a 20 percent discount on all merchandise, but it didn't work. On July 28 the strike ended with a decisive victory for the union. Wage increases of $4 to $8 a week were won, but the most impressive feature of the settlement was retroactive pay for 73 weeks, back to March 1951. Thus employees recovered most of the wages lost during the strike, and went on to higher pay in future. Other gains were time and one-half for overtime after 40 hours, and a seniority clause.[14] The collective agreement, covering all of the firm's retail employees, was renewed over a 26-year period.[15]

One might have expected that the gains won through the militance of Dupuis Frères workers would have had a salutary effect on Eaton's employees' union. Although, whenever the subject of another vote was raised it was agreed that Local 1000 would win it "hands down," by summer the percentage of re-signed members was well below the 45 percent needed to make another application for certification. As in the initial campaign, employees who were in occupations closer to blue- rather than white-collar work, in Mail Order, restaurants, maintenance, delivery and warehouse, were in the lead.

September, our best organizing month, was approaching, and ideas for injecting more enthusiasm, optimism and momentum into the campaign were discussed with our key people.

It was agreed that a small Local 1000 Organizing Committee be formed of members who would periodically issue their views in a bulletin, *"Speak-Up,"* and otherwise provide leadership. This new approach was intended to allay employee fears about the risk of participating in the union, and also to demonstrate that Local 1000 consisted of Eaton employees and not "outsiders."

The first issue of *Speak-Up* appeared on September 11, 1952, with the names and departments of 14 members of the Organizing Committee, headed by such stalwarts as Doris Griffiths, Phil Murphy, Maude Fisher, Sid Moffat and Otto Klingbeil, who was subsequently named chairman. While it appeared that representation came from all divisions, as five worked in the Main Store, five in Mail Order, two in Delivery-Dispatch and two in restaurant departments, a closer look revealed that only one Main Store member was a salesclerk: the other four were from Caretaking, Shoe Repair, Groceries and Elevators.

This first issue of *Speak-Up* set the tone for special distributions throughout the month:

> We are confident that the next vote will be the *Victory Vote*. We will be meeting to draw up plans and carry them into action. Your help will be essential. We will welcome . . . any who wish to help in any capacity.
>
> Like yourselves, we felt, when Local 1000 narrowly missed out in the vote last fall, that we would give the Company an opportunity to prove its statements that we would receive better treatment without a union . . .
>
> Divided, as we have plainly been this past year, we will go forward only when and if it suits management. Together, we will have the strength to build a better future, both for ourselves and for the T. Eaton Company.

This was followed by a leaflet, "Quarter-Century Employee Says: I'm for the Union Because . . . ." Otto Klingbeil, a specialist in Mail Order farm equipment repair, spoke of the need for higher pay and proper job classification which had been revealed in the union's salary survey while he was chairman of the Contract Committee. But he also stressed that a union could achieve "better co-operation between the staff and the Company," because:

> Nearly everyone I know in Mail Order feels that the staff counsellors are Company men, and hesitates to go to them. They would be far more likely to talk things over with their Union Steward, once they knew they had the protection of a Union . . .

The banner slogan adopted for leaflets was: ON TO THE VICTORY VOTE. Most of the publicity repeated the fact that, for the first time since Local 1000 began organizing in 1948, the $2 a week increases had come to a halt, the last having been in September 1951, a full year previous.

To create shop talk on a lighter side, we tried a "gimmick" which required painstaking advance preparation by members. Thousands of the then prevalent drugstore variety of pill capsules were purchased, to be filled with "directions" printed in small type on a narrow strip of paper. This was inserted in the capsule by first rolling it around a small stick, with the label, VITAMIN U, on the outside, followed by:

> Sagging paycheck? Bills making you bilious?
> Aching back from doing three jobs? Sleepless nights from rentitis?
>
> TRY VITAMIN U
>
> It takes U to make a Union. U will bring relief... from low pay, no raises, quack counsellors. Union men across Canada are standing by U... Start VITAMIN U today by signing a Union card.

The futility of the counsellor plan to secure pay increases became apparent when a group of Mail Order women went to see a counsellor to ask why they were left out of the raises received by a few in their department, in a return to the old "Private and Confidential" manner. The counsellor arranged individual interviews with the department supervisor so that they could be informed, one by one, why no increase was forthcoming.[16]

Another success story was provided in October when the Textile Workers Union of America, CIO-CCL, was certified to represent some 900 employees at Eaton Knitting in Hamilton, one of the factories owned by the Eatons. Their first application had been denied a year previously. The reason it went through this time without the need for a vote was related to our executive in a joint meeting with the TWUA delegation, headed by their president, Jim McConnell, who had worked 28 years for the Company.

On the plea of difficult conditions in the textile industry, the Knitting Company introduced a number of cutbacks in benefits over the summer of 1952. Paid statutory holidays were reduced from eight to four a year, annual vacations cut to the one week required by law instead of two, and premium pay eliminated for second and third shifts. The last straw which led to a TWUA majority was a reduction in pension plan benefits by the amount of the government Old Age Security pension. We publicized the success of the Textile Workers' second bid for certification, and in the same leaflet asked Toronto employees, "Is *Your* Pension Secure?" pointing out Section 18 of the T. Eaton Co. plan in which "the Company... reserves the right to change, modify or discontinue it [the plan] at any time."[17]

By fall, turnover extended to key members of Local 1000's executive. Larry Nielsen, vice-president, returned to Vancouver. Margaret Morton, recording secretary, and her husband moved to Kingston, and the president, Charlie Norman, left to become an electronics inspector with the Department of National Defense.

Taking leave of the union which he had served so well in so many capacities, Charlie's parting words at the October meeting were characteristically constructive:

> Given an opportunity, plus a good reason to exercise these talents which lie dormant in so many of us, it is truly amazing what people can accomplish in fields entirely foreign to their normal experience. The Union has given both the opportunity and the reason, and those who have accepted the challenge have surprised themselves with their own accomplishments, and have lived a richer life in consequence. I urge every one of you to seek every opportunity to serve the Union in some capacity.
>
> Those of us who manned the ship these past few years have charted the course. We sailed into unknown waters, but for you the course is marked.... You do not have to guess how many members you need to achieve certification... your whole effort must be concentrated on attaining that figure.

His appeal was echoed by Otto Klingbeil in reporting for the Organizing Committee, who added with an authentic ring as an employee with almost 30 years of service at Eaton's: "We can't all be fortunate enough to leave for a better job, so let's try to make our present jobs better."

On November 10, 1952, the Department Store Organizing Committee met in Ottawa to consider the report of a committee appointed by the CCL to explore alternatives concerning the future of the Eaton Drive and department store organization in Canada.

RWDSU was the logical union, but Millard reported that he had been informed by T. B. MacLachlan, Canadian director, that his union could not undertake the costs involved. It was then agreed that the CCL officers in attendance at the forthcoming CIO convention be asked to arrange meetings with the heads of the CIO's Department Store Organizing Committee to discuss the matter. Failing a solution through that avenue, Dowling proposed that the CCL assume responsibility for Local 1000 for the time being.

By year's end, Local 1000 had regained 1,558 members. About 25 percent of the potential in Mail Order, Delivery and Warehouses had joined. Although the Stores accounted for some 700 members, this was only 12 percent of those eligible. The Local 1000 Organizing Committee of Eaton employees was still meeting regularly, and about 100 key people were taking an active part in the union, which, after losing a vote, would have been remarkable in any firm except the Eaton mammoth. It was not an impressive "comeback" but neither could it be written off. There was a moral obligation to sustain these people to see if Eaton's would provide issues to spark a revival of unionism. The situation, as I had reported it earlier to the DSOC, still obtained:

> Union sentiment is building up due to lack of wage increases and speed-up, but it is not reflecting in card inflow due to lack of stewards. Between the three of us on staff, we average more than 100 phone contacts a week, and canvassers are seeing 15 to 20 at home. If promises to sign over the phone were immediately followed up by cards, we'd be well away, but without stewards at work, much of this contact has to be repeated time and again before the card comes in. Members report that employees are still too afraid to talk openly at work about the union.

Unless this atmosphere changed, it appeared to me that it would remain a holding operation for some time to come. At this point, I decided it was time for me to return to the Steelworkers, before I became part of the problem. I did not share Lynn's optimism about Local 1000's future, nor his undaunted enthusiasm to tackle other organizational possibilities in the department store field.

The two-year campaign which I had anticipated when we opened the office at 572 Bay Street in September 1947 had stretched into five and one-half years. Chronic fatigue had set in, and I was badly in need of a change. Lynn was not only well-qualified to take over the direction, but I think welcomed the opportunity. Just back from England, Olive Richardson agreed to rejoin our group.

Since this is a memoir of the period during which I was directly involved, it should end as of February 1953. For the sake of continuity, I shall risk a brief reference to subsequent developments, with the warning that those who were on the scene could give a more complete and accurate picture.

For the first part of 1953, organizational efforts concentrated on Mail Order. Once again the possibility of applying for certification for this division of some 1,700 employees was considered. By June, membership was within 200 cards of a majority.

In May, Eaton's provided the union with an issue by announcing that in September, the Stores would open six days a week, instead of five and one-half. Employees would work all day Saturday, with a day off during the week. Daily hours would be extended by a half hour to 5:30 p.m.

During the vote campaign, the Company had implied that if the union were defeated, the half-day off on Saturday would remain unchanged, and Loyal Eatonians had circulated petitions to this effect.

Now the Company instituted the change, and many employees felt double-crossed.

The proposed change in hours, along with the lack of a wage increase, boosted membership to 2,155 by June 30.

Efforts to interest the CIO in department store organization in Canada met with a series of frustrations. A move was afoot in the United States to consolidate its fragmented retail union membership. But Local 1000's pressing need for funding could no longer be postponed. The CCL placed Lynn, Ernie and Olive on their payroll, and assumed a limited amount of expenses at 572 Bay Street.

By the end of 1953, Local 1000 was transferred from the RWDSU to a CCL-chartered local, and operations were moved to the regional office at 137 Bond Street.

The original momentum of the Local 1000 campaign was never achieved again. In my opinion, this was due more to internal factors in the workplace, than to lack of external support.

For me, the most rewarding part of any union campaign, won or lost, was the friendship of the wonderful people who surfaced along the way, those whose courage, sparkle, humour and compassion made it all worthwhile. There were one or two memorable people in every Union campaign. In the Eaton Drive, every one of our staff must have known at least a dozen. One of the incalculable losses for the labour movement was this wealth of potential leadership. At least, there were many who, social consciousness aroused and confidence acquired, went on to make valuable contributions to society in political and other activites.

As for our small organizing staff, our years of working together forged a deeper bond, which has endured these 30 years. Although we are now widely separated geographically, we keep in touch by correspondence and never miss an opportunity to hold a "reunion party," whether in Ontario or British Columbia.

CHAPTER TWENTY-TWO

Epilogue

BEFORE CONCLUDING this narrative from labour's past and noting briefly some of the momentous changes that have taken place in retail unionism in the intervening years, there are some features of the Local 1000 experience which, to my mind, deserve to be emphasized.

The loss of the vote should not be allowed to obscure the fact that the Eaton Drive did demonstrate that even the largest of department store operations in Canada *could be organized*. In the three years from September 1947 to October 1950, more than 9,000 Eaton employees applied for membership in Local 1000: 3,000 or about one-third of these left the Company. Nevertheless, Local 1000 retained a sufficient net membership to apply for certification.

The cost of the three-year organizing campaign was about $100,000. The expense of the additional year until the vote was finally held, the legal fees, extra publicity during the vote campaign, and the assistance to Local 1000 for a further two years after the vote, brought the total still to less than $250,000.[1] Granted, this was exceptional for a union campaign in the Fifties, but Eaton's was an exceptional target. Had the total been distributed over the million Canadian unionists of the day, the cost per member would have come to 25¢.

In economic terms, of course, Eaton's Toronto employees were the prime beneficiaries, whether or not they joined Local 1000. Increased salaries, pensions and welfare during the Drive took many millions of dollars out of the coffers of the Eaton family (Appendix A).

And not least, there was the "social dividend," derived from the enhancement of personal qualities and leadership ability in scores of Local 1000 members, and manifested in their subsequent contribution to other organizations. The value of this contribution is impossible to quantify; that made by some of our staff has been summarized in Appendix C.

There is no doubt that the loss inhibited attempts of similar magnitude in other leading department stores, and put an end to the then favourable prospects for organizing Simpsons across the road. While collective agreements have been concluded with such stores, including Eaton's, for operating engineers or other highly-skilled occupations, the sales force of the giants — Sears, Simpsons-Sears, Hudson's Bay, Simpsons and Eaton's — remain outside the ranks of Canadian labour.

Variety, apparel or home furnishing stores of smaller chains have been organized in various cities: Zellers, Woolco, K-Mart, Bonimart, Marks & Spencer, and the furniture stores of Legaré and Woodhouse, to mention but a few. Another group of contracts covers employees of co-operative associations in Western Canada. As only agreements covering 200 or more employees are processed by Labour Canada, a complete picture for general merchandise stores could only be gathered through provincial labour departments.

The fact remains that so long as the dominant department stores are not organized, unions in this sector are in the same position as the Steelworkers would be without Algoma Steel or Stelco, or the Auto Workers without GM, Ford and Chrysler. On the other hand, retail trade is so widely dispersed throughout Canada that there is no "jugular vein" similar to the basic steel and auto industries. Therefore, store organization requires a wider, if more localized, approach.

Are prospects in the Eighties more favourable? To provide some answers, it might help to review the major stumbling blocks encountered in the Eaton Drive, and to see to what extent these have since been overcome or mitigated.

- inadequate resources, particularly in the initial period;
- delay in certification proceedings;
- lack of acceptance of unions among white-collar workers, particularly women and part-time employees;
- muzzling of the press through the influence of advertising revenue;
- anti-union propaganda by the Company during the vote campaign.

From the outset, there was not enough staff. The full-time organizer's role is to find the stewards who will sign up their fellow employees. With an original target of 13,000, in hundreds of departments, twelve organizers instead of four (and half of them women), might have developed a more effective steward body and in much less time.

The "blitz," successfully used for a few months in 1949 and 1950, could have been employed sooner, staff and funds permitting. When turnover exceeds 25 percent annually, speed is of cardinal importance.

The problem of insufficient resources was compounded by changes in sponsorship, from the RWDSU to the ACW, and finally to the

Department Store Organizing Committee which the Congress set up to *assist*, without contemplating that its members, top officers of their own unions, would have to assume full responsibility for the Eaton campaign.

Today, these impediments no longer appear to exist. Retail unionism has a stable base in Canada with ample resources and the capacity to mount large-scale organizing drives.

In 1954, a study of 285 collective agreements then on file with the federal labour department, covering some 26,000 in retail trade, indicated that more than half worked in the food sector, compared with 11 percent in department stores. At that time, the three leading unions were the Teamsters, RWDSU and RCIA in that order.[2] Since then, there has been a spectacular, if little publicized, growth in retail unions, exceeding many times over the rate of increase in Canadian unions as a whole. (Table 7).

The change in the ranking between retail unions has been equally dramatic. In 1977, five unions embraced almost 80 percent of organized retail workers; the Retail Clerks accounted for about half of these (Table 8).

In June 1979, two large Internationals, the Retail Clerks and Butcher Workmen, merged to form the United Food and Commercial Workers (UFCW). With 1.3 million members, UFCW became the third largest in the United States.[3] The Canadian counterparts, RCIA and the Canadian Food & Allied Workers (CFAW) followed suit the same year, with 100,000 members placing it in sixth place among Canadian unions.[4]

Merger talks continued in early 1981 between RWDSU and the Service Employees International Union (SEIU) in the United States. Should this merger be consummated and extended to Canada where SEIU has some 57,000 members, it would create another strong affiliate of the CLC. The traditional base of SEIU has been in janitorial and maintenance services in the private sector, including some department stores, especially in Chicago. The SEIU has now been greatly diversified in Canada, while the RWDSU is about equally divided between wholesale and retail trade.

A breakdown of membership into sub-classifications of retail trade clearly shows that food store employees are still the most amenable to organization, comprising three-quarters of the total, whereas the next largest category is department stores with 7 percent (Table 9).

Impressive as the growth of membership in retail unions has been in absolute numbers, one should not lose sight of the potential. In 1977, of 1.5 million paid workers in trade (retail and wholesale), only eight percent were union members, compared with 45 percent in manufacturing.[5]

A crucial element in the loss of the Eaton vote was the delay in certification proceedings. The 14 months, which dragged on between our application and the vote, cost nearly one thousand members in turnover. Unlike previous years, this attrition was not offset by gains, for once application is made, a "wait and see" attitude quickly develops. The three months it took Eaton's to provide payroll lists pushed the voting into the Christmas rush, the worst season for our stewards.

More importantly, the delays engineered by J.C. Adams gave the Company time to prepare a complete reversal of strategy: from trying to "buy" employee satisfaction with improved benefits to open hostility peaking just prior to the vote. Neither the provisions of labour law nor its administrative regulations gave the Ontario Labour Relations Board any way to cope with such tactics.

Lynn Williams credits the Eaton experience with giving impetus to the OFL to seek ways of eliminating such frustrating delays.

> Of course, we were not alone. The destructive effect of delay was a general complaint, in bargaining units large and small. But the Eaton experience provided a focus and example which loomed large in everyone's mind.
>
> One of the results of these efforts was the pre-hearing vote, which came into effect in 1960. I know that I and others used it to good advantage in a number of situations.

Subsequent amendments to the Ontario Labour Relations Act gave a trade union the right to request a pre-hearing vote at the time of filing its application for certification. The Board was then authorized to determine the "voting constituency," and if the union could show 45 percent or more as members, the Board was empowered to order a vote. The ballot boxes were then sealed and not counted until after hearings on the bargaining unit. Once this was completed, if the union could still show 45 percent or more members in the approved bargaining unit, the results of the pre-hearing vote became final.[6]

Had a representation vote been held shortly after Local 1000's application was filed, I feel confident that the high enthusiasm at that time would have swung the balance in favour of Local 1000.

More recently, the Nova Scotia Board has introduced an alternative option to certification on the basis of membership cards. Whenever a union believes it has majority support, it may apply to the Board for a vote within a maximum of five days. The employer's opportunity for a full-blown counterattack is thereby limited, and the debilitating effect of a long antagonistic vote campaign avoided. According to reports, unions are winning about 80 percent of these "quickie" votes.[7]

If government is to give more than lip service to the right of workers to bargain collectively, then its legislation should facilitate the free expression of employees with regard to union representation. After all, certification is only the first test of a union's strength; it must then succeed in the more demanding key to survival, the negotiation of a first collective agreement with the employer.

In retrospect, organized labour's protest over Eaton's delay should have been mobilized earlier, and more persuasively than leaflet distributions at stores across the country, and wires and letters to the Company.

When discussing this with me recently, Don Montgomery, who worked with us during the vote campaign and is now secretary-treasurer of the CLC, remarked on how much more sophisticated the labour movement has become. The Canadian Imperial Bank of Commerce was to learn this in 1980 when the CLC threatened to withdraw its several millions of dollars on deposit unless the bank concluded an agreement with a local of the Union of Bank Employees containing a union security clause which it considered essential.

Very few Eaton employees, apart from supervisors, were actively hostile to the union and they were not much in evidence until a few weeks before the vote, when the Loyal Eatonians started up. Those who were least interested were, broadly speaking: women employed as salesclerks or office workers, particularly part-time employees; those nearing pension age; commission salesmen in "big ticket" merchandise departments; and those who had personally received generous treatment during illness or in other circumstances.

Apart from the work environment, the attitude of an Eaton white-collar employee toward the union tended to be influenced by family and friends. If an employee's husband was a union member, she was more likely to join Local 1000. However, because so few were organized at the time, contacts with members of other white-collar unions, which might have produced favourable attitudes, were virtually non-existent. Eaton employees might regard the wages and other gains of blue-collar unionists with envy, but they were afraid that strike action might be the only way to obtain them. Union gains achieved without a strike, then as now, were rarely publicized.

Since the Fifties, the composition of both the labour force and the trade unions has undergone radical change. As employment shifts from goods-producing industries to the service sector, a majority of the labour force is now in trade, finance, public administration, and community, business and personal services. All of these employ large numbers of women. By 1980 the proportion of women in the labour force had almost doubled from 30 years ago. One out of two women either had a job or was looking for one. The participation of married women had risen at the same rate; about half are now working, and this upward trend is continuing.[8]

These changes have been partially reflected in the union membership. There are now as many union members in service-related groups as in manufacturing and construction; each comprises about 40 percent of the total. The growth of unions in community, business and personal services and in public administration has been responsible; together they account for 36 percent of union members in Canada. Trade and finance represent only four percent.[9]

White-collar unionists, from professionals to clerks, are highly visible in public administration. Sixty percent of more than 500,000 union members in community, business and personal services are women.[10] Occupations range from hotel and restaurant workers, janitorial and maintenance employees, to teachers, nurses and musicians.

Women in trade unions have become more aggressive on their own behalf, as in other spheres. In Quebec, women employees, skilled and unskilled, in provincial hospital, educational and social institutions, enjoy the best maternity leave protection in Canada. They won these benefits by participating in negotiations through the Common Front, a joint bargaining committee of all Quebec labour centrals.[11] In 1980, clerical workers, one of the largest categories in the federal civil service, backed their salary demands with an unprecedented nationwide strike. Their militancy may have surprised officials of the Public Service Alliance as much as it did the Treasury Board.

The added purchasing power represented by the steady influx of women into the work force is being pursued through increased retail advertising, and department stores are devoting much research to ways and means of attracting their share. In a news report on rising profits of the Hudson's Bay Company, its president, Donald McGiverin, referred to the influence that "the two-income family, declining birth-rate and changing lifestyle" is having on retail patterns. "Shopping... must be a form of entertainment," he stated, "...our new spacious department stores are designed to emphasize the theatrical."[12] As competition leads to ever more expensive ways to woo the "upwardly mobile" woman, the employees who are part of the "props" in this new scenario may not find their own roles so entertaining.

At the time of the Eaton Drive, newspapers and radio competed as purveyors of news. Television had not yet made its appearance. It came as no surprise to us that any news of Local 1000's progress, any reports of enthusiastic labour support at CCL conventions, Labour Councils or other events, were ignored by the Toronto dailies. Since Timothy's time, publishers had recognized the source of their bread and butter.

Coupled with the prominence given to the Eatons as public benefactors, world travellers, patrons of the arts, and "enlightened" employers, the failure of the press to acknowledge the existence of Local 1000, let alone the aims and objectives of thousands of Eaton employees who made up its membership, undoubtedly contributed to the effectiveness of Eaton's campaign.

More significant was the traditional role of the press as a corporate mouthpiece, seeking to turn public opinion against the labour and socialist movements.

With the advent of television, the stranglehold on the mass media by advertising agencies and their corporate clients tightened. It has been well documented in the reports of the Senate Committee on Mass Media: "The major course... of revenue is advertising, and the economics of advertising ultimately determines all other decisions basic to the operation of a newspaper or broadcasting station."[13]

In September 1980, yet another media inquiry, The Royal Commission on Newspapers, was charged with examining corporate concentration in Canada's newspaper industry, in which the field had narrowed to three major interests (as contrasted with competitors): Thomson Newspapers, Southam Inc. and K. C. Irving in the Maritimes.

Over the previous year, the Thomson family had acquired 73 percent of Hudson's Bay Company, to add to its 71 percent control of its newspaper organization, which in 1980 bought FP Publications, a chain of papers with the second largest circulation in Canada. Thomson owns close to 50 newspapers, and there is now competition between separate owners in only four English-language cities. Testifying at hearings of the Royal Commission of Newspapers, Lord Thomson denied that his department store and newspaper holdings would lead to preferential business deals. "Before that happened, I would soon divest myself," he stated.[14]

The same sessions were enlivened by the disclosure of a "confidential" memorandum to Thomson circulation managers, setting forth recruitment guidelines. They were cautioned to avoid those seeking temporary work during strikes, summer students, moonlighters and "most important — guard against factory workers who will agitate for union rates and conditions." Housewives are the best prospects, the memo advised. "If during an interview a prospect asks.... Do I receive minimum wages? Union rates? Fringe benefits? Regular step-up increases? etc., the interview should be pleasantly terminated, and the prospect not contracted.''[15]

It goes without saying that concentration of power in such corporate hands will have a bearing on future unionization of Hudson's Bay and its subsidiary department stores.

This brings me to the fifth and final factor which, in my view, was decisive in defeating Local 1000: Eaton's virulent propaganda during the vote campaign itself (Chapter 19).

Eaton's and their legal advisors had always offered self-righteous explanations for their obstruction. Their ''intervention'' ploy of telling union members how to resign was merely by way of ''informing'' employees of their legal rights; for three months, their ''best efforts'' were devoted to the ''big job'' of producing a payroll list, and so forth. But for the final stage, no holds were to be barred. In preparing leaflets, every prejudice likely to create confusion, mistrust and division in union ranks was played upon.

In bald terms, the Company appeal was: make your choice between the small group of outside professional organizers, who are only after money and power, and your future job security with Eaton's. No person was named and, hence, there were no grounds for libel suits.

In choosing J.C. Adams' law firm, the Eaton family did not err. As the best known anti-union lawyers in Ontario, their performance in the Eaton case proved to be well worth their fees. Nevertheless, reports reached us that, even as late as the night that the ballots were to be counted, there were still doubts among the family clan who had gathered at Lady Eaton's estate in King, Ontario to await the results. And with good reason. Of the 8,900 valid votes cast, a shift of just 500 votes from ''no'' to ''yes'' would have given Local 1000 a majority. In retrospect, it is remarkable that the union vote held as well as it did.

Ontario labour law at the time required a union to obtain a majority of those eligible to vote in order to be certified. Neither the pro nor the anti forces secured a majority of the 9,900 eligible in the Eaton case. By now, most jurisdictions have amended their legislation to make a simple majority of those actually casting ballots the criterion.

According to Lynn Williams, whose position as International Secretary of the United Steelworkers of America gives him an overview of the industrial relations climate in both the U.S. and Canada: ''The type of attack we experienced (at Eaton's) is still a major problem today. Professional groups marketing services to help employers fight unions has become a growth industry in the United States, and to a lesser degree, in Canada.''

The techniques offered by most management consultants are not as crude as those used by J. P. Stevens, but tend to rely on brainwashing and manipulation. Their wares range from screening procedures to weed out "troublemakers" before they are hired, attitudes surveys, aids for sessions with new employees on the benefits of a "union-free" work environment, to ways to nip unionism in the bud at the first sign of activity. As one such anti-union expert told a management seminar, "Any company that gets a union deserves what it gets."[16]

A prominent authority on labour law, Paul Weiler, former chairman of the Labour Relations Board in British Columbia, and now a professor of Canadian Studies at Harvard Law School, concurs that "the technique for beating unions in representation campaigns has been developed almost into an art form."[17] Weiler has observed that few employers can resist entering into vote campaigns, using their advantage of superior resources and easier access to employees. He asserts: "...surely that collective employee choice should be as off limits to the employer as the employer's choice of vice-president of industrial relations is off limits to the employees."[18] These views, reinforced by experience on the B.C. Board, have led Weiler to favour signed membership applications over representation votes as criteria in certification cases.[19]

A few of the innovations in certification procedures in various provincial jurisdictions have been mentioned, and undoubtedly experimentation will continue. The Seventies have also seen some new concepts introduced, either by legislative amendment or administrative precedent, to assist unions in establishing collective bargaining relationships with "bad faith" employers. For example, the decision of the Canada Labour Relations Board in dealing with charges of unfair labour practices brought by the Union of Bank Employees (UBE), CLC, against the Canadian Imperial Bank of Commerce must have raised eyebrows not only in the banking community, but among employers across the country.

The Commerce was found guilty of contravening the Canada Labour Code on a number of counts. This was the fourth time the Board had found the employer guilty of anti-union activity. Among the remedial measures, in themselves a new departure, the CLRB ordered the bank to reimburse the employees in three of UBE-certified branches retroactively for salary increases withheld during negotiations, but given to non-union employees in other branches. The bank was also ordered to post the full text of the Board's decision with reasons in its 2,000 branches in Canada, and was further told to "cease and desist" from such interference in future.[20]

Granted that labour legislation will not organize a single worker nor is it a substitute for a strong union membership in collective bargaining, it is well to recall that the greatest strides in union growth in this century have followed legislation which put the stamp of approval on collective bargaining. The Wagner Act in 1935 gave impetus to the CIO. P.C. 1003, a federal wartime regulation passed in 1944, did the same, if belatedly, for Canadian unions. In 1967, the Public Service Staff Relations Act was followed by the transformation of separate and ineffectual federal department employee associations into meaningful collective bargaining instruments for the first time.

As further improvements continue to be incorporated into Canadian labour law, unorganized department store workers will find the path a little less rocky should they decide to unionize.

People join unions for diverse reasons. Initially, I suppose, most are attracted by the prospect of better pay. Union rates in an industry or community have a spill-over effect on non-union employers who must offer wages high enough to recruit new employees. But just as wage increases generally lag behind price increases, so do earnings of unorganized employees lag behind those of union members. Moreover, continuing inflation is creating greater pressure on workers to organize in order to keep abreast of rapidly rising living costs.

In the long term, there are advantages to union membership which outweigh the economic gains, as we repeatedly stressed in Local 1000 publicity. These derive from the change in employee-employer relationships. The individual acquires more dignity and security in the knowledge that his job tenure does not depend on arbitrary use of managerial prerogatives. Before he can be dismissed, the union contract requires that just cause be shown, to an outside arbitrator, if need be. Before he can be laid off, his seniority must be taken into account. For women, it puts an end to demeaning sexual favours, the present-day analogy to slipping the foreman a mickey on Fridays.

For the employees as a group, the union introduces the beginnings of democracy in the workplace. To maintain a functioning union is in itself a valuable exercise in self-government. The opportunity for its elected leaders to participate in decision-making with management can be a very important by-product of collective bargaining.

Arthur Kube, former CLC director of white-collar organization, and now its regional education director in Western Canada, believes that the changing nature of work in department stores will make employees more amenable to union organization. The increasing use of technology and computerization, where every function is centralized and impersonalized, has made it impossible to maintain a semblance of paternalism in employee relations.

Kube contends that:

> ...unorganized workers in the private service sector are coming to realize that Gunnar Myrdal's "organizational society" has arrived, and that the only way an individual can effectively participate in decision-making, whether at the corporate or government level, is through group representation. It may take some time yet, but I'm confident that enlightened self-interest will convince them that unions are the answer to their feeling of hopelessness, as workers in a monolithic enterprise, and as citizens confronted with broader issues: housing, energy needs versus environmental controls, pensions without poverty, and a host of others.

As for the Eaton Drive, Kube's view is that:

> ...no organizing campaign or strike is ever entirely lost. In each one, people develop who give leadership in other union or political campaigns and social action movements. Each struggle creates its own dynamics, its own leadership, because it contains the three main ingredients for social progress: agitation, organization and education.

If Canada's 180,000 department store employees are to be assisted in organizing, it cannot be accomplished by *ad hoc* campaigns here and there. It will require the best efforts of the Canadian Labour Congress and its affiliates to mount carefully-planned, adequately-funded, well-coordinated organizational drives. Will union leaders have the vision and initiative to meet the challenge?

In my last job as a researcher in the federal labour department, I seem to recall that studies were almost invariably expected to conclude by pointing to the need for further study. Writing this memoir has brought me to a different conclusion. *There is need for further action.* My warmest wishes for success go to all who undertake it.

TABLE 1

Union Membership in Canada, Selected Years
and Estimated Total Non-Agricultural Paid Workers

Year	(1) Union Membership 000's	(2) Total Non-Agricultural Paid Workers 000's	(3) (1) as % of (2)
1935	281	1,941	14.5
1939	359	2,079	17.3
1941	462	2,566	18.0
1943	665	2,934	22.7
1945	711	2,937	24.2
1947	912	3,139	29.1
1949	1,006	3,326	29.5
1951	1,029	3,625	28.4
1961	1,447	4,578	31.6
1971	2,231	6,637	33.6
1976	3,042	8,158	37.3
1980	3,397	9,027	37.6

Source: *Labour Organization in Canada*, Labour Canada. *Directory of Labour Organizations in Canada*, Statistics Canada, 1980.

TABLE 2

Sales Volume of Department Stores
and Selected Commodity Groups in Retail Trade
(in dollars and as percentage of total retail sales, Canada)

	1941		1951		1961		1971		1977	
	$ (000,000)	%	$ (000,000	%	$ (000,000)	%	$ (000,000)	%	$ (000,000)	%
Total Retail Sales	3,442	100.0	10,661	100.0	16,777	100.0	30,646	100.0	61,564	100.0
Dept. Stores (a)	378	11.0	915	8.6	1,503	9.0	3,184	10.4	6,940	11.3
Food Stores (b)	647	18.8	2,076	19.5	4,825	28.8	7,914	25.8	15,560	25.3
Automotive Products (c)	565	16.4	2,363	22.2	3,700	22.1	7,620	24.9	18,227	29.6
Apparel & Shoes	269	7.8	694	6.5	957	5.7	1,867	6.2	3,302	5.4

(a) From 1966, mail order sales were excluded from department store sales; concession sales were included.
(b) Includes grocery, combination food and other commodities, meat stores.
(c) 1977 data includes car dealers, service stations and garages, automotive parts and accessories; 1971 data lists only car dealers, service stations, garages.

Source: 1941 and 1951 data: CanadaYear Book, 1954, p. 931
1961 " " " " 1966, p. 865
1971 " " " " 1975, p. 718
1977 " " " " 1978-79, p. 747

TABLE 3

Retail Locations by Kind of Business
1961 and 1971, Canada

	1961		1971	
All retail locations [a]	152,620		156,532	
General merchandise group [b]	11,686		9,363	
Department stores		139		430
Food group	47,313		42,256	
Automotive group	35,237		37,768	
Apparel and accessories group [b]	19,213		20,356	
Hardware and home furnishings group [b]	15,445		17,376	
All others	23,726		29,413	
	152,620		156,532	

(a) Locations refer to physical outlets, not establishments which for census purposes mean the principle reporting unit or accounting entity. Thus, in 1971, there were 430 department store locations pertaining to 34 establishments.

(b) The data are not strictly comparable; the change in outlets included in the groups was made in the 1966 census. The number of department stores as shown in comparable.

Source: *Census of Canada*, 1971. *Retail Trade*. Vol. VII
Establishments (7-6) Table 14
Locations (7-1) Table 16

TABLE 4

Employment and Average Weekly Earnings in Retail Trade by Commodity Group, Canada, January 1980 (a)

	Number of Employees (000)	% Female %	Average Weekly Earnings %	As % of Dept. Stores %
Retail Trade	611.4	51.0	191.14	116.3
Automotive	96.2	19.1	251.20	152.8
Liquor, wine & beer	21.3	16.9	246.67	150.0
Food, combination & meat	123.0	44.1	210.84	128.2
Household furniture & appliances	16.1	33.3	198.73	120.7
Dept. Stores	187.2	66.7	164.42	100.0
Apparel & shoes	50.0	65.3	155.71	94.7
Variety stores	41.9	63.1	144.15	87.7
All others	75.7	n/i	n/i	n/i

(a) The month of January was chosen as it represents the annual low point in employment in department stores, particularly of part-time and casual categories, both of which distort the average earnings in the department store sub-group.

Source: *Statistics Canada*, Catalogue 72-002, February, 1980.

TABLE 5

Age and Marital Status of Female Salesclerks (a)
Canada, 1951, 1971

	1951		1971	
Total Number	95,443	100.0%	159,825	100.0%
24 and younger		31.3		31.6
25-34		23.9		11.1
35-44		19.0		18.5
45 and over		25.7		38.7
single		55.0		30.1
married		38.2		62.2
widowed, divorced		6.8		7.7

(a) Based on census occupation 5137, sales clerks, commodities. In 1971 there were 82,275 males and 159,825 females in this occupation.

Source: 1951 *Census* Vol. IV, Table 11, pp. 17-18.
1971 *Census Catalogue* 94-733 Vol. III, Bulletin 3.3-6, January 1975, pp. 7-8.

TABLE 6

Average Weekly Earnings in Retail Trade[a] and Selected Industries[b]
City of Toronto, Ontario
(all data are for the month of January)

	1951	As % of R.T.	1961	As % of R.T.	1971	As % of R.T.	1980	As % of R.T.
	$		$		$		$	
Retail Trade	41.61	100.0	65.72	100.0	100.50	100.0	200.58	100.0
Finance, insurance and real estate	48.44	116.4	77.91	118.5	137.43	136.7	301.73	150.4
Manufacturing	47.60	114.4	82.94	126.2	142.93	142.2	324.40	161.2
Industrial Composite[c]	46.80	112.5	80.42	122.4	137.54	136.9	297.80	148.5

Notes

(a) The trade industry is subdivided into wholesale and retail trade. In January 1951, average earnings in wholesale trade exceeded those in retail trade by 20 percent, and by January 1980, by 55 percent. To the extent that it occurs, part-time employment distorts average *weekly* earnings. The month of January was chosen for all data because seasonal part-time employment is usually lowest.

(b) The finance, insurance and real estate industry employs a large proportion of women; in January 1980, 60.4 percent of employees were female.

(c) The industrial composite excludes agriculture, fishing, public administration, and non-profit activity such as education, health and welfare, and religious organizations.

All data are based on returns from employers having 20 or more employees in the month of the report.
Source: *Statistics Canada*, Monthly Catalogue 72-002; January 1951, 1961; February 1971, 1980.

TABLE 7

Increase in Union Membership, Retail Clerks International Union, Retail Wholesale & Department Store Union, and Canada, 1948-1978

	1948	1958	% Inc.	1968	% Inc.	1978	% Inc.
RCIA	1,096	4,041	269	21,123	448	52,000	146
RWDSU[(a)]	5,000	11,500	130	20,000	74	28,000	40
All Unions	978,000	1,454,000	49	1,736,000	19	3,278,000	89

(a) RWDSU entered Canada in 1944. About half its current membership is employed in wholesale trade.

Source: Membership data supplied by Labour Canada, Labour Data Branch, Ottawa, taken from various editions of *Labour Organizations in Canada*.

TABLE 8

Unions comprising more than 5% of the Total Membership in Retail Trade, 1977

Union	Affiliation	Number of Members	% of Total in Retail Trade
RCIA	AFL/CIO/CLC	41,646	40.0
Canadian Food & Allied Workers	AFL/CIO/CLC	14,032	13.5
Union of Canadian Retail Employees	Independent	6,255	6.6
RWDSU	AFL/CIO/CLC	14,842	14.3
Commerce Federation	CNTU	5,686	5.4

Notes: 1. The first three unions merged in 1979 into UFCW. A majority of CFAW members work in meat packing plants. About half RWDSU members work in wholesale trade. Commerce Federation membership is in the province of Quebec.

2. Of a total of 103,802 union members, 21,341 or 20.8 percent are fragmented into about 40 other unions. This total includes 6,948 employees in motor vehicle repair shops, who are represented by 15 unions other than those above.

Source: Calculated from unpublished data from "Corporate and Labour Union Returns Report," Part II, 1977, supplied by Labour Canada, Labour Data Branch, Ottawa, Canada.

TABLE 9

Union Membership in Canadian Retail Trade
By Commodity Classification, 1977

S.I.C.[a] Code	Commodity	No. Union Members	% Total Members	% Female Members
631	Food Stores	76,553	73.7	46.2
642	General Merchandise, incl. Department Stores	7,470	7.2	60.7
652	Tire & Battery	1,414	1.4	(
654	Gas Service Stations	133	*	(4.8
656	Auto Dealers	3,672	3.5	(
696	Liquor Stores	3,465	3.3	8.6
673	Hardware Stores	1,919	1.8	4.3
681	Drug Stores	1,034	1.0	83.2
676	Household Furnishing Stores	586	*	37.0
Misc.	8 Commodity Classifications with less than 500 members in each, e.g. Shoes, Men's Clothing, Books, Jewellery, Tobacco	608	*	
658[b]	Motor Vehicle Repair	6,948	6.7	1.1
		103,802	98.6	

* Less than one (1) percent.

(a) SIC Codes refer to those used by Statistics Canada to denote sectors of economic activity. A description of the above, which fall under Retail Trade, may be found in the *Standard Industrial Classification Manual.*

(b) This activity is classified under Retail Trade. However, the employees are MVR mechanics and are not members of the predominant retail unions.

Source: Calculated from unpublished data from returns on file under the Corporate and Labour Union Returns Act, Part II, 1977, supplied by Labour Canada, Labour Data Branch, Ottawa, Canada.

APPENDIX A

Major Improvements in Wages and Working Conditions, 1947-1951
T. Eaton Company, Toronto, Ontario

"I still think back to the happy days of helping to organize our staff. Too bad we lost, but we did improve wages and conditions just by trying."

Bill Lewin, formerly employed in Main Store Bake Shop, Chief Steward, Restaurant Division, Local 1000.

Fall, 1947	
	General wage increase of $2 per week. Time and one-half for overtime, after first 30 minutes of overtime.
1948	
Various times	Departmental wage increases. Almost all employees received at least one $2 per week increase. Skilled trades had higher increases. Drivers had a $2 raise in April and another $2 in November.
July	Factory vacations changed to two weeks after two years' service instead of after 5 years.
October	Eaton Retirement Annuity Plan instituted (see Chapter 9).
1949	
Various times	Increases of $1 to $3 by departments; more for certain skilled trades.
1950	
September	Mail Order hours of work reduced from 42 to 41½. General wage increase of $3 per week for men, $2 for women and $1 for part-time employees. Health Plan, employee paid; Blue Cross and Associated Medical Services (Toronto only).
October	Uniform basis for welfare (sick pay) placed on record for first time.
1951	
February	General increase of 5%.
April	Straight commission salesmen to receive pay for all statutory holidays, based on average earnings (previously paid for Christmas Day only).
June	General increase of $2 per week ($1 part-timers).
September	Mail Order hours reduced to 40, Monday to Friday. General increase of $2 week (1 for part-timers).

Note: In a bargaining unit of about 10,000 employees, a $2 general wage increase would represent approximately $1,000,000 annually. After Local 1000 lost the vote in December, 1951, there were no general increases in 1952. Increases to employees on an individual basis resumed in 1953.

APPENDIX B

Bargaining Unit as determined by the Ontario Labour Relations Board
in the case of
Local 1000, Department Store Employees Union – and –
The T. Eaton Company

The Board... finds that all employees of The T. Eaton Co. Limited at Toronto who regularly work at least three full-time or part-time days per week throughout the year, save and except

> first assistants, persons above the rank of first assistant, and persons below the rank of first assistant a part of whose duties it is to recommend alterations in the employment status of employees;
>
> persons employed in offices and bureaus other than those of store merchandise departments, mail order merchandise departments, customer service departments, and mail order operating departments with the exception of mail order office and order office management; persons employed in factory departments and in printing, cheque book printing, photoengraving, and multi-typing workrooms;
>
> persons employed in city advertising and art, and mail order advertising, art and sales promotion departments;
>
> persons employed in the investigation department, night watchmen and floor superintendents;
>
> persons at present represented for collective bargaining purposes by International Union of Operating Engineers, Local 796. Amalgamated Clothing Workers of America, Local 212, and Commercial Artists and Photographers Association, Local 24515, A. F. of L.;
>
> persons employed in the employment department; and
>
> persons who come within the terms of section 1 (3) (a) of The Labour Relations Act, and registered nurses

constitute a unit of employees of The T. Eaton Co. Limited appropriate for collective bargaining.

May 28, 1951

(signed) P. M. Draper
for the Board.

APPENDIX C

Biographical Notes 1954-1981

1954-1955: Lynn Williams and Ernest Arnold organized Smith's department store in Windsor, Ontario and negotiated first agreement. With Olive Richardson, organized Simpson-Sears Mail Order in Regina, Saskatchewan and applied for certification. Company took court action to challenge Board decision that the mail order was an appropriate bargaining unit, and were upheld. CCL would not authorize an appeal to the Supreme Court.

ARNOLD, ERNEST F. 1956-1975: General representative, Canadian Labour Congress, Toronto area, until retirement. Active on executive and election campaigns for CCF/NDP in Toronto-Woodbine. Member, Canadian Council of Retirees, CLC. Volunteer rehabilitation work at Donwood Institute, Toronto. Married Rita Jean Badgley in 1937: sons, Robert and Edward, daughter, Linda, seven grandsons.

CHESTER (RICHARDSON) OLIVE 1957-1969: Business representative, Local 343, Office & Professional Employees International Union; conducted negotiations for employees of more than 100 union offices in Ontario; 1969-1977: Office supervisor, New Democratic Party caucus, Ontario Legislature. Convention secretary for provincial and federal conventions. 1977- : Conciliation officer, Ontario Ministry of Labour. Married Richard Chester in 1953: two daughters, Toni and Diane.

ROSS, WALTER S. 1952: Representative, United Steelworkers of America, organization and negotiations, office workers' locals in Ontario. 1953-1957: directed organizing campaign, Aluminum Company, Kitimat, B.C.; assisted in contract negotiations. 1958: organizing campaign, Denison Uranium Mines, Elliott Lake, Ontario; second vote won. 1960: troubleshooter, strikes, Dominion Bridge, Alberta, Wabash Engineering, Toronto. 1961: headed local union committee organizing small plants, Toronto area. 1963: organizing campaign, International Minerals & Chemicals, Esterhazy, Saskatchewan. 1964: International Nickel, Sudbury-Steel/Mine Mill dispute. 1966: Ontario NDP organization director, on leave from Steelworkers, 1968-1970: Provincial secretary, NDP, British Columbia. 1971- Real estate salesman, Lower Mainland, B.C. Participated in all elections for NDP. Married Mary Walker in 1944: sons, Michael and Gary, daughters, Nancy and Susan.

SUFRIN (TALLMAN) EILEEN 1953-1956: Head, Office Workers' Department, National Office, United Steelworkers of America. June, 1953: Represented Canadian Congress of Labour at International Confederation of Free Trade Unions' Women's School at La Brevière, France. 1957-1958: Studied Italian trade unions, Canada Council grant; wrote articles for Canadian labour press. 1959-1964: Industrial Relations Administrator for Crown corporations in Saskatchewan, Government Finance Office. 1965-1966: Editor, Canadian Packinghouse Worker, Toronto. 1967-1972: Department of Labour, Ottawa. Legislation Branch, "Labour Relations Legislation in Canada" (1969); Economics & Research Branch, studies for Women's Bureau and Federal Industries Division. 1972: Moved to White Rock, B.C. Active in local NDP. October, 1979:

Governor-General's Persons Award for efforts to improve conditions of Canadian working women. Married Bert Sufrin, 1960.

WILLIAMS, LYNN R. 1956: Representative, United Steelworkers of America, District 6. Area supervisor, Niagara Peninsula. Assistant to District Director Larry Sefton. 1964: Delegated by CLC to three-month programme, International Institute for Labour Studies, Geneva, Switzerland. Headed negotiations in nickel and copper industries in Canada. 1973: Elected Director of District 6. 1976: Member, Ontario Economic Council. Director, University of Toronto. 1977: Honorary law degree, McMaster University. Elected International Secretary, United Steelworkers of America. Moved with his family to Pittsburgh. Delegate, 24th World Congress of International Metalworkers Federation in Munich, Germany. Chaired IMF World Aluminum Conference, and World Nickel Conference. At union headquarters, monitors following departments: By-laws & Elections, Data Processing, Public Relations, Personnel & Local Union, New Members, International Affairs, Education. Married Audrey Hansuld, 1946: children, Judith, David, Barbara and Brian.

APPENDIX D

"We, the undersigned One Hundred Committee Members...."

Local 1000 is now nearing the final stages of union organization.

Over 5,000 employees of the T. Eaton Company, believing that the program of the Union will benefit ALL Eaton employees, have joined Local 1000, Dept. Store Employees' Union.

In order to negotiate with the management on a collective bargaining agreement on behalf of all Eaton employees, the Union must show a clear majority of employees signed as members, in accordance with the regulations of the Ontario Labour Act.

THEREFORE, WE, THE UNDERSIGNED ONE HUNDRED COMMITTEE MEMBERS OF LOCAL 1000, Department Store Employees' Union, ask you to join Local 1000 without delay. If you are already a member, we ask you to help in signing up employees who have not yet joined.

NAME	DEPARTMENT
L.A. Nillsen	Hayter Upholstery
Fred Tucker	M.S. Bedding & Linens
Rita Le Gard	Louisa Cafeteria
R.W. Dennie	Annex Linoleums
P.B. Lennon	Piano Workroom
S. Allen	M.S. Foundation Garments
Anne Stone	M. O. Adjusting
Margaret Brown	M. O. Circulation
Celia Bell	M. S. Groceries 5th
Steve Hrabets	Overseas Packing
Marge Kope	Budget Plan
Pat E. Houlahan	Christie Furn.Fin.
Ernest M. Cooper	Caretaking
H.C. Norman	M.S. Bedding & Linens
G. M. Cowan	Housewares Stock
Elna Anderson	M. O. Correspondence
Pat Rooney	M. O. Hardware
Kay Sefton	Fur Factory
[illegible] Roy	M. O. Hardware
A. Sauvé	M.O.Corresp.
Samuel Lucy	Painters
Frances Rate	M. O. Shipping
Lorna Miller	Annex Elevators
Arthur E. Edwards	Drapery Workroom
W. J. Guyton	Fact. Men's Clothing
Ellen Macdonald	M. O. Dresses
Chris Graham	M. O. Shipping
Maud Fisher	M. O. Dresses
Enid G. Mould	Annex Purses
J. Kavin	Pipe Shop
R.J. Bond	M. O. C.O.D.
S.R. McShane	M.O. Boy's Clothing
T. A. Foley	Radio Repair
Jean E. Fitzsimmons	College Hosiery
Elizabeth Burdick	Annex Candies
C. Coffey	Budget Plan
P. A. Honson	Radio
[illegible]	M.S. Sportswear
C.J. Richardson	College St. Shoes
E. G.A. Mowat	Men's Clothing
Evelyn Treadway	M. S. Drugs
Christine Walford	6th Coffee Shop
O. Boxall	Georgian Room
Andy MacDonald	M.S. Elevators
Edwin Lake	Georgian Room

(over)

Nicholas Beckwith Hayter Delivery
A. Hoyle Dye House
H. W. Hart Night Caretaking
C. O'Reilly Louisa Cafeteria
James Geo McKee Fact. Men's Clothing
R. Savage M.S. Housewares
K. Clark Lansdowne Drivers
[illegible] Elevators
Mark Robbins Round Room
Frank L. Jones Leaside Warehouse
Augustus Parsons Georgian Rm.
Percy Sandford Annex Shoes
Alice Stevens Georgian Room
[illegible] Louisa Cafeteria
G. H. Slater College Rugs
Bill Edwards C. D. S.
H. Dennison Basement Groceteria
A. Burbage Organ Factory
Kay Hunt M. S. Hosiery
Albert Topliss Fur Factory
J. B. McManus Albert St. Packers
A. J. Simeral Ticket Writing
Shelby E. [illegible] 5th Fl. Groceries
Lawrence Smith Georgian Room
Beatrice Flint Drapery Workroom
J. R. Breck M. O. China
A. Abbott Round Room

W. B. Thomas M.S. Budget Plan
G. Joyner M. S. Girls' Wear
R. Morton Toy Stockroom
E. J. McComb Hayter Del
Frank Brown Christie Furn.
Audrey Williams Comparison Of
James [illegible] M.S. Bedding &
R. Gilmer M. O. Adjusting
J. Easdale Central Shippin
Bill Taylor M.S. Bake S
T. Brickman Factory Shirts
James Mill College Luncheon
Edith McWaery M. S. Chi
Ernest Jones M. S. Piece G
Phil Murphy Mdse. Ret
J. Keenan 5th Floor Groceteria
C. Marchment Shoe Rep
Frank E. Skelton Factory Men's Cl
Morley L. Janes Service Bu
[illegible] College Elec
Margaret McWilliam Georgian R
James Roberts Electrical W
E. G. Packman College Av
W. [illegible] M. O. Budget
Geo. Hallows Business Mach. M
Florence Neale Hub
Chas. W. Perrett M.S. Ha
Dorothy Wright College Elev

Issued by: Local 1000, Department Store Employees' Union, 572 Bay St. AD.8581

Footnotes

Prologue

1. Stephenson, William. *The Store That Timothy Built*, McClelland & Stewart, Toronto, 1969, p. 98.
2. For an account of background to formation of Committee for Industrial Organization and major industrial union conflicts in U.S. industries, see: Levinson, Edward, *Labour On The March*, Harper Bros., New York, 1938. Reference to white-collar unions is on p. 325.
3. Levinson, op. cit., p. 315.
4. For a comprehensive account of the entry of CIO unions into Canada, see: Abella, Irving M. *Nationalism, Communism and Canadian Labour*, University of Toronto Press, Toronto, 1973.
5. Logan, Harold A. *Trade Unions in Canada*, MacMillan Co. of Canada, Toronto, 1948, p. 386.
6. Logan, op. cit., pp. 379-82.
7. Canadian Congress of Labour, Convention Proceedings, 1940, p. 20.
8. Dominion Order-in-Council P.C. 1003, Wartime Labour Relations Regulations, February 17, 1944.
9. Logan, op. cit., p. 391.
10. Estey, Marten S. "Patterns of Union Membership in The Retail Trades" in Industrial & Labor Relations Review, Vol. 8, No. 4, July 1955, pp. 557-564.
11. Levinson, op. cit., pp. 250-251.
12. Estey, op. cit., p. 560.

Chapter One

1. *Maclean's*, August 27, 1979, "The Leviathan of Yonge Street" 92: 28
2. *Financial Post*, May 24, 1975, C-8, Susan Goldenberg, "After 1,800 shopping centres, they've run out of locations."
3. Bryant, George. *Department Store Disease*, McClelland & Stewart, Toronto, 1977, p. 120. For factors leading to Eaton's decline as Number One Canadian retailer, see the chapter, "The Competitors," pp. 99-124.
4. *Globe & Mail*, January 2, 1979.
5. Ph.D. Thesis, University of Toronto, 1978, Gene Howard Homel. "James Simpson and the Origins of Canadian Social Democracy," ch. 8.
6. Canada Department of Labour. *Part-time Employment in Retail Trade*, Queen's Printer, Ottawa, 1969, pp. 27-37.
7. Royal Commission on the Status of Women. Marianne Bossen, *Patterns of Manpower Utilization in Canadian Department Stores*, Information Canada, Ottawa, 1971, Table 3 and Table 6.
8. Harrington, Michael. *The Retail Clerks*, John Wiley & Sons, New York, 1962, Ch. 1, pp. 1-4.
9. *Labour Gazette*, January 1950, "The Canadian Labour Force." p. 28.
10. See George Sayers Bain, "Union Growth & Public Policy in Canada," Labour Canada, October 1978, pp. 47, for a discussion of the factors which promote or inhibit union growth.
11. Bossen, op. cit., pp. 73-75.

Chapter Two

1. *New Liberty*, Toronto, October, 1948, Frank Hamilton, "Young Mr. Eaton," pp. 14-15, 75-76.
2. Nasmith, George C. *Timothy Eaton*, McClelland & Stewart, Toronto, 1923, pp. 20-67.
3. Nasmith, op. cit. Cash and fixed price policies had been in effect much earlier in A.T. Stewart's New York store; it was not known if Timothy Eaton heard of this or adopted the same policies independently. pp. 98-99.
4. Ibid., p. 87.
5. Logan, Harold A. op. cit., pp. 39-41.
6. Stephenson, op. cit., p. 30.
7. Brecher, Jeremy. *Strike*! Straight Arrow Books, San Francisco, 1972, pp. 28-31.
8. Logan, op. cit., p. 57.
9. Nasmith, op. cit., pp. 219-223.
10. Kirstein, Geo. C. *Stores & Unions*, Fairchild Publications, N.Y., pp. 15-24.
11. *Financial Post Magazine*, Toronto, May 1978, Ian Brown, "The Empire That Timothy Built," p. 18.
12. *Labour Gazette*, May 1902, p. 647.
13. Nasmith, op. cit., p. 303.
14. Starowicz, Mark. "Eaton's: An Irreverent History." One of a series of articles in *Last Post* combined in *Corporate Canada*, James, Lewis & Samuels, Toronto, 1972, p. 7.
15. Speisman, Stephen A. *The Jews of Toronto: A History to 1937*, McClelland & Stewart, Toronto, 1979, p. 193.
16. *World*, Toronto, March 25, 1912.
17. Speisman, op. cit., p. 194.
18. *Weekly Bulletin of the Clothing Trades*, Toronto, February 23, 1912. Cited in Wayne Roberts "Labour and Reform in Toronto, 1896-1914," Ph.D. thesis, University of Toronto, 1978.
19. *Financial Post Magazine*, Brown, "The Empire...," p. 20.
20. Stephenson, op. cit., p. 74.
21. Starowicz, op. cit., pp. 10-11.
22. Eaton, Flora. *Memory's Wall*, Clarke, Irwin & Co., Toronto, 1956, p. 73.
23. Report. Royal Commission on Price Spreads and Mass Buying, 1935, pp. 207-208.
24. *Financial Post Magazine*, Brown. "The Empire...," p. 25.
25. Report. Price Spreads Commission. pp. 406-407.
26. Starowicz, op. cit., pp. 13-18.
27. Horn, Michiel. *The Dirty Thirties*, Copp Clark Publishing Co., Toronto, 1972. pp. 133-134.
28, *Maclean's*. June 1968. Alexander Ross, "What It's Like to Live in Toyland," p. 15.
29. *Financial Post Magazine*, Brown. "The Empire...," p. 34.
30. *Toronto Star*. August 8, 1969.

31. Newman, Peter C. *The Canadian Establishment, Vol. 1*, McClelland & Stewart, Toronto, 1975. p. 220.
32. *Financial Post Magazine*, Brown. "The Empire...," p. 31.

Chapter Three

1. Minutes of executive and membership meetings, Local 540, Retail Clerks International Protective Association, 1944-1946.

Chapter Four

1. Logan, H. A. *Trade Unions in Canada*... p. 396.
2. Office & Professional Workers Organizing Committee. "The First Canadian Bank Strike," 1942. Public Archives, Ottawa.
3. Eaton's. "What Are They Selling?" November 13, 1951.
5. Eaton's. "Watch For the Worms in These Local 1000 Apples," November 22, 1951.

Chapter Six

1. R.S.O. Chapter 29, 1944; Ch. 44,
   1946: Ch. 54, 1947: Ch. 51, 1948.
2. P.C. 1003 Wartime Labour Relations Regulations, Sec. 19 (2). R.S.O. Chapter 228, 1980, Section 66.
3. Local 1000 Broadcast, January 25, 1950. Incident reported in leaflet, undated, "Mr. Palmer — You're Out of Step."
4. R.S.O. Chapter 34, April 6, 1950.
5. R.S.O. Chapter 34, 1950, Sec. 53. Ch. 228, 1980, Sec. 79.
6. CCH Canadian Limited. Case 17,006. International Chemical Workers Union AFL and Sifto Salt Co. Limited, and International Union, UAW-CIO Local 456. Decision: October 26, 1949, pp. 1356-57.
7. R.S.O. Chapter 232, 1970 Section 7 (3). Ch. 228, 1980. Sec. 7 (3).
8. R.S.O. Chapter 54, 1960 Sec. 7a. Ch. 228, 1980, Sec. 9.

Chapter Seven

1. George Luscombe is internationally known for his work as director of the Toronto Theatre Workshop.
2. Hugh Webster is now a prominent actor, appearing frequently on CBC programmes.
3. Stephenson, Wm. *The Store That Timothy Built*... p. 153. The author reports that Eaton's spent some $14,000 per day on ads in Toronto's three newspapers. Publication date of this book was 1969.

Chapter Eight

1. Local 1000, CKFH, May 15, 1951.
2. Mills, C. Wright. *White Collar*, Oxford University Press, New York, 1951, p. 241.
3. Ibid, p. 241.
4. *Unionize*, March 6, April 17, 1951.
5. Stephenson, Wm. *The Store That Timothy Built*, op. cit., p. 120.

6. *Unionize*, January 25, 1949.
7. *Unionize*, August 10, 1948, May 1, 1950.
8. *Unionize*, July 11, 1950.
9. *Unionize*, June 1, 1948.
10. *Unionize*, September 9, 1948.

Chapter Nine

1. *Unionize*, September 21, November 9, November 23, 1948; April 26, June 7, 1949.
2. CKEY, March 1, 1950. *Unionize*, March 14, 1950.
3. *Unionize*, April 3, 1950.
4. Macpherson, Mary-Etta. *Shopkeepers to a Nation*. McClelland & Stewart, Toronto, 1963. p. 106-107.
5. *Unionize*, April 18, 1950.
6. *Unionize*, May 9, 1950.

Chapter Ten

1. A "spiff" is commission paid on articles priced over a certain amount. I do not have data on comparable prices in New York and Toronto at that time. From *Women's Wear Daily*, our "Bible" on retail trade, we must have assumed that Eaton employees would be knowledgeable about comparable prices and hence that higher pay for department store workers in New York represented a better standard of living. This was confirmed by visits to New York stores made by Marjorie Gow in 1948 and by Lynn and myself in 1951. Most clothing items in the New York stores cost less than comparable items in Toronto; restaurant meals were more reasonable.

Chapter Eleven

1. For background information on RWDSU, I have relied on George C. Kirstein, *Stores & Unions*. Fairchild Publications, New York, Chapter VII, The History of the CIO's Retail Union, 1937-1950, pp. 75-88.
2. In 1940 the name was changed to United Retail, Wholesale and Department Store Employees.

Chapter Twelve

1. *Unionize*. February 7, 15, March 1, 1949.
2. *Unionize*. February 15, March 22, June 7, 1949.
3. Eaton, Flora. *Memory's Wall*, op. cit., pp. 199-200.
4. *Unionize*. April 19, 1949.
5. Ibid.
6. Anne (Stone) Coy left Eaton's in 1952, and was employed by the Canadian Broadcasting Corporation. She joined the Association of Radio and Television Employees of Canada (ARTEC) at CBC and served as steward, local grievance chairman, local president and member of national negotiating team. Retired from CBC in 1978. Was co-founder of and still active in the Patients' Rights Association, a volunteer group assisting

patients with a health care problem to gain redress through the relevant health College.

7. *Unionize*. August 5, 1949.

Chapter Thirteen

1. Loans were advanced by Local 2251, USWA (Algoma Steel) and Local 114, UPWA (Canada Packers).
2. John Gilbert was elected NDP MP for the federal riding of Broadview in Toronto in 1965. He held the seat until his appointment as Judge of the Ontario Court in 1978.

Chapter Fourteen

1. Statistics Canada. Catalogue 72-002, July 1980. Average weekly earnings for Industrial Composite in Toronto, June 1980, were $309.01.
2. *Unionize*, October 5, 1950.
3. *Financial Post*, October 14, 1950, "Here's Why CIO-CCL Spent $100,000 on Drive to Organize T. Eaton Co."

Chapter Fifteen

1. Regulations 236, Consolidated Regulations of Ontario, 1950.
2. R.S.O. Chapter 34, 1950. Section 7 (5).
3. The interveners representing other unions were: International Union of Operating Engineers, Local 796; Local 33, International Jewellery Workers' Union, AFL; Toronto Allied Printing Trades Council; Toronto Photo Engravers' Union, Local 35; Locals 212 and 132, Amalgamated Clothing Workers of America.
4. *Toronto Daily Star, Telegram, Globe & Mail*. December 6, 1950.
5. Provision for employee, as distinct from union, interventions is now made under Regulations to the Ontario Act by means of petitions signed by employees, which must be patently free of employer influence. For a review of petitions in certification cases processed by the Ontario Labour Relations Board in 1978, see D. D. Carter and J. W. Woon, "Union Recognition in Ontario" available from Labour Canada, Ottawa. pp. 16-18.
6. R.S.O. Chapter 34, 1950. Section 1 (1) (a).
7. For full description of the unit as determined by the OLRB in the Local 1000 application for Eaton's, Toronto, see Appendix B. For a discussion of current practices of the OLRB with respect to part-time workers and bargaining units, see Wendy Weeks "Collective Bargaining and Part Time Work in Ontario." Industrial Relations Vol. 33, No. 1, 1978, pp. 80-91.
8. *Certiori* involves a plea for a writ requiring re-examination of a case by a higher court, or to quash a decision of a lower tribunal (in the Eaton case, this might have been the Labour Board's decision). *Mandamus* is a writ issued by a superior tribunal to an inferior one, requiring the production of certain documents or other evidence. In the Eaton case, such a writ might have jeopardized the confidentiality of certain documents deposited with the Labour Board.

Chapter Seventeen

1. Local 1-S, United Retail Workers, "Local 1-S Is Your Union." January, 1950.
2. T. Eaton Co. "An Open Letter to Employees." September 27, 1950.
3. *Women's Wear Daily*, New York. "CIO Mapping New Campaign in Store Field." October 16, 1950.
4. For an account of membership participation in a very large retail local, see Michael Harrington, *The Retail Clerks*, pp. 47-50. Local 770, RCIA, in California.
5. Local 1000. "She Knows the Value of a Union." September 13, 1951.

Chapter Eighteen

1. *Canada Year Book*, 1962. pp. 928-929.

Chapter Nineteen

1. T. Eaton Co., *"What Are They Selling?"* November 13, 1951.
2. *Unionize* Supplement, November 22, 1951.
3. Eaton, Flora McCrea. *Memory's Wall*, Clarke, Irwin & Co., Toronto, 1956, pp. 150-151.
4. Ibid.
5. T. Eaton Co., *"Your Future Is At Stake"* November 8, 1951.
6. T. Eaton Co., *"What Are They Selling"...*
7. Ibid.
8. T. Eaton Co. "*Some Reminders*" November 27, 1951.
9. T. Eaton Co. *"Your Future..."*
10. Ibid.
11. T. Eaton Co., *"Watch for the Worms in Those Local 1000 Apples"* November 22, 1951.
12. T. Eaton Co., *"What Are They Selling . . ."*
13. For 1951, RWDSU reported 42 locals and 6,000 members in Canada. Labour Organizations in Canada, Labour Canada, Ottawa.
14. T. Eaton Co., *"What Are They Selling . . ."*
15. T. Eaton Co., *"Watch for the Worms . . ."*
16. Local 1000, "*Union Dues Bring Union pay,"* November 13, 1951.
17. Local 1000, "*Union Pay Is On Record,"* November 24, 1951.
18. T. Eaton Co., *"That Macy Contract"*, November 23, 1951.
19. Local 1000, "*Eaton's Give You a HALF TRUTH So They Can Hand You a HALF LOAF,"* Undated, but after November 23, 1951.
20. T. Eaton Co., *"Will They Give You Your Money Back?"* November 16, 1951.
21. Local 1000, *"Less Sleep Lost if Your Job's Secure"*, November 23, 1951.
22. T. Eaton Co., *"Watch for Worms . . ."* and Local 1000 *"Nail It Down,"* November 27, 1951.
23. Ibid.
24. T. Eaton Co., *"Watch for the Worms . . . ."*
25. Len Horrocks. Tape recording, Local 1000 Reunion, April 25, 1980.
26. *Unionize*, May 7, 1951.

Chapter Twenty

R.S.O. Chapter 232, 1970, Section 7(3); Ch. 228, 1980, Sec. 7(3).

Chapter Twenty-one

1. *Financial Post*, "Shuffle in Big Store League," January 26, 1952.
2. Correspondence. RWDSU: MacLachlan-Simon, November 6, 1950. CCL-CIO: Conroy-Haywood, March 12 and 19, 1951. CCL-RWDSU: Conroy-MacLachlan, March 29, 1951. Minutes, Department Store Organizing Committee, CCL, November 10, 1952, Public Archives, Ottawa.
3. *Unionize*, March 13, 1952.
4. Ibid.
5. Eaton's, "*Will They Give You Your Money Back?*" November 16, 1951.
6. Local 1000, Special Leaflet, August 19, 1952.
7. In 1948 Eaton's purchased nine stores from David Spencer Limited in the province of British Columbia.
8. Local 1000, "*The Polite Brush-Off,*" April 18, 1952.
9. Eaton's, "*A Message from the President about your Staff Counsellors,*" May 14, 1952.
10. *Unionize*, September 17, 1952.
11. Dominion Bureau of Statistics, Annual Review, Employment and Payrolls, 1952.
12. The name of the organization was changed in 1960 to Confédération Nationale des Travailleurs Unis (CNTU).
13. *Unionize*, Supplement, June 12, 1952.
14. *Unionize*, August 7, 1952.
15. The last collective agreement between Dupuis Frères and the Commerce Federation expired January 31, 1978, four days after the Company closed its doors and ceased operations.
16. Local 1000, "*Is Your Pension Secure?*" November 6, 1952.
17. Ibid.

Chapter Twenty-two

1. From annual financial statements submitted to the Department Store Organizing Committee, CCL, for 1949, 1950, 1951; author's estimates for 1947-48, 1952-53.
2. *Labour Gazette*, October 1954, pp. 1457-1460.
3. *Financial Post*, June 2, 1979, John Duffy, "Merged Retail Union Will Have Muscle to Push for New Members."
4. *Globe & Mail*, June 20, 1979, Wilfred List's column.
5. Corporate and Labour Union Returns Act (CALURA) Report, 1977, Part II, pp. 74-75. See also Table 4.
6. R.S.O. Ch. 54, 1960, Section 7a; Ch. 228, 1980, Section 9. In 1978 pre-hearing votes were requested in 138 cases, or 14.0 percent of all certification applications disposed of by the OLRB for that year. For a tabulation and analysis of results of these vote requests, see Carter-Woon, op. cit., pp. 8-9, 19.

7. Weiler, Paul. *Reconciliable Differences: New Directions in Canadian Labour Law*, The Carswell Company Ltd., Toronto, 1980, pp. 44-45.
8. Statistics Canada. Catalogue 71-001, December 1980, Labour Force. See also : *Women in the Labour Force: Facts and Figures*. Various editions. Labour Canada, Ottawa.
9. CALURA, op. cit., Table 27A, p. 69.
10. Ibid.
11. Canadian Advisory Council on the Status of Women. Julie White, *Women and Unions*, pp. 110-111. This work deals with historical and current participation of Canadian women in the labour force and in unions.
12. *Vancouver Sun*, April 22, 1980, "Hudson's Bay Profits Rise."
13. Senate Committee on Mass Media, Report II: 119, 1970. See also: Wallace Clement, *The Canadian Corporate Elite*. McClelland & Stewart, Toronto, 1975, Chapters 7 and 8, pp. 270-324.
14. *Vancouver Sun*, April 14, 1981, Patrick Nagle, "'I Don't Play Favorites,' Thomson tells Newspaper Probers."
15. Ibid., April 15, 1981, Nagle, "Shy Thomson Tycoon goes on Defensive for Newspaper Chain."
16. *Saskatchewan Commonwealth*. June 18, 1980, Michelle Celarier, "Union Busting by Any Other Name."
17. Weiler, op. cit., p. 40.
18. Ibid, p. 46.
19. Ibid, pp. 37-48.
20. Canada Labour Relations Board. Decision dated November 30, 1979, in the case of Union of Bank Employees, Locals 2104 and 2100, CLC, and Canadian Imperial Bank of Commerce operating at the following branches: Niagara and Scott Street, St. Paul and McDonald Street, St. Catharines, Ontario and Creston, B.C. See also: *Canadian Labour*, December 14, 1979, p. 3.

Index

Part A — by Name

Part B by Subject

The Eaton Drive

THE EATON DRIVE is the story of one of the most intensive a sustained organizing campaigns in Canadian labour history.

With 30,000 employees, post-war Eaton's was the country's th largest employer, surpassed only the railways and the federal government. Because its stores and mail order operations extend across Canada, Eaton's influenced retail wages nationwide.

Eaton's Toronto operations, dispersed over a dozen work loca and embracing 16,000 employees at peak seasons, presented a for challenge to Local 1000 of Retail Wholesale and Department Sto Union and the Canadian Congress of Labour. When it applied fo certification in October, 1950, the Ontario Labour Relations Boar faced with the largest and most complex bargaining unit ever to c before it.

The labour movement considered the success of the Eaton Dri central to removing the threat of a large, lower-paid, constantly s work force to their wage standards and supported it with unprece generosity.

Eileen Tallman Sufrin, who was one of the organizers, describ campaign from the union viewpoint in the hope that the insight it provides will assist retail workers in organizing in the future.

Eileen Tallman Sufrin became active in socialist politics in the '30s. Her career in the trade union movement began in 1940. She helped to organize bank clerks, munition plant workers, office staff in steel mills, and led the long, spectacular, but unsuccessful, drive to unionize Eaton employees in Toronto. This is her memoir of that extraordinary chapter in retail unionism and Canadian labour history. In October 1979 she was one of seven women awarded the Governor-General's medal, commemorating the 50th anniversary of the "Persons Case".

Fitzhenry & Whiteside Limited

ISBN 0-889